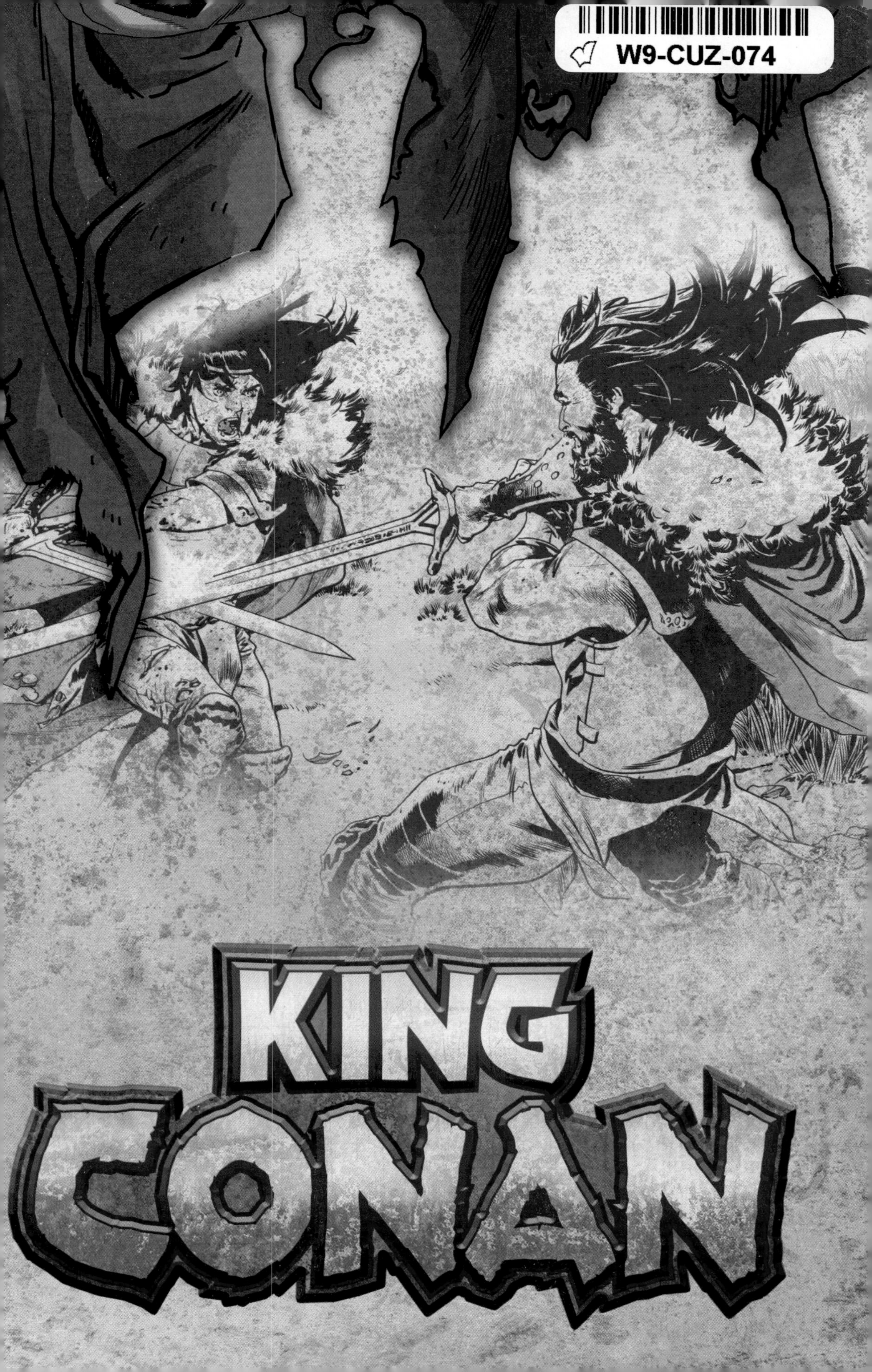
KING
CONAN

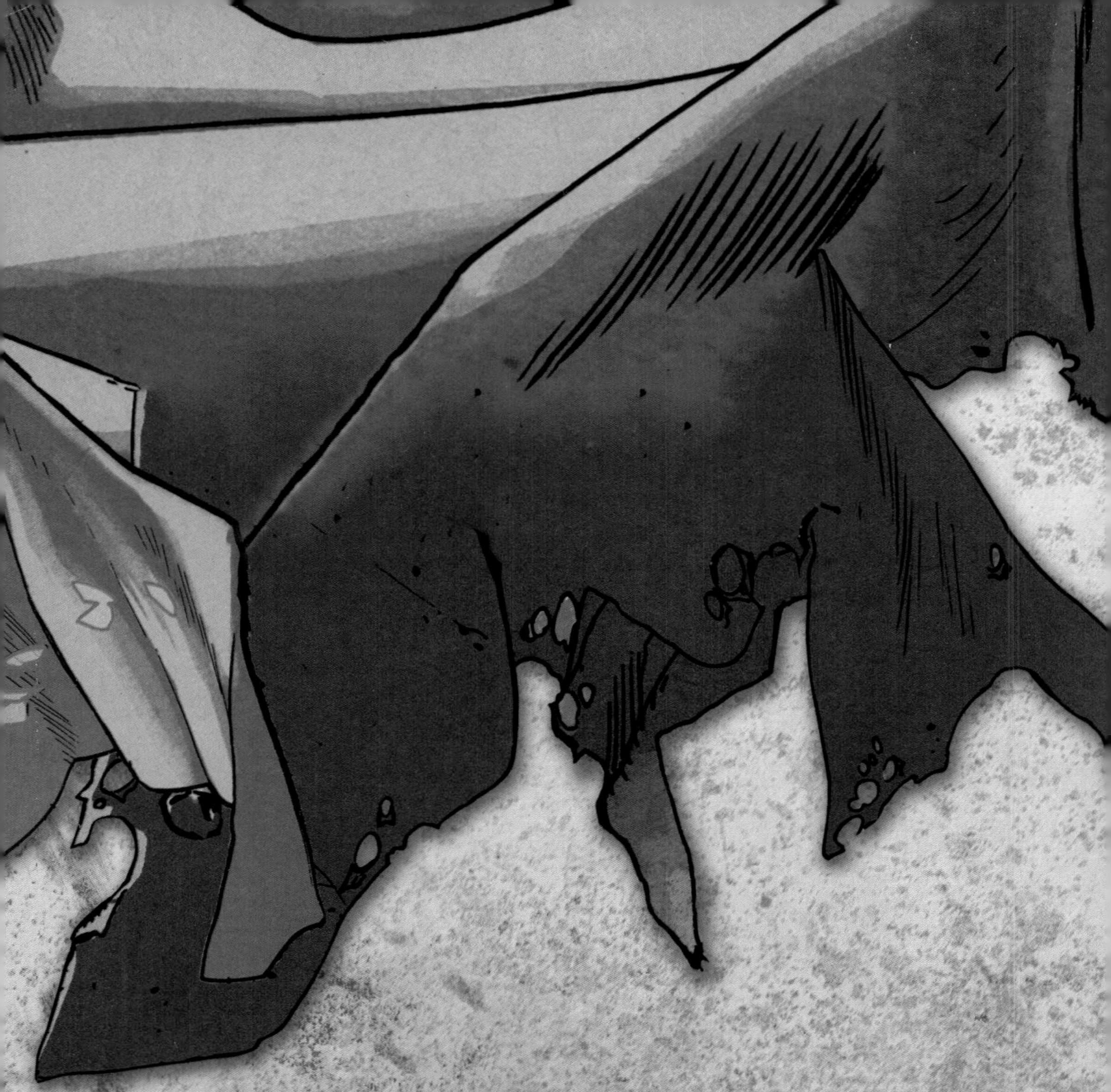

FOR CONAN PROPERTIES INTERNATIONAL

FREDRIK MALMBERG △ PRESIDENT
JOAKIM ZETTERBERG △ EXECUTIVE VICE PRESIDENT
STEVE BOOTH △ CHIEF OPERATING OFFICER

CONAN CREATED BY **ROBERT E. HOWARD**

COLLECTION EDITOR: **DANIEL KIRCHHOFFER**
ASSISTANT MANAGING EDITOR: **MAIA LOY**
ASSOCIATE MANAGER, TALENT RELATIONS: **LISA MONTALBANO**
DIRECTOR, PRODUCTION & SPECIAL PROJECTS: **JENNIFER GRÜNWALD**
VP PRODUCTION & SPECIAL PROJECTS: **JEFF YOUNGQUIST**

BOOK DESIGNER: **STACIE ZUCKER**
SENIOR DESIGNER: **ADAM DEL RE**
SVP PRINT, SALES & MARKETING: **DAVID GABRIEL**
EDITOR IN CHIEF: **C.B. CEBULSKI**

KING CONAN. Contains material originally published in magazine form as KING CONAN (2021) #1-6. First printing 2022. ISBN 978-1-302-93055-4. Published by MARVEL WORLDWIDE, INC., a subsidiary of MARVEL ENTERTAINMENT, LLC. OFFICE OF PUBLICATION: 1290 Avenue of the Americas, New York, NY 10104. © 2022 Conan Properties International LLC ("CPI"). CONAN, CONAN THE BARBARIAN, HYBORIA, THE SAVAGE SWORD OF CONAN and related logos, characters, names, and distinctive likenesses thereof are trademarks or registered trademarks of CPI. No similarity between any of the names, characters, persons, and/or institutions in this magazine with those of any living or dead person or institution is intended, and any such similarity which may exist is purely coincidental. Marvel and its logos are TM Marvel Characters, Inc. **Printed in Canada.** KEVIN FEIGE, Chief Creative Officer; DAN BUCKLEY, President, Marvel Entertainment; JOE QUESADA, EVP & Creative Director; DAVID BOGART, Associate Publisher & SVP of Talent Affairs; TOM BREVOORT, VP, Executive Editor; NICK LOWE, Executive Editor, VP of Content, Digital Publishing; DAVID GABRIEL, VP of Print & Digital Publishing; SVEN LARSEN, VP of Licensed Publishing; MARK ANNUNZIATO, VP of Planning & Forecasting; JEFF YOUNGQUIST, VP of Production & Special Projects; ALEX MORALES, Director of Publishing Operations; DAN EDINGTON, Director of Editorial Operations; RICKEY PURDIN, Director of Talent Relations; JENNIFER GRÜNWALD, Director of Production & Special Projects; SUSAN CRESPI, Production Manager; STAN LEE, Chairman Emeritus. For information regarding advertising in Marvel Comics or on Marvel.com, please contact Vit DeBellis, Custom Solutions & Integrated Advertising Manager, at vdebellis@marvel.com. For Marvel subscription inquiries, please call 888-511-5480. **Manufactured between 6/10/2022 and 7/12/2022 by SOLISCO PRINTERS, SCOTT, QC, CANADA.**

10 9 8 7 6 5 4 3 2 1

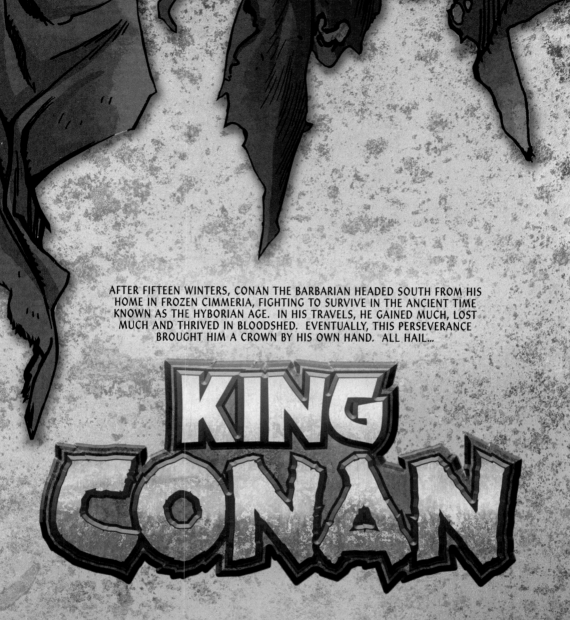

AFTER FIFTEEN WINTERS, CONAN THE BARBARIAN HEADED SOUTH FROM HIS
HOME IN FROZEN CIMMERIA, FIGHTING TO SURVIVE IN THE ANCIENT TIME
KNOWN AS THE HYBORIAN AGE. IN HIS TRAVELS, HE GAINED MUCH, LOST
MUCH AND THRIVED IN BLOODSHED. EVENTUALLY, THIS PERSEVERANCE
BROUGHT HIM A CROWN BY HIS OWN HAND. ALL HAIL...

KING CONAN

WRITER △ JASON AARON

ARTIST △ MAHMUD ASRAR

COLOR ARTISTS △ MATTHEW WILSON
WITH MAHMUD ASRAR (FLASHBACKS, #1-2)

LETTERER △ VC's TRAVIS LANHAM
COVER ARTISTS △ MAHMUD ASRAR & MATTHEW WILSON

EDITOR △ MARK BASSO
ASSISTANT EDITORS △ LAUREN AMARO & DREW BAUMGARTNER
CONSULTING EDITOR △ RALPH MACCHIO

SPECIAL THANKS TO BRIAN OVERTON

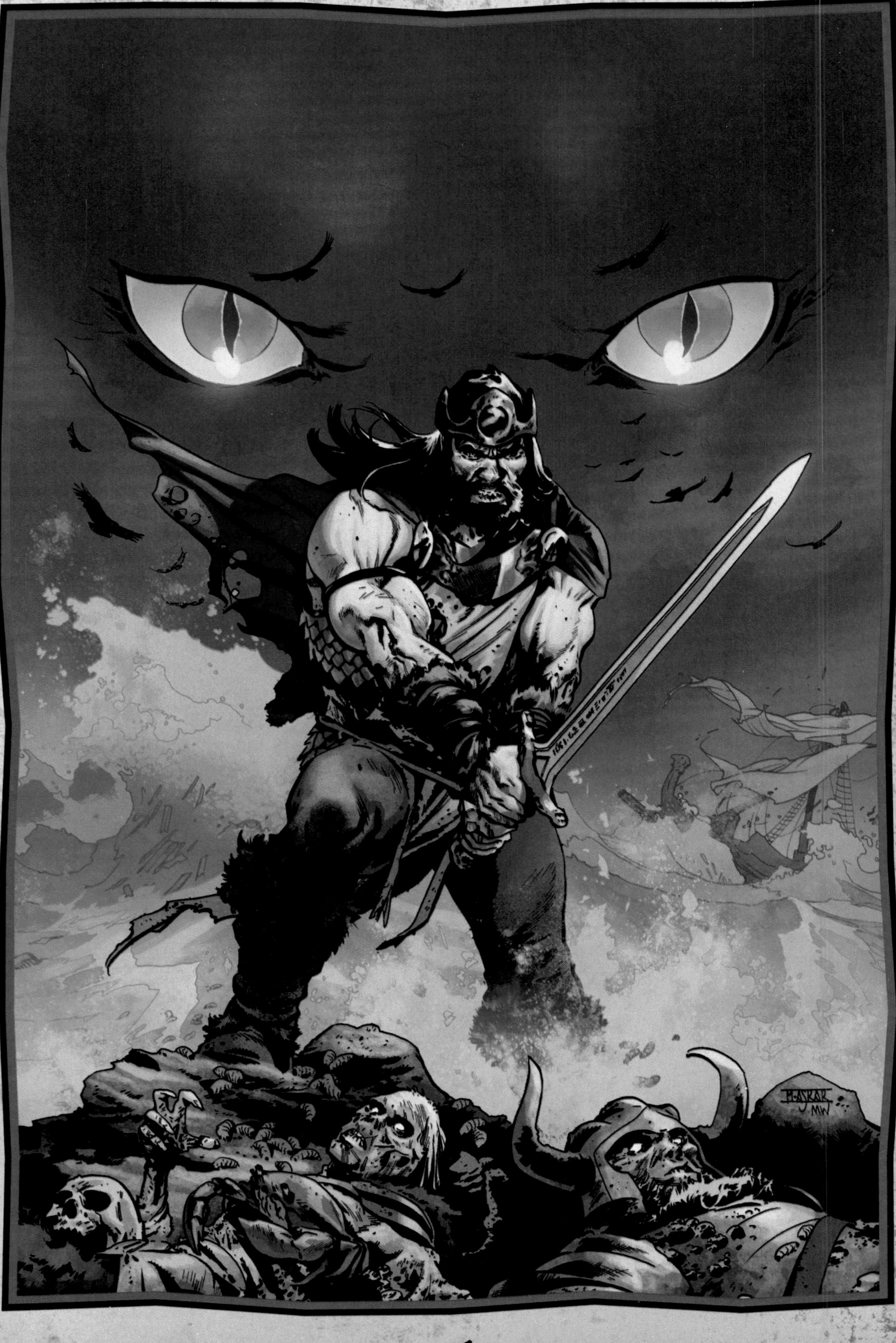

1

Know, oh prince, that between the years when the oceans drank Atlantis and the gleaming cities, and the years of the rise of the Sons of Aryas, there was an age undreamed of, when shining kingdoms lay spread across the world like blue mantles beneath the stars...Hither came Conan, the Cimmerian, black-haired, sullen-eyed, sword in hand, a thief, a reaver, a slayer, with gigantic melancholies and gigantic mirth, to tread the jeweled thrones of the Earth under his sandaled feet."

--The Nemedian Chronicles

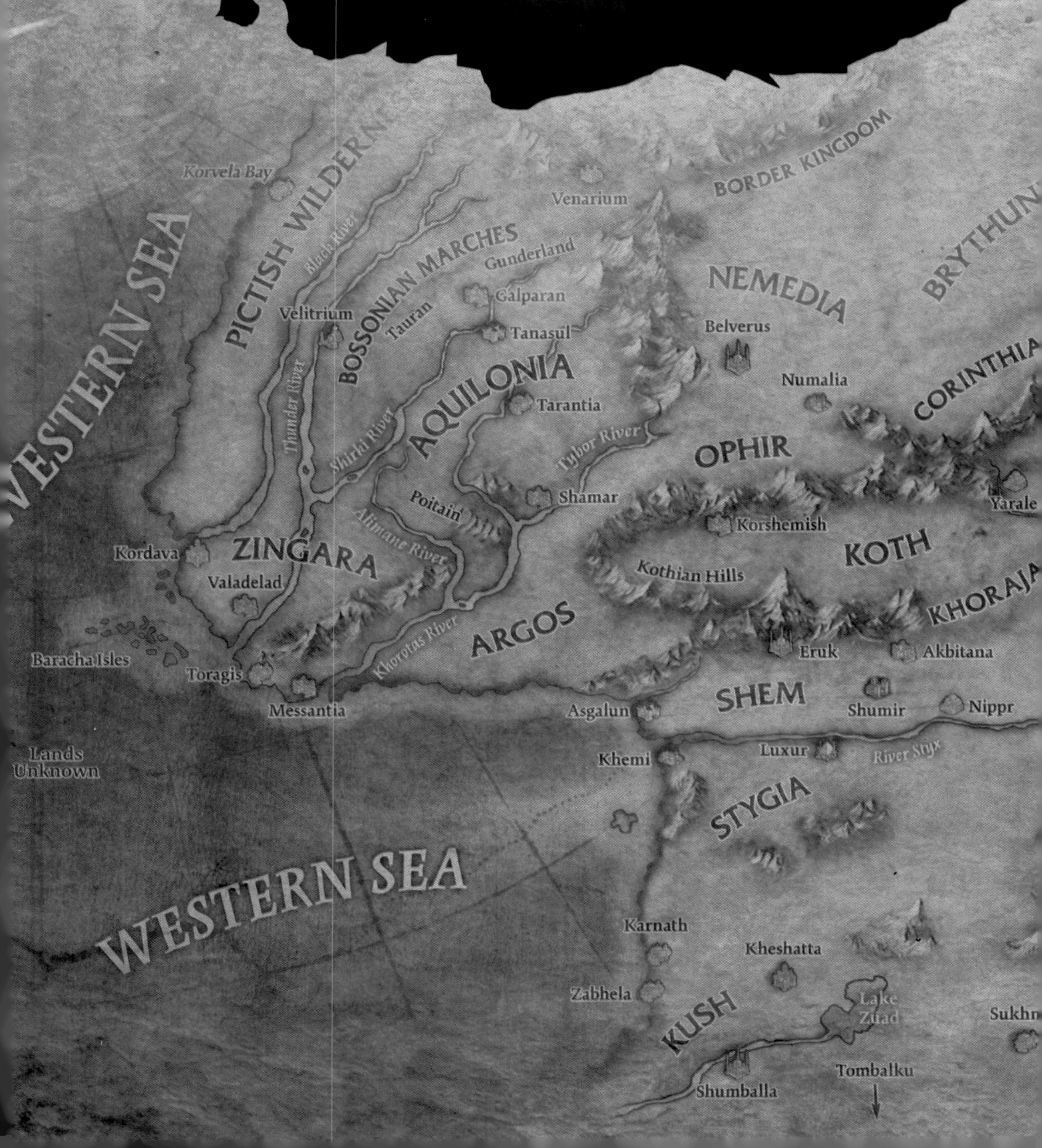

Korvela Bay
Venarium
BORDER KINGDOM
WESTERN SEA
PICTISH WILDERN
Black River
BOSSONIAN MARCHES
Gunderland
Galparan
Tauran
Velitrium
Tanasul
NEMEDIA
BRYTHUN
Belverus
Thunder River
AQUILONIA
Numalia
Tarantia
CORINTHIA
Shirki River
Tybor River
OPHIR
Poitain
Shamar
Yarale
Alimane River
Korshemish
Kordava
ZINGARA
KOTH
Valadelad
Kothian Hills
KHORAJA
ARGOS
Khorotas River
Baracha Isles
Eruk
Akbitana
Toragis
SHEM
Messantia
Asgalun
Shumir
Nippr
Luxur
River Styx
Lands Unknown
Khemi
STYGIA
WESTERN SEA
Karnath
Kheshatta
Zabhela
KUSH
Lake Zuad
Sukhm
Tombalku
Shumballa

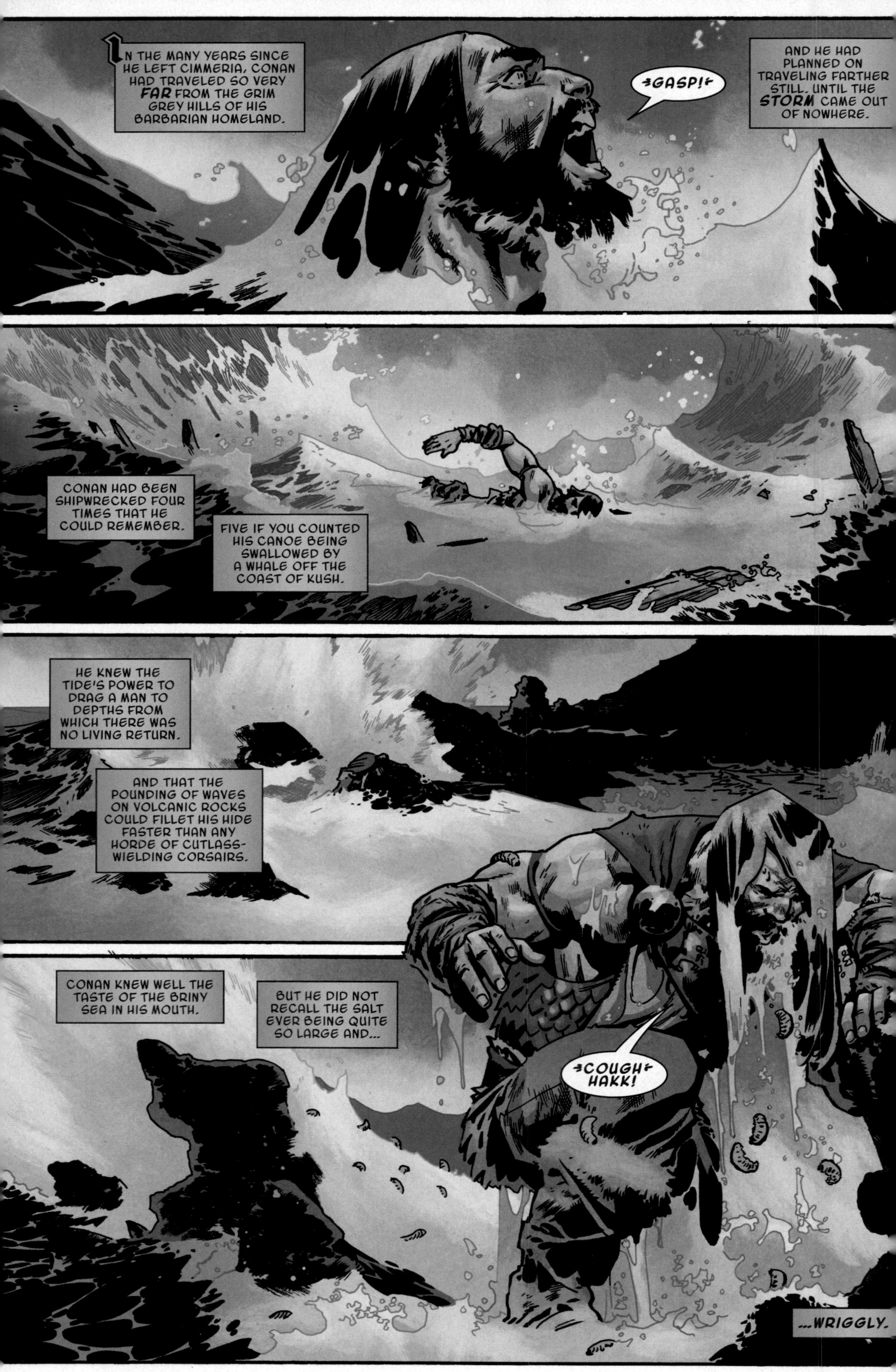
IN THE MANY YEARS SINCE HE LEFT CIMMERIA, CONAN HAD TRAVELED SO VERY FAR FROM THE GRIM GREY HILLS OF HIS BARBARIAN HOMELAND.
GASP!
AND HE HAD PLANNED ON TRAVELING FARTHER STILL. UNTIL THE STORM CAME OUT OF NOWHERE.
CONAN HAD BEEN SHIPWRECKED FOUR TIMES THAT HE COULD REMEMBER.
FIVE IF YOU COUNTED HIS CANOE BEING SWALLOWED BY A WHALE OFF THE COAST OF KUSH.
HE KNEW THE TIDE'S POWER TO DRAG A MAN TO DEPTHS FROM WHICH THERE WAS NO LIVING RETURN.
AND THAT THE POUNDING OF WAVES ON VOLCANIC ROCKS COULD FILLET HIS HIDE FASTER THAN ANY HORDE OF CUTLASS-WIELDING CORSAIRS.
CONAN KNEW WELL THE TASTE OF THE BRINY SEA IN HIS MOUTH.
BUT HE DID NOT RECALL THE SALT EVER BEING QUITE SO LARGE AND...
COUGH HAKK!
...WRIGGLY.

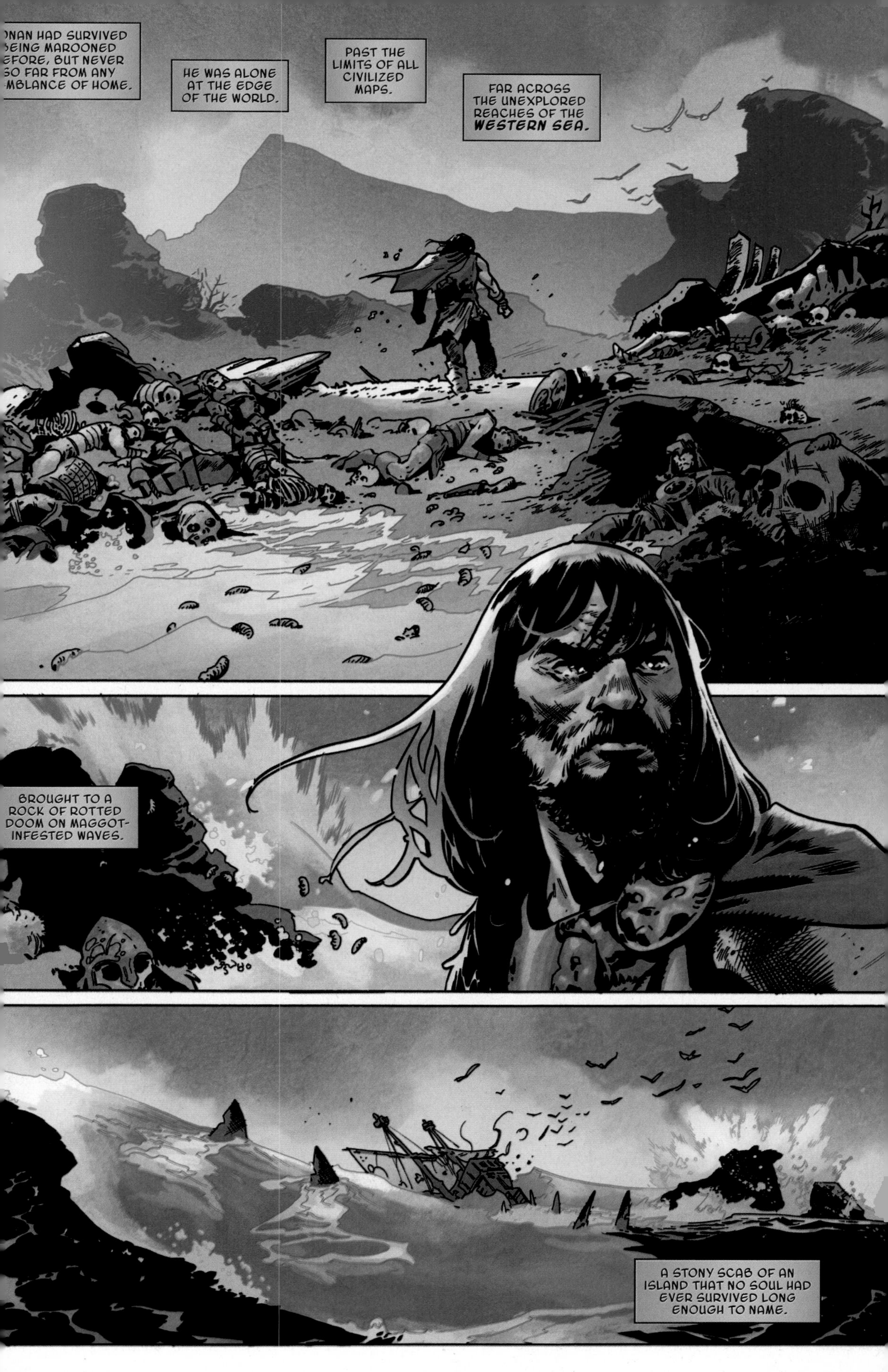
ONAN HAD SURVIVED BEING MAROONED BEFORE, BUT NEVER SO FAR FROM ANY MBLANCE OF HOME.
HE WAS ALONE AT THE EDGE OF THE WORLD.
PAST THE LIMITS OF ALL CIVILIZED MAPS.
FAR ACROSS THE UNEXPLORED REACHES OF THE WESTERN SEA.
BROUGHT TO A ROCK OF ROTTED DOOM ON MAGGOT-INFESTED WAVES.
A STONY SCAB OF AN ISLAND THAT NO SOUL HAD EVER SURVIVED LONG ENOUGH TO NAME.

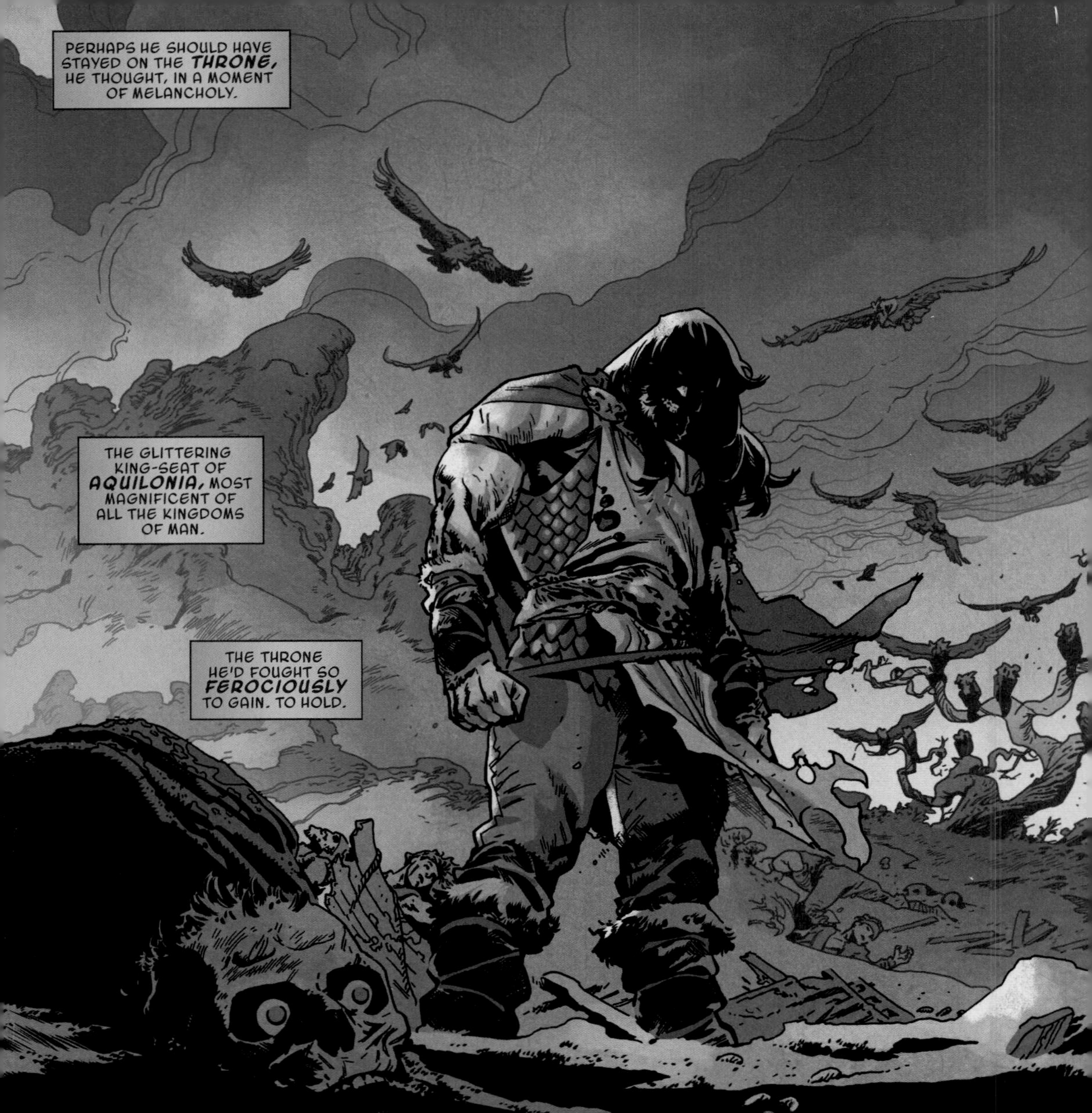
PERHAPS HE SHOULD HAVE STAYED ON THE **THRONE,** HE THOUGHT, IN A MOMENT OF MELANCHOLY.
THE GLITTERING KING-SEAT OF **AQUILONIA,** MOST MAGNIFICENT OF ALL THE KINGDOMS OF MAN.
THE THRONE HE'D FOUGHT SO **FEROCIOUSLY** TO GAIN. TO HOLD.
THE THRONE... CONAN HAD **ABANDONED.**

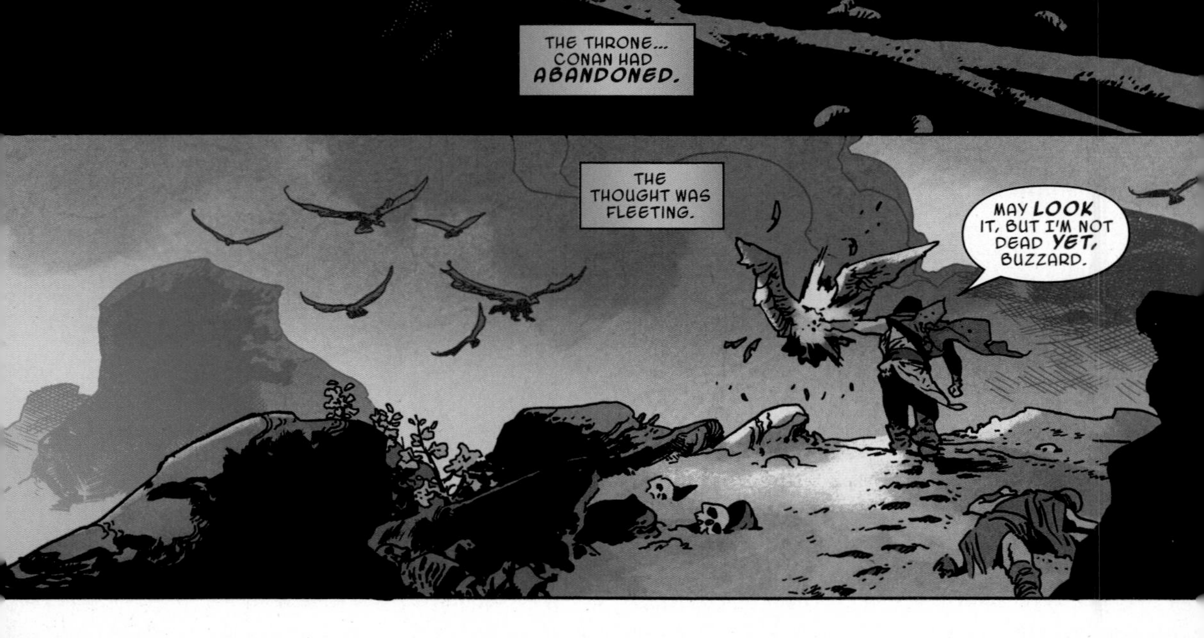
THE THOUGHT WAS FLEETING.
MAY **LOOK** IT, BUT I'M NOT DEAD **YET,** BUZZARD.

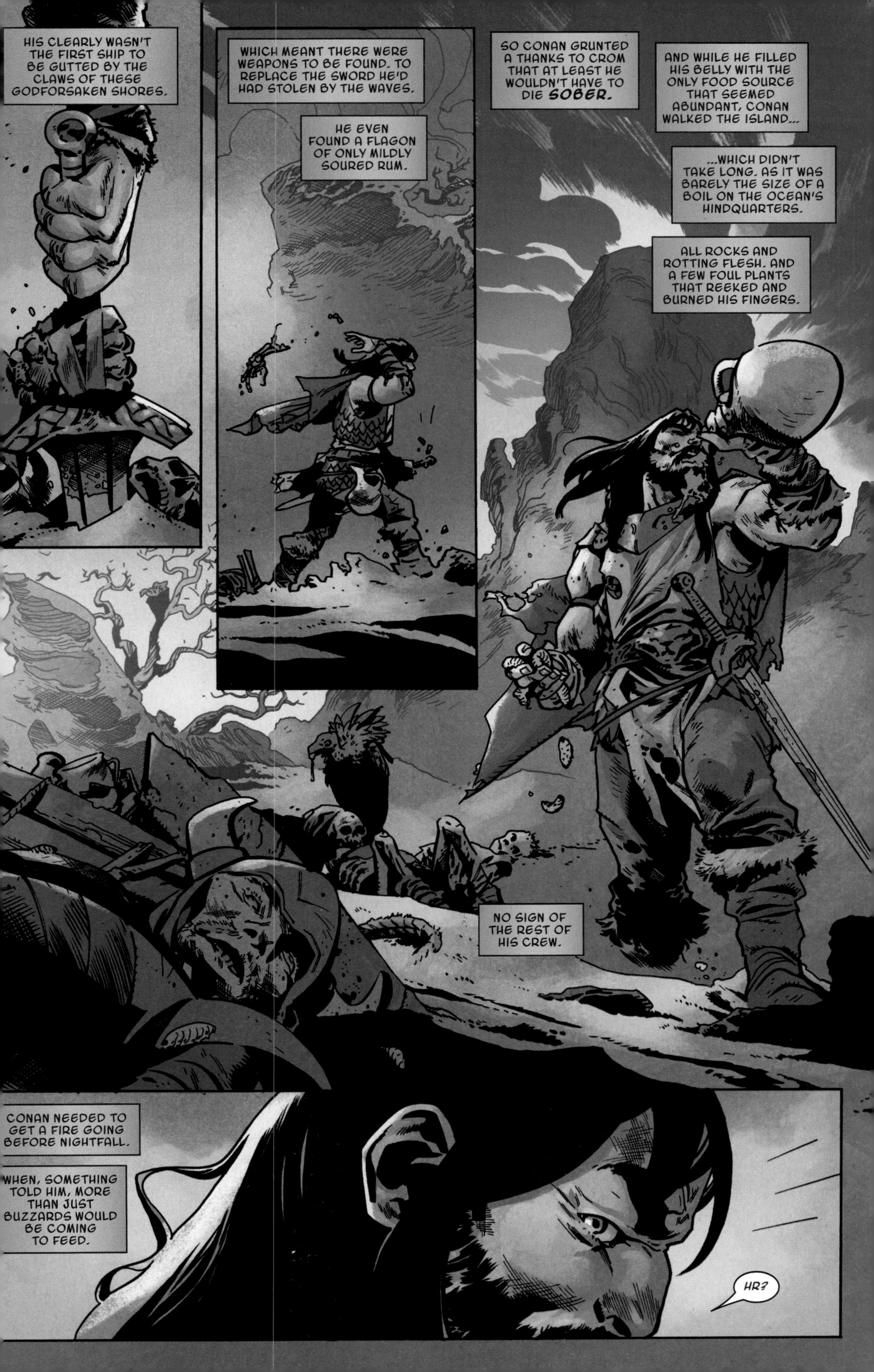
HIS CLEARLY WASN'T THE FIRST SHIP TO BE GUTTED BY THE CLAWS OF THESE GODFORSAKEN SHORES.
WHICH MEANT THERE WERE WEAPONS TO BE FOUND. TO REPLACE THE SWORD HE'D HAD STOLEN BY THE WAVES.
HE EVEN FOUND A FLAGON OF ONLY MILDLY SOURED RUM.
SO CONAN GRUNTED A THANKS TO CROM THAT AT LEAST HE WOULDN'T HAVE TO DIE SOBER.
AND WHILE HE FILLED HIS BELLY WITH THE ONLY FOOD SOURCE THAT SEEMED ABUNDANT, CONAN WALKED THE ISLAND...
...WHICH DIDN'T TAKE LONG. AS IT WAS BARELY THE SIZE OF A BOIL ON THE OCEAN'S HINDQUARTERS.
ALL ROCKS AND ROTTING FLESH. AND A FEW FOUL PLANTS THAT REEKED AND BURNED HIS FINGERS.
NO SIGN OF THE REST OF HIS CREW.
CONAN NEEDED TO GET A FIRE GOING BEFORE NIGHTFALL.
WHEN, SOMETHING TOLD HIM, MORE THAN JUST BUZZARDS WOULD BE COMING TO FEED.
HR?

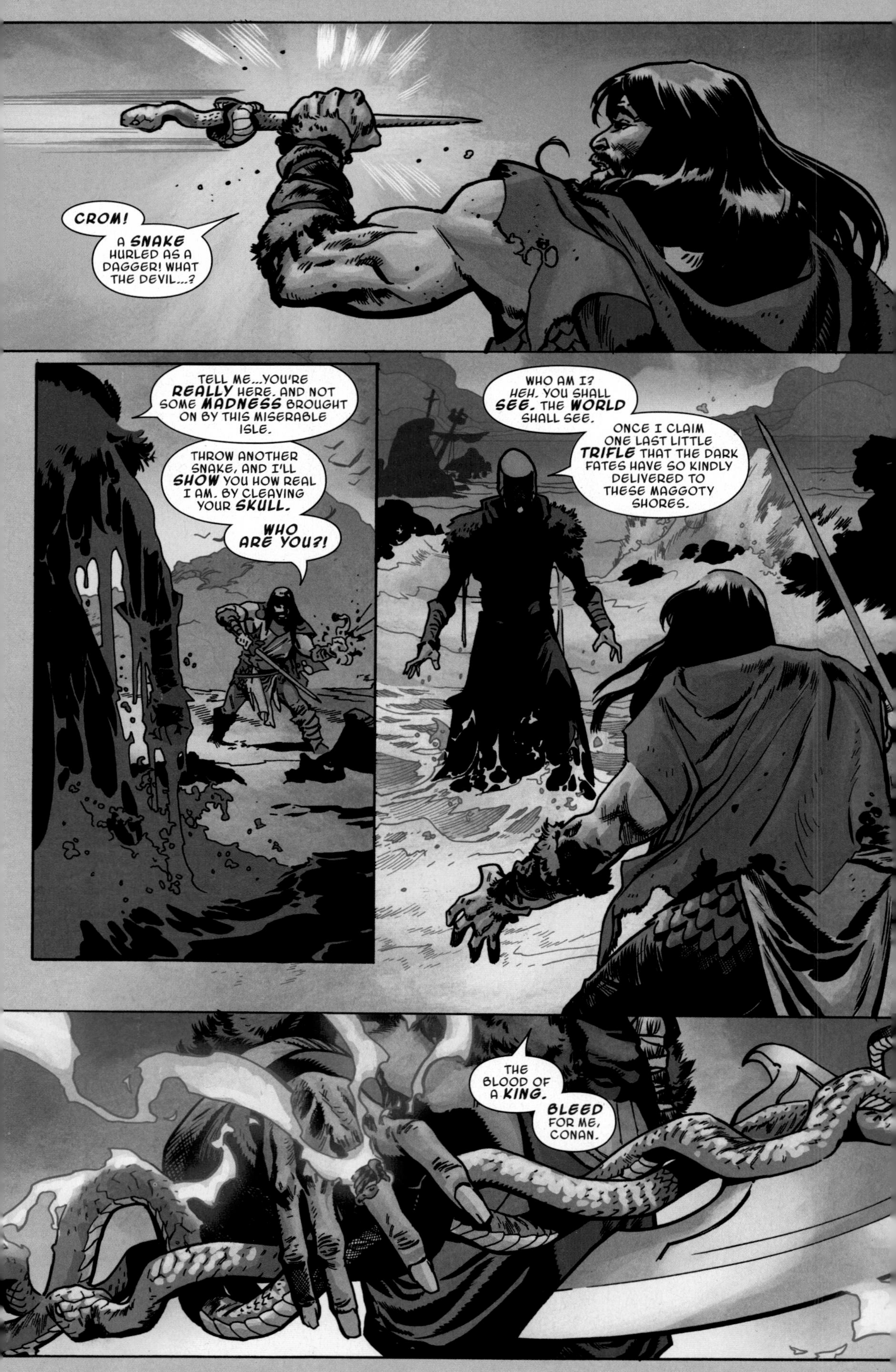
CROM!
A SNAKE HURLED AS A DAGGER! WHAT THE DEVIL...?
TELL ME...YOU'RE REALLY HERE. AND NOT SOME MADNESS BROUGHT ON BY THIS MISERABLE ISLE.
THROW ANOTHER SNAKE, AND I'LL SHOW YOU HOW REAL I AM. BY CLEAVING YOUR SKULL.
WHO ARE YOU?!
WHO AM I? HEH. YOU SHALL SEE. THE WORLD SHALL SEE.
ONCE I CLAIM ONE LAST LITTLE TRIFLE THAT THE DARK FATES HAVE SO KINDLY DELIVERED TO THESE MAGGOTY SHORES.
THE BLOOD OF A KING.
BLEED FOR ME, CONAN.

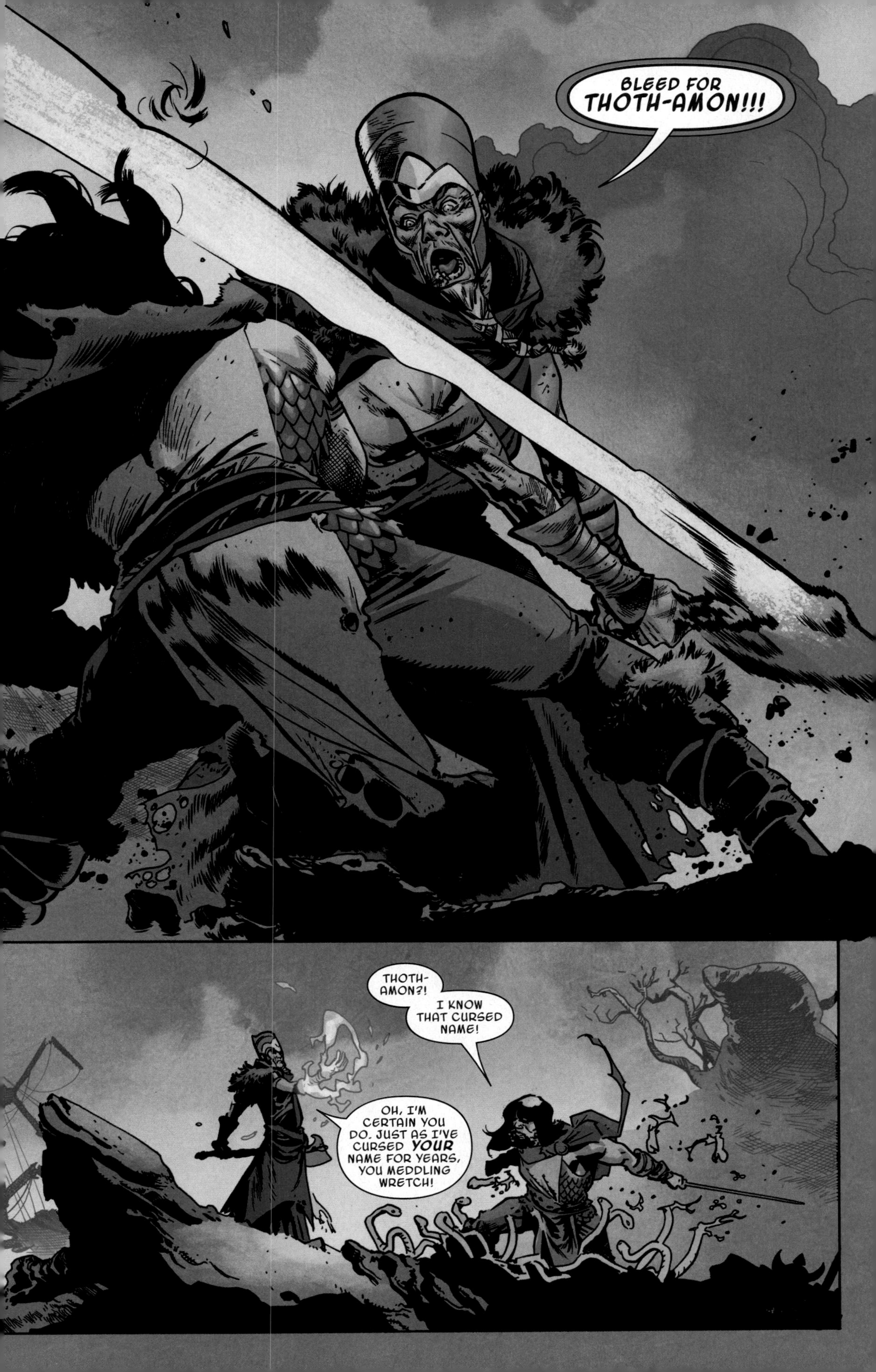
BLEED FOR THOTH-AMON!!!
THOTH-AMON?!
I KNOW THAT CURSED NAME!
OH, I'M CERTAIN YOU DO. JUST AS I'VE CURSED YOUR NAME FOR YEARS, YOU MEDDLING WRETCH!

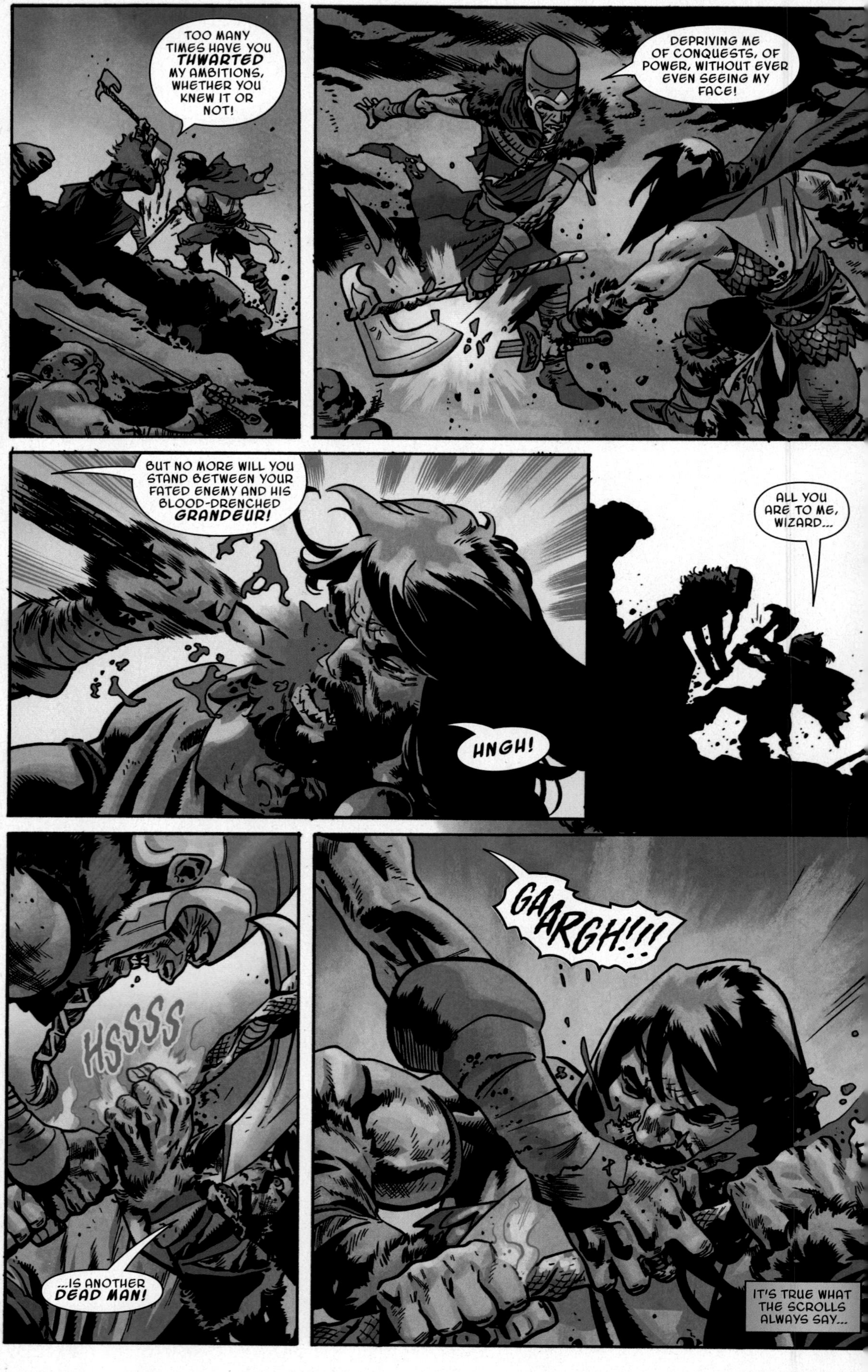
TOO MANY TIMES HAVE YOU THWARTED MY AMBITIONS, WHETHER YOU KNEW IT OR NOT!
DEPRIVING ME OF CONQUESTS, OF POWER, WITHOUT EVER EVEN SEEING MY FACE!
BUT NO MORE WILL YOU STAND BETWEEN YOUR FATED ENEMY AND HIS BLOOD-DRENCHED GRANDEUR!
HNGH!
ALL YOU ARE TO ME, WIZARD...
HSSSS
...IS ANOTHER DEAD MAN!
GAAARGH!!!!
IT'S TRUE WHAT THE SCROLLS ALWAYS SAY...

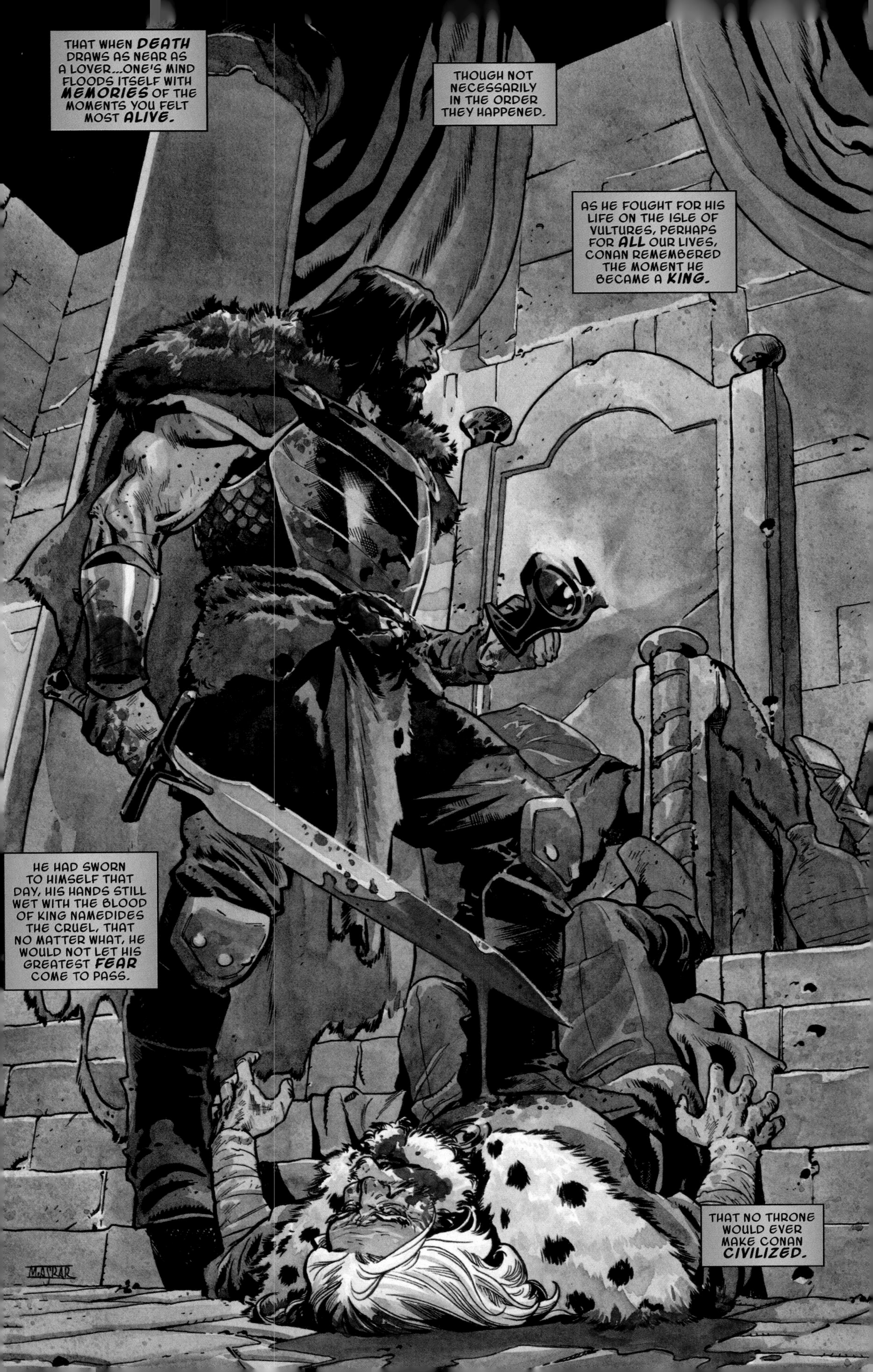
THAT WHEN DEATH DRAWS AS NEAR AS A LOVER...ONE'S MIND FLOODS ITSELF WITH MEMORIES OF THE MOMENTS YOU FELT MOST ALIVE.
THOUGH NOT NECESSARILY IN THE ORDER THEY HAPPENED.
AS HE FOUGHT FOR HIS LIFE ON THE ISLE OF VULTURES, PERHAPS FOR ALL OUR LIVES, CONAN REMEMBERED THE MOMENT HE BECAME A KING.
HE HAD SWORN TO HIMSELF THAT DAY, HIS HANDS STILL WET WITH THE BLOOD OF KING NAMEDIDES THE CRUEL, THAT NO MATTER WHAT, HE WOULD NOT LET HIS GREATEST FEAR COME TO PASS.
THAT NO THRONE WOULD EVER MAKE CONAN CIVILIZED.
M. ASRAR

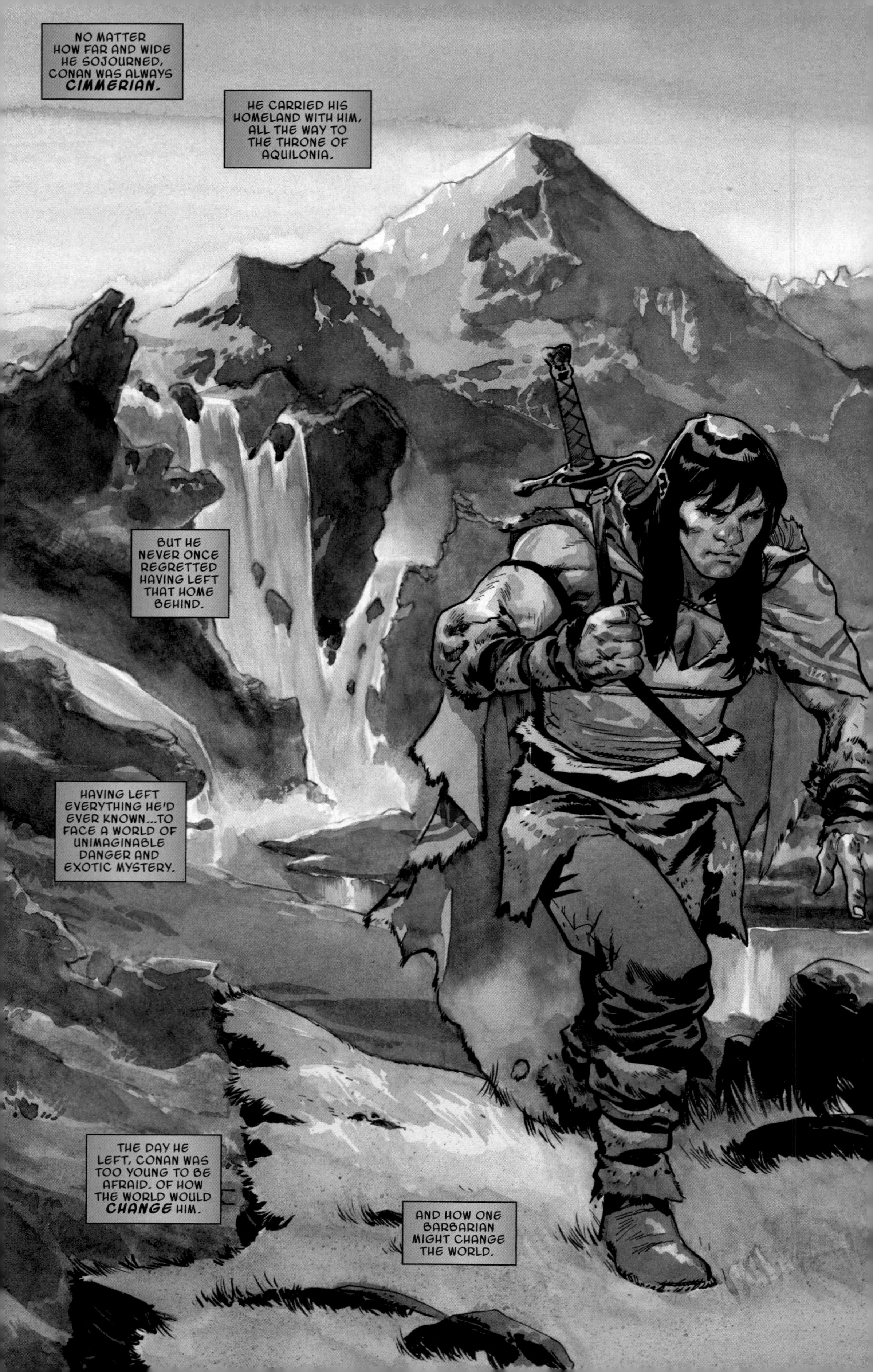
NO MATTER HOW FAR AND WIDE HE SOJOURNED, CONAN WAS ALWAYS CIMMERIAN.
HE CARRIED HIS HOMELAND WITH HIM, ALL THE WAY TO THE THRONE OF AQUILONIA.
BUT HE NEVER ONCE REGRETTED HAVING LEFT THAT HOME BEHIND.
HAVING LEFT EVERYTHING HE'D EVER KNOWN...TO FACE A WORLD OF UNIMAGINABLE DANGER AND EXOTIC MYSTERY.
THE DAY HE LEFT, CONAN WAS TOO YOUNG TO BE AFRAID. OF HOW THE WORLD WOULD CHANGE HIM.
AND HOW ONE BARBARIAN MIGHT CHANGE THE WORLD.

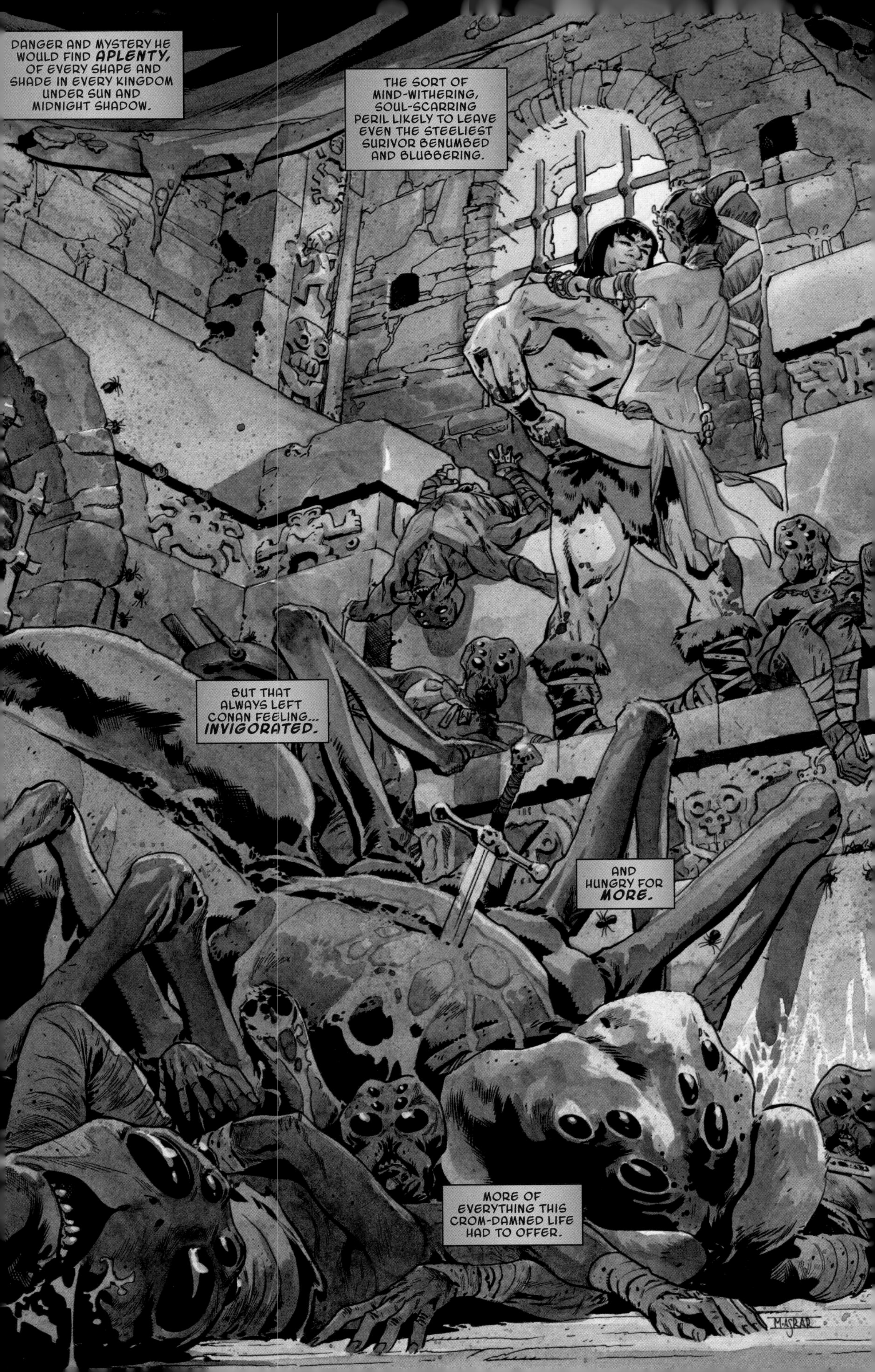
DANGER AND MYSTERY HE WOULD FIND **APLENTY,** OF EVERY SHAPE AND SHADE IN EVERY KINGDOM UNDER SUN AND MIDNIGHT SHADOW.
THE SORT OF MIND-WITHERING, SOUL-SCARRING PERIL LIKELY TO LEAVE EVEN THE STEELIEST SURIVOR BENUMBED AND BLUBBERING.
BUT THAT ALWAYS LEFT CONAN FEELING... **INVIGORATED.**
AND HUNGRY FOR **MORE.**
MORE OF EVERYTHING THIS CROM-DAMNED LIFE HAD TO OFFER.
M. ASRAR

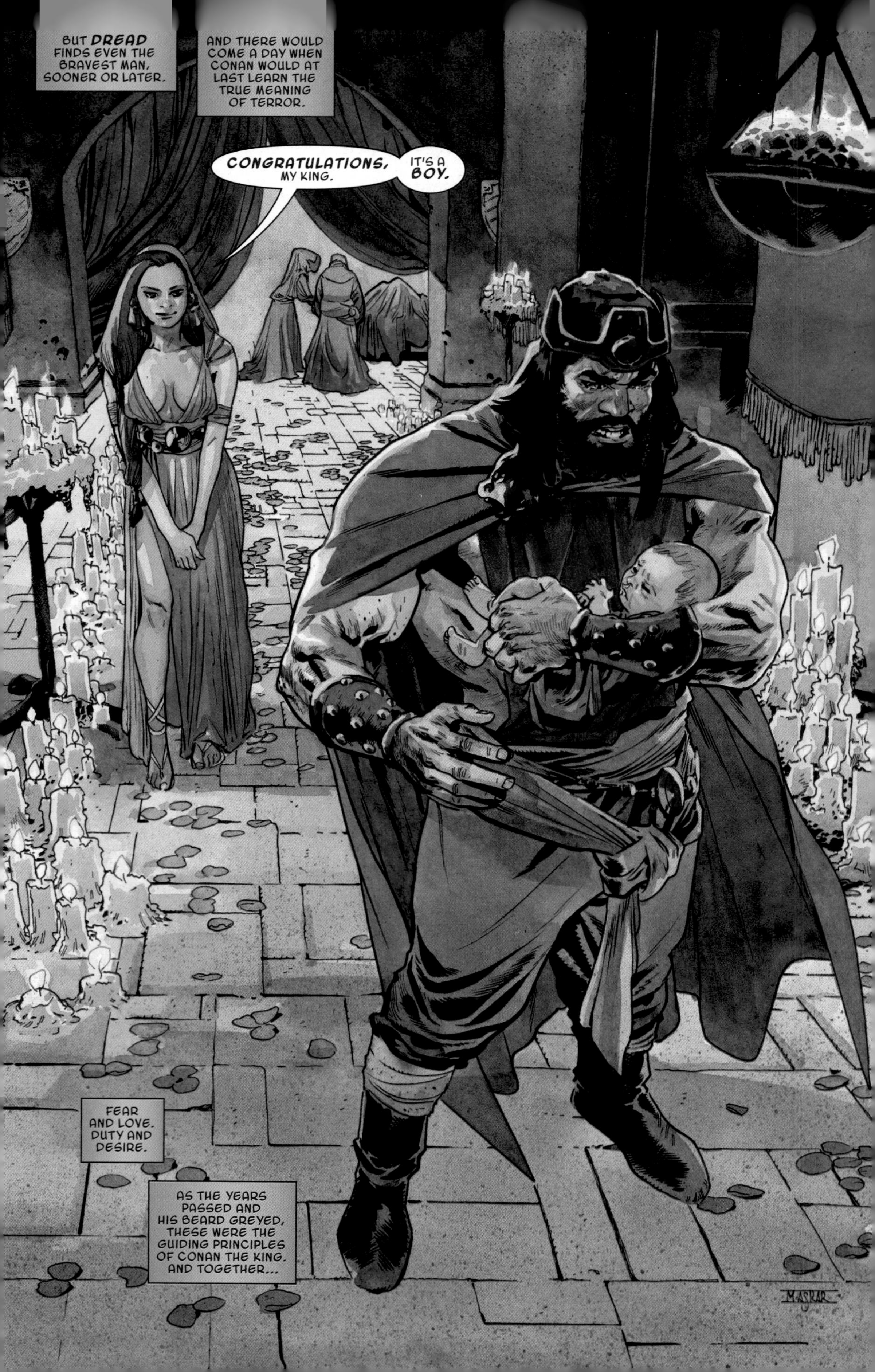
BUT DREAD FINDS EVEN THE BRAVEST MAN, SOONER OR LATER.
AND THERE WOULD COME A DAY WHEN CONAN WOULD AT LAST LEARN THE TRUE MEANING OF TERROR.
CONGRATULATIONS, MY KING.
IT'S A BOY.
FEAR AND LOVE. DUTY AND DESIRE.
AS THE YEARS PASSED AND HIS BEARD GREYED, THESE WERE THE GUIDING PRINCIPLES OF CONAN THE KING. AND TOGETHER...
MASRAR

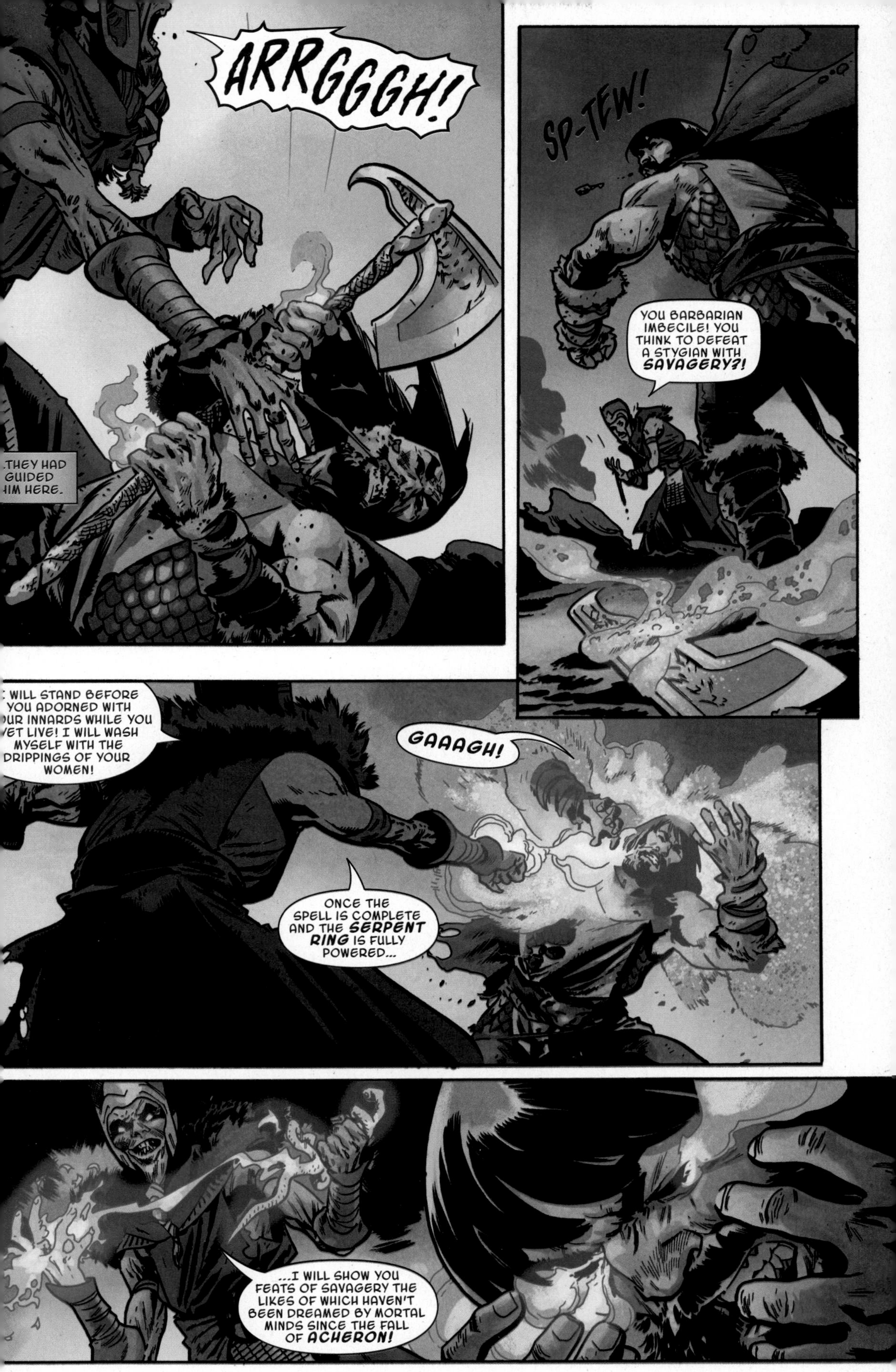
ARRGGGH!
...THEY HAD GUIDED HIM HERE.
SP-TEW!
YOU BARBARIAN IMBECILE! YOU THINK TO DEFEAT A STYGIAN WITH SAVAGERY?!
I WILL STAND BEFORE YOU ADORNED WITH YOUR INNARDS WHILE YOU YET LIVE! I WILL WASH MYSELF WITH THE DRIPPINGS OF YOUR WOMEN!
GAAAGH!
ONCE THE SPELL IS COMPLETE AND THE SERPENT RING IS FULLY POWERED...
...I WILL SHOW YOU FEATS OF SAVAGERY THE LIKES OF WHICH HAVEN'T BEEN DREAMED BY MORTAL MINDS SINCE THE FALL OF ACHERON!

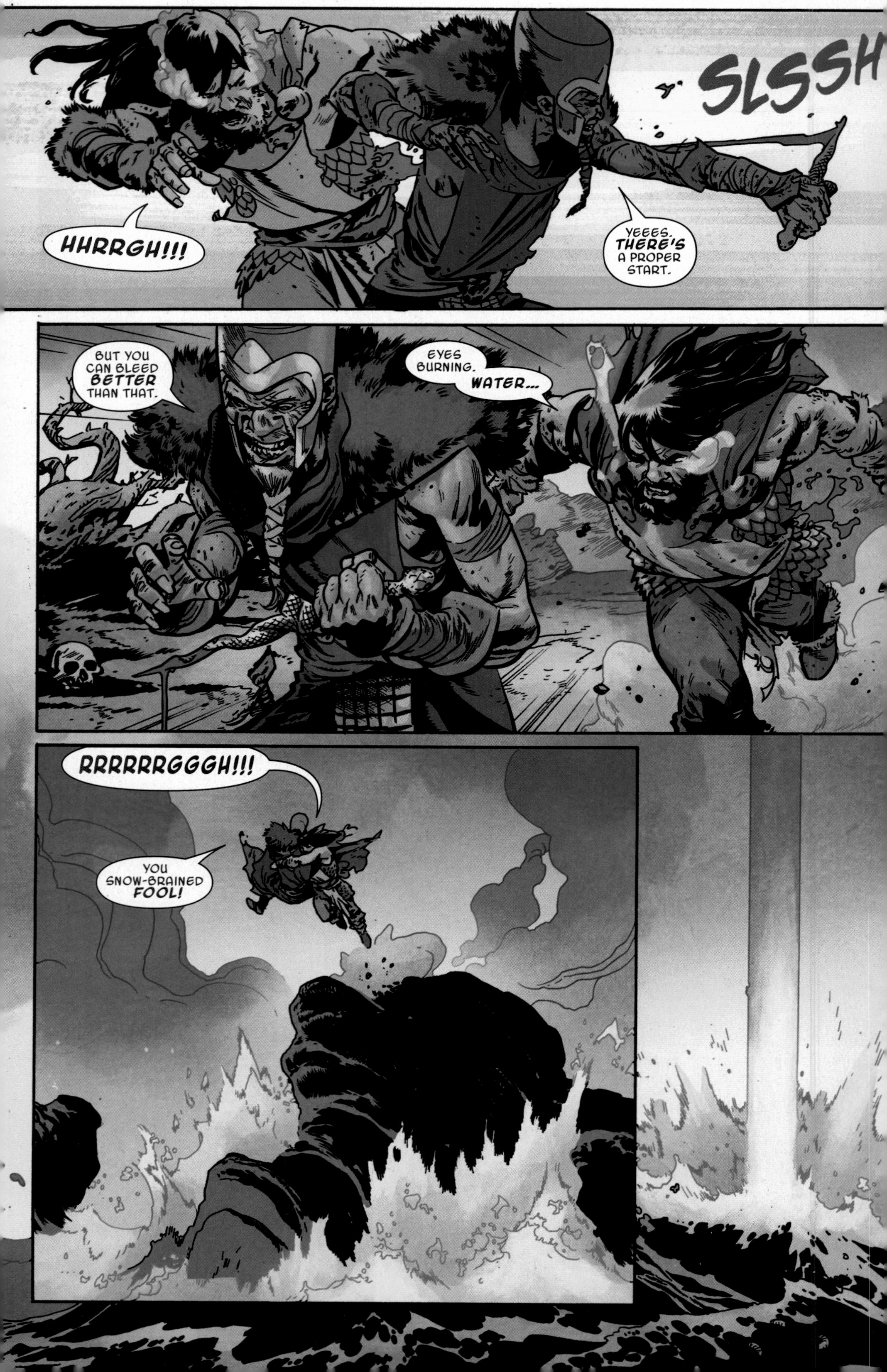
SLSSH
HHRRGH!!!
YEEES. THERE'S A PROPER START.
BUT YOU CAN BLEED BETTER THAN THAT.
EYES BURNING. WATER...
RRRRRRGGGH!!!
YOU SNOW-BRAINED FOOL!

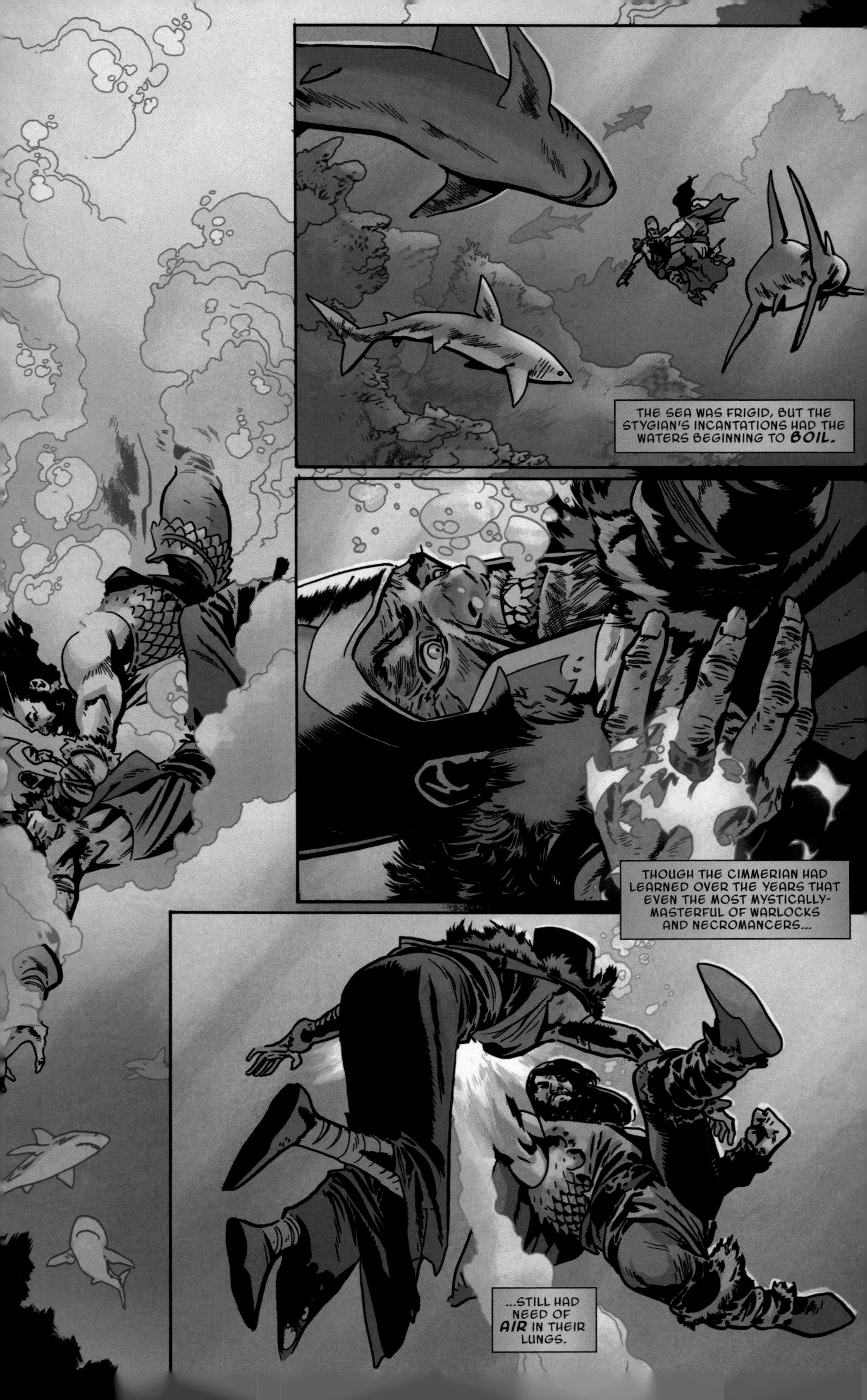
THE SEA WAS FRIGID, BUT THE STYGIAN'S INCANTATIONS HAD THE WATERS BEGINNING TO BOIL.
THOUGH THE CIMMERIAN HAD LEARNED OVER THE YEARS THAT EVEN THE MOST MYSTICALLY-MASTERFUL OF WARLOCKS AND NECROMANCERS...
...STILL HAD NEED OF AIR IN THEIR LUNGS.

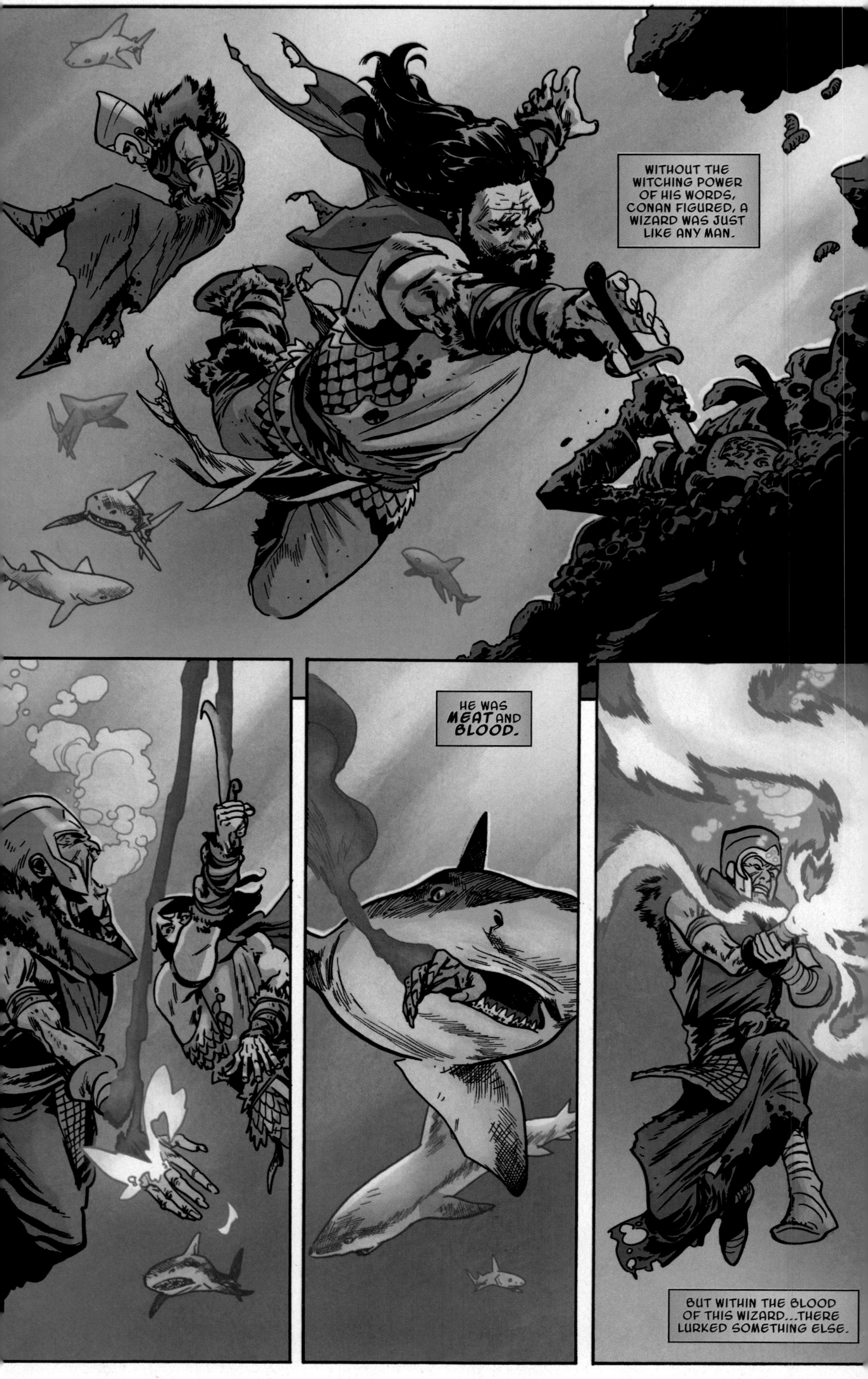
WITHOUT THE WITCHING POWER OF HIS WORDS, CONAN FIGURED, A WIZARD WAS JUST LIKE ANY MAN.
HE WAS MEAT AND BLOOD.
BUT WITHIN THE BLOOD OF THIS WIZARD...THERE LURKED SOMETHING ELSE.

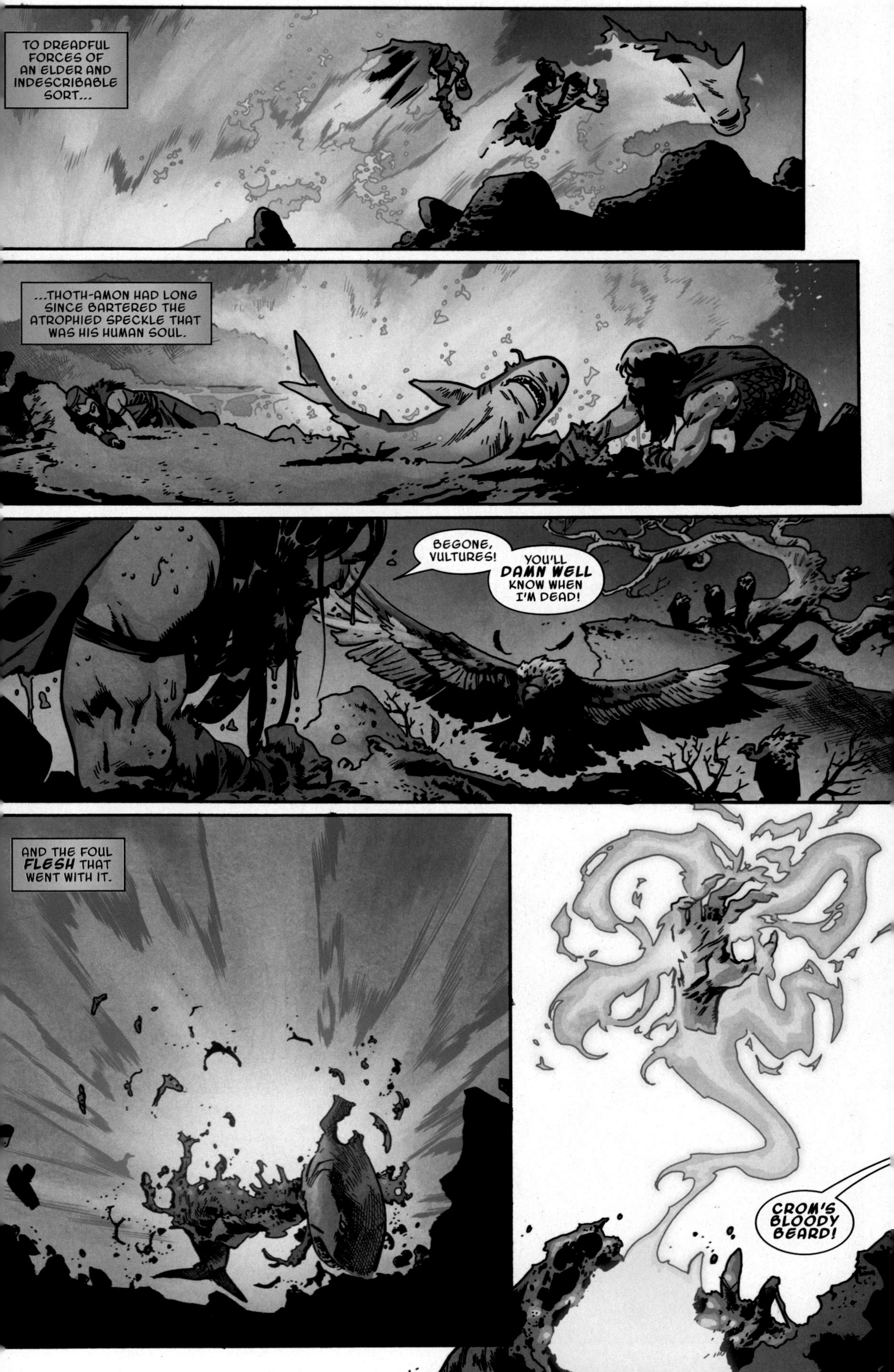
TO DREADFUL FORCES OF AN ELDER AND INDESCRIBABLE SORT...
...THOTH-AMON HAD LONG SINCE BARTERED THE ATROPHIED SPECKLE THAT WAS HIS HUMAN SOUL.
BEGONE, VULTURES!
YOU'LL DAMN WELL KNOW WHEN I'M DEAD!
AND THE FOUL FLESH THAT WENT WITH IT.
CROM'S BLOODY BEARD!

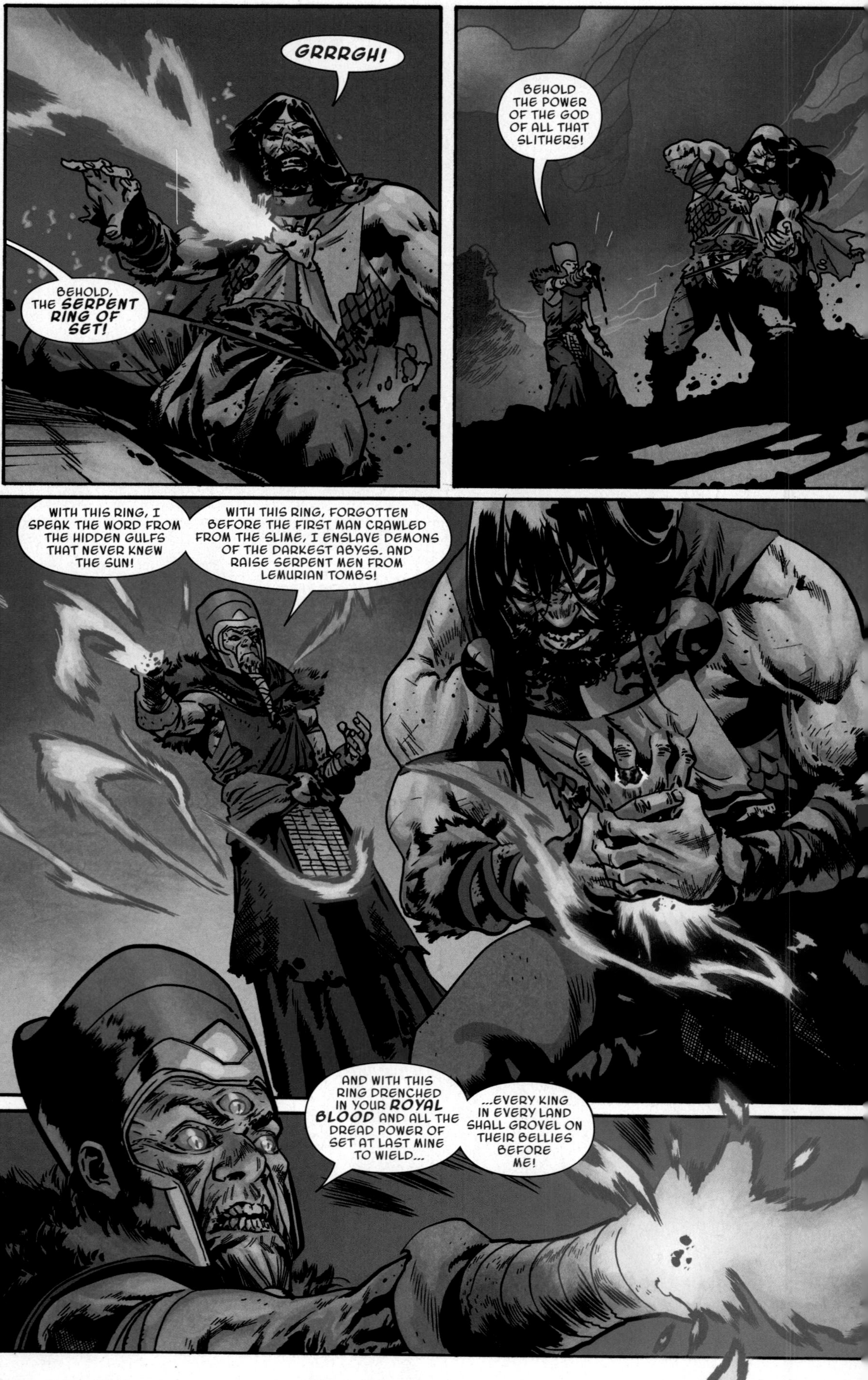
GRRRGH!
BEHOLD, THE SERPENT RING OF SET!
BEHOLD THE POWER OF THE GOD OF ALL THAT SLITHERS!
WITH THIS RING, I SPEAK THE WORD FROM THE HIDDEN GULFS THAT NEVER KNEW THE SUN!
WITH THIS RING, FORGOTTEN BEFORE THE FIRST MAN CRAWLED FROM THE SLIME, I ENSLAVE DEMONS OF THE DARKEST ABYSS. AND RAISE SERPENT MEN FROM LEMURIAN TOMBS!
AND WITH THIS RING DRENCHED IN YOUR ROYAL BLOOD AND ALL THE DREAD POWER OF SET AT LAST MINE TO WIELD...
...EVERY KING IN EVERY LAND SHALL GROVEL ON THEIR BELLIES BEFORE ME!

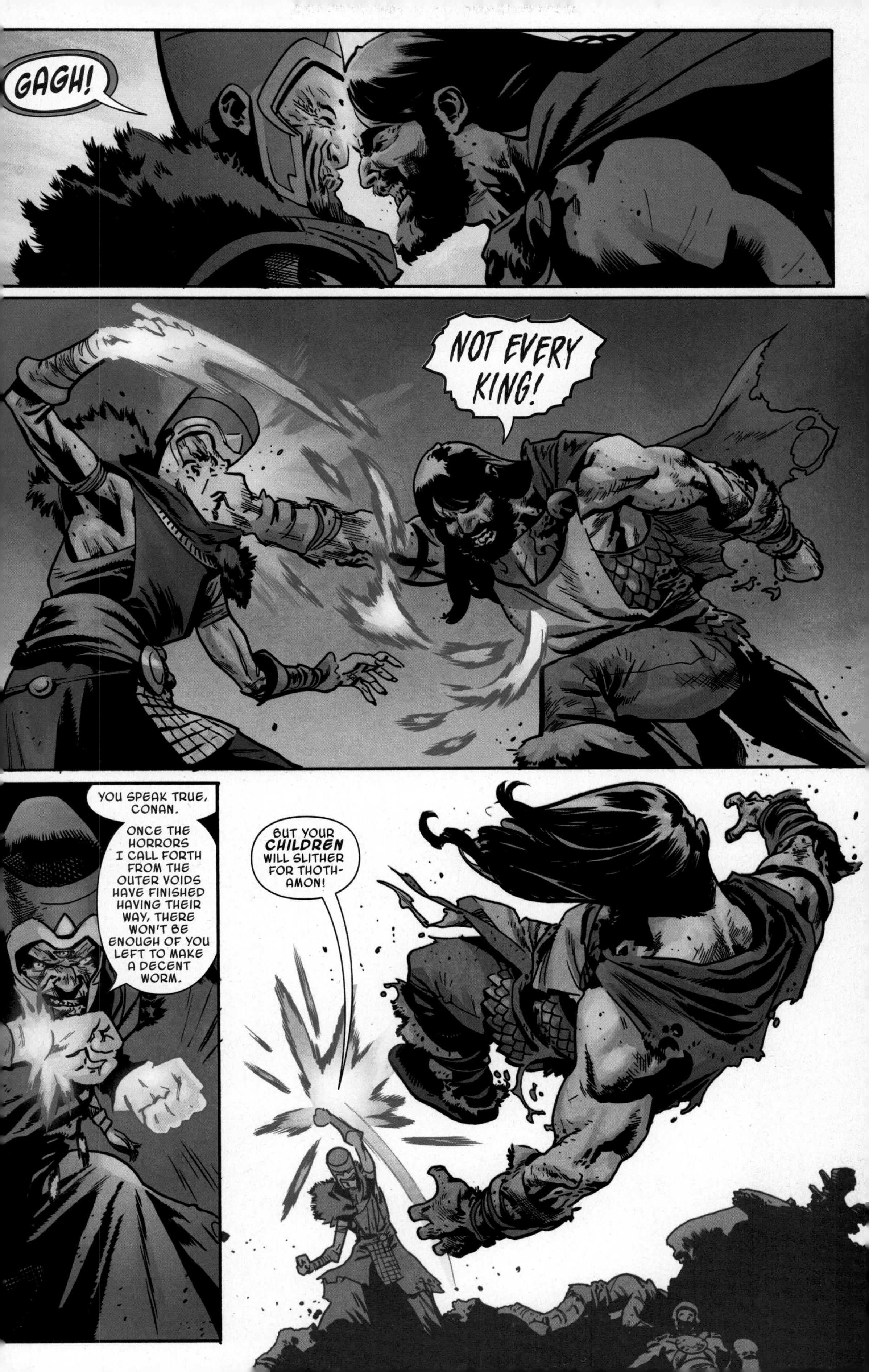
GAGH!
NOT EVERY KING!
YOU SPEAK TRUE, CONAN.
ONCE THE HORRORS I CALL FORTH FROM THE OUTER VOIDS HAVE FINISHED HAVING THEIR WAY, THERE WON'T BE ENOUGH OF YOU LEFT TO MAKE A DECENT WORM.
BUT YOUR CHILDREN WILL SLITHER FOR THOTH-AMON!

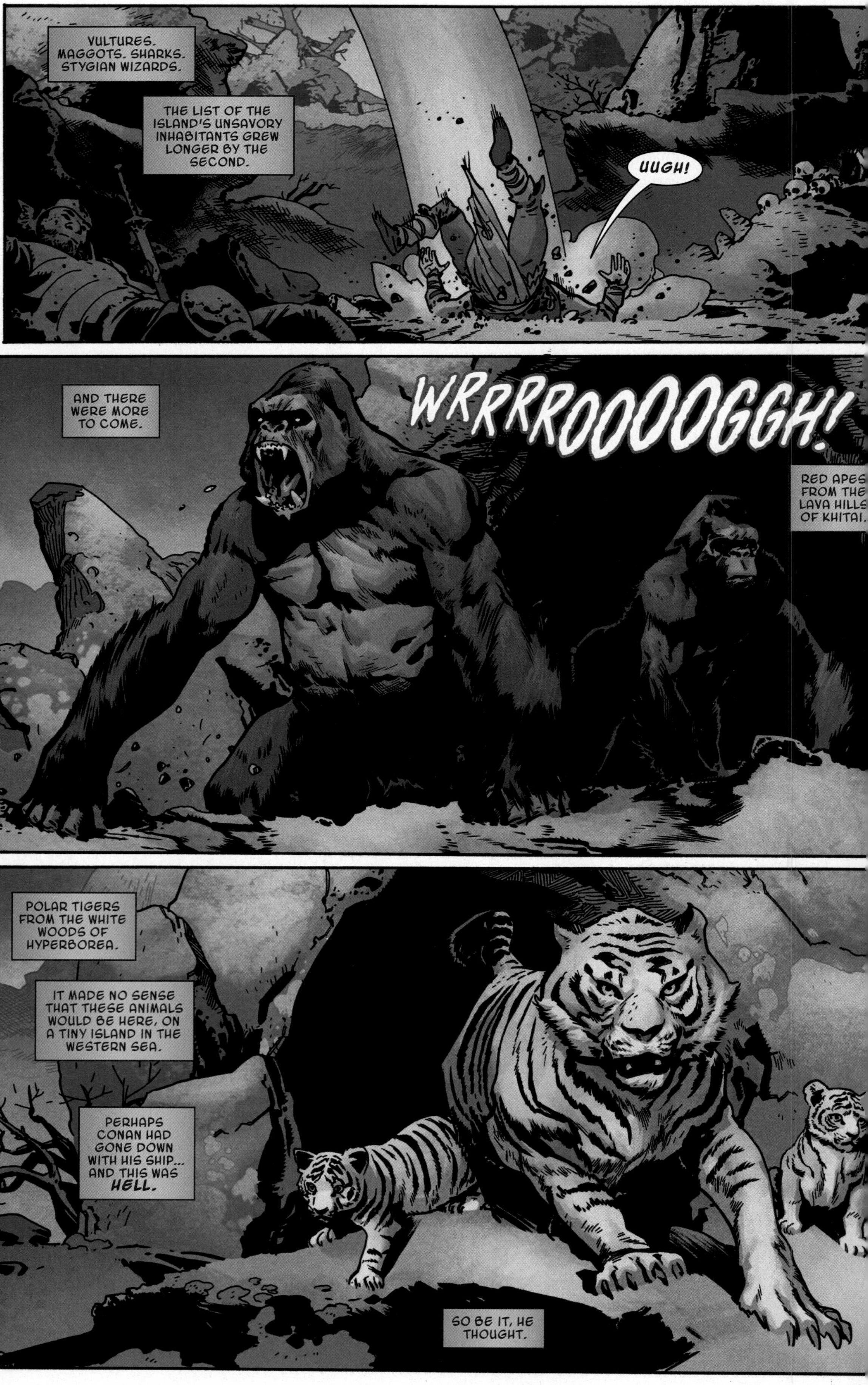
VULTURES. MAGGOTS. SHARKS. STYGIAN WIZARDS.
THE LIST OF THE ISLAND'S UNSAVORY INHABITANTS GREW LONGER BY THE SECOND.
UUGH!
AND THERE WERE MORE TO COME.
WRRRROOOOOGGH!
RED APES FROM THE LAVA HILLS OF KHITAI...
POLAR TIGERS FROM THE WHITE WOODS OF HYPERBOREA.
IT MADE NO SENSE THAT THESE ANIMALS WOULD BE HERE, ON A TINY ISLAND IN THE WESTERN SEA.
PERHAPS CONAN HAD GONE DOWN WITH HIS SHIP... AND THIS WAS HELL.
SO BE IT, HE THOUGHT.

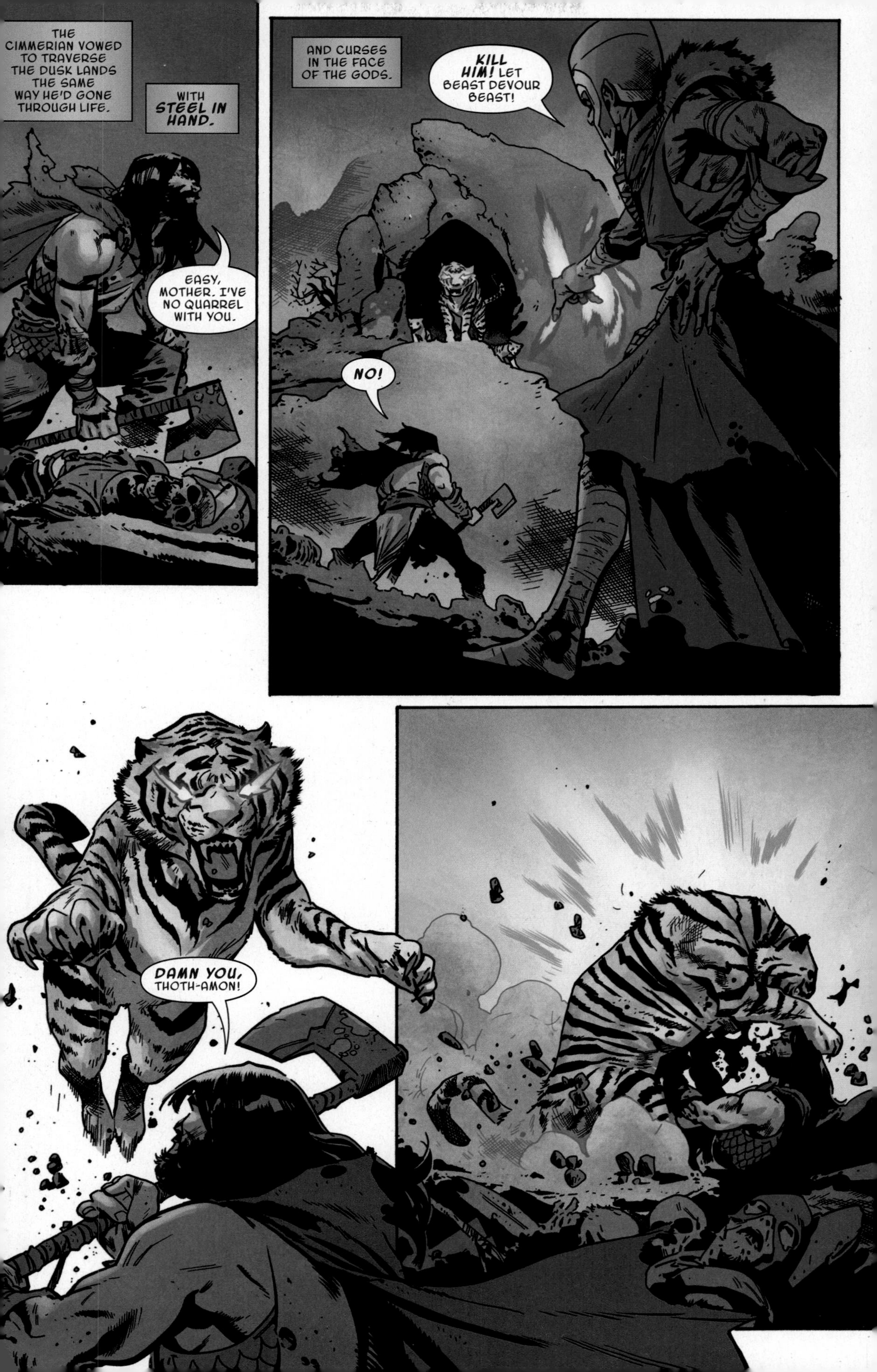
THE CIMMERIAN VOWED TO TRAVERSE THE DUSK LANDS THE SAME WAY HE'D GONE THROUGH LIFE.
WITH STEEL IN HAND.
EASY, MOTHER. I'VE NO QUARREL WITH YOU.
AND CURSES IN THE FACE OF THE GODS.
KILL HIM! LET BEAST DEVOUR BEAST!
NO!
DAMN YOU, THOTH-AMON!

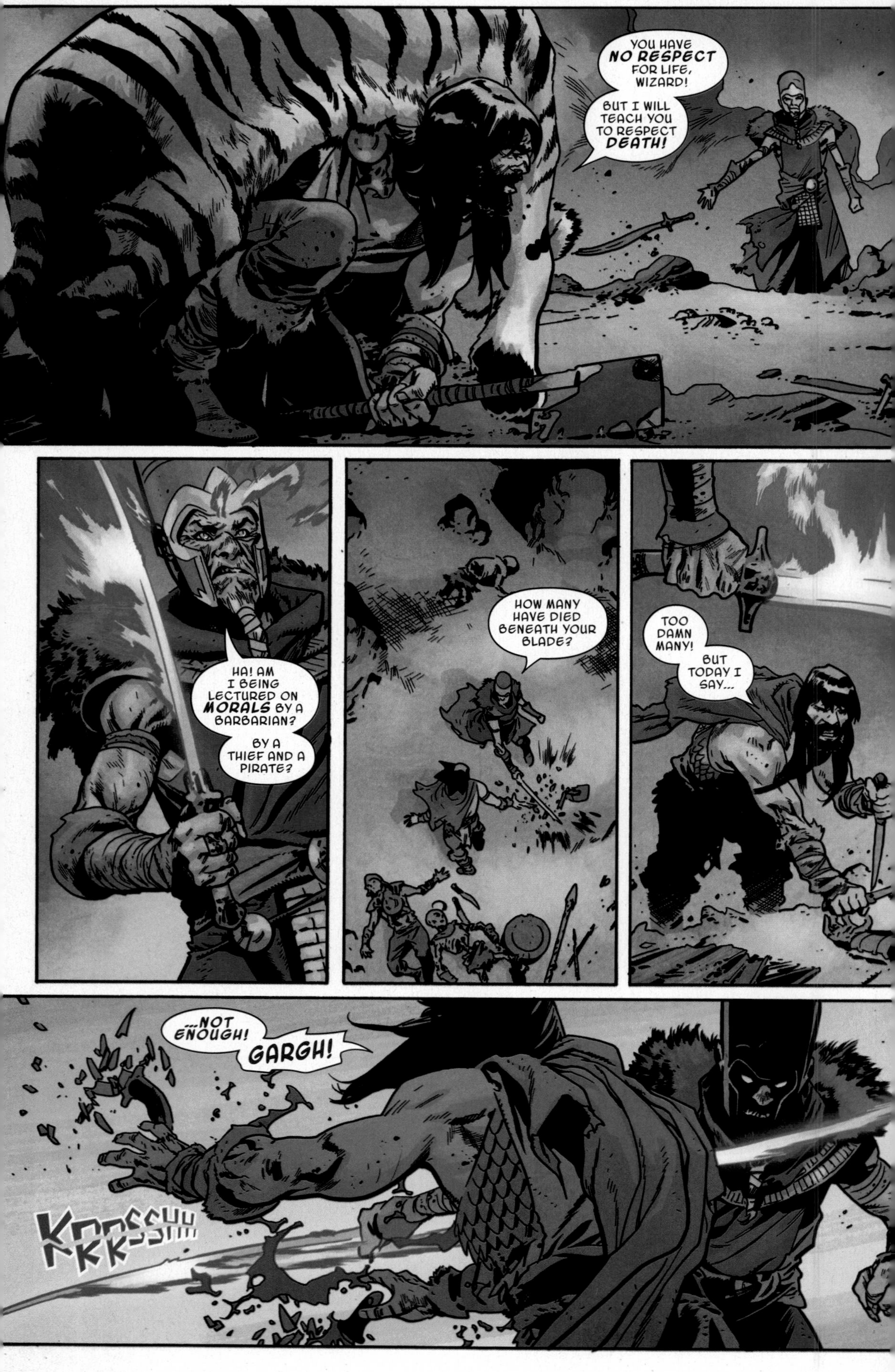
YOU HAVE NO RESPECT FOR LIFE, WIZARD!
BUT I WILL TEACH YOU TO RESPECT DEATH!
HA! AM I BEING LECTURED ON MORALS BY A BARBARIAN?
BY A THIEF AND A PIRATE?
HOW MANY HAVE DIED BENEATH YOUR BLADE?
TOO DAMN MANY!
BUT TODAY I SAY...
...NOT ENOUGH!
GARGH!

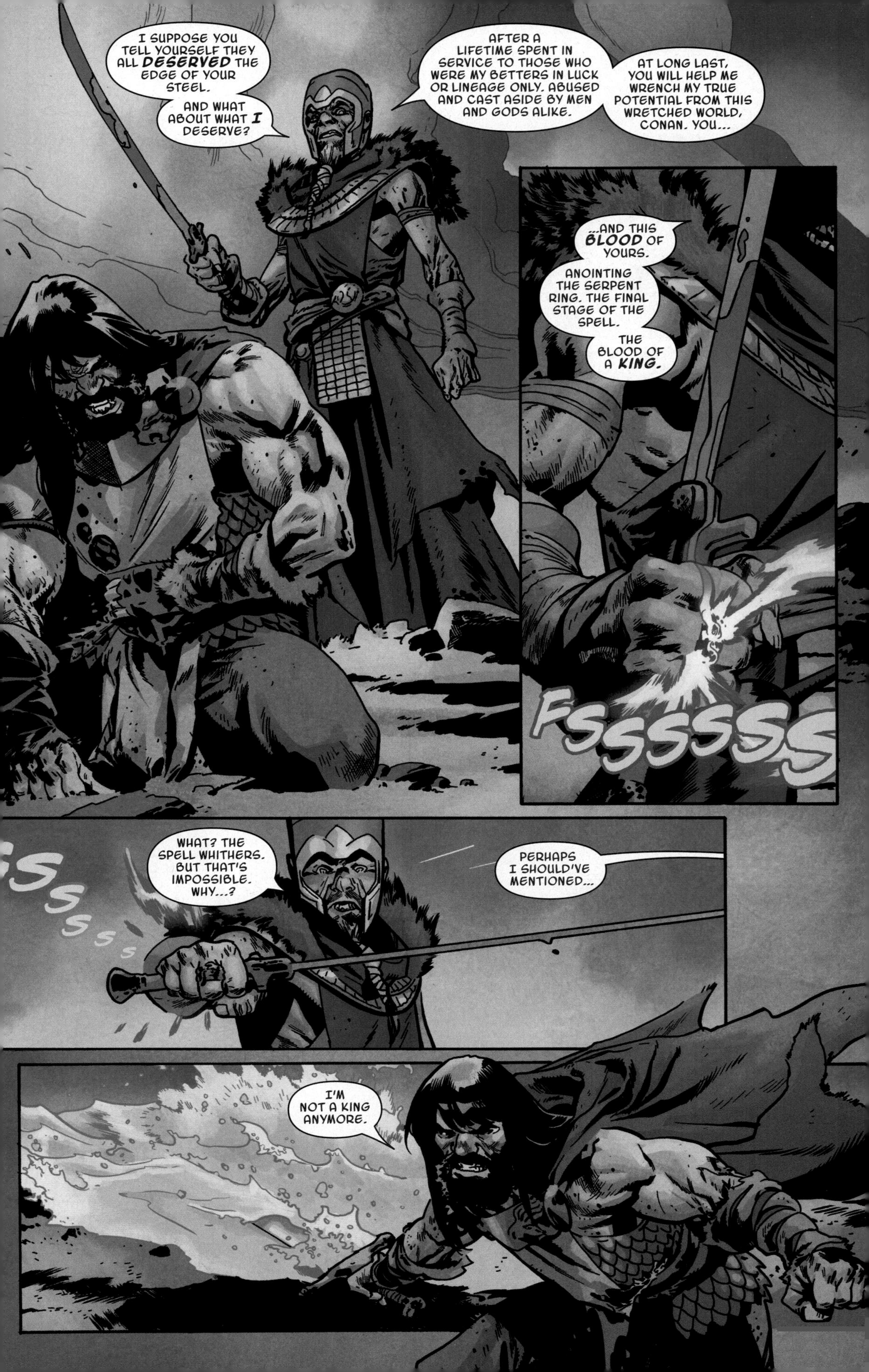
I SUPPOSE YOU TELL YOURSELF THEY ALL DESERVED THE EDGE OF YOUR STEEL.
AND WHAT ABOUT WHAT I DESERVE?
AFTER A LIFETIME SPENT IN SERVICE TO THOSE WHO WERE MY BETTERS IN LUCK OR LINEAGE ONLY. ABUSED AND CAST ASIDE BY MEN AND GODS ALIKE.
AT LONG LAST, YOU WILL HELP ME WRENCH MY TRUE POTENTIAL FROM THIS WRETCHED WORLD, CONAN. YOU...
...AND THIS BLOOD OF YOURS.
ANOINTING THE SERPENT RING. THE FINAL STAGE OF THE SPELL.
THE BLOOD OF A KING.
FSSSSSS
SSSSSS
WHAT? THE SPELL WHITHERS. BUT THAT'S IMPOSSIBLE. WHY...?
PERHAPS I SHOULD'VE MENTIONED...
I'M NOT A KING ANYMORE.

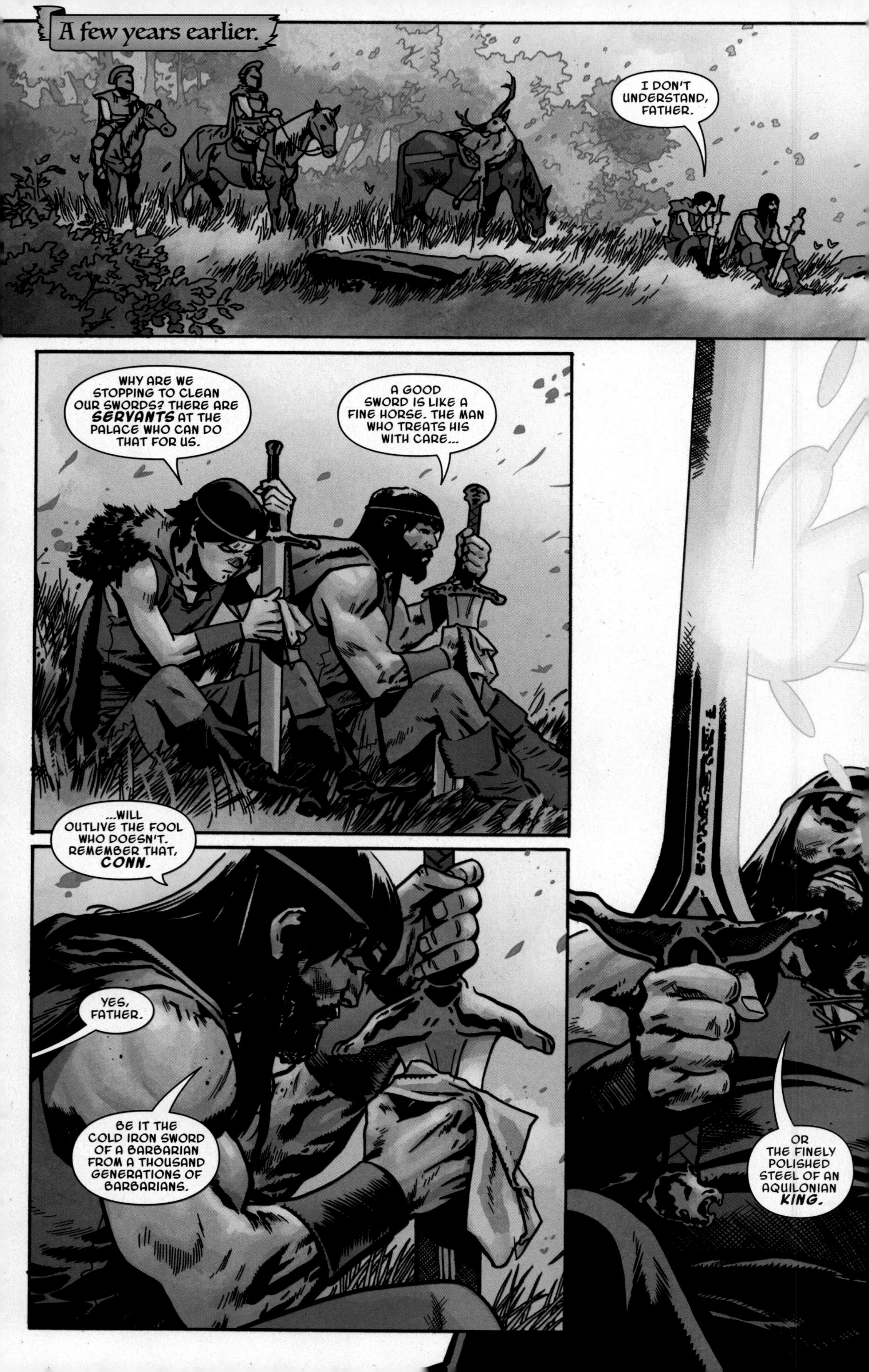
A few years earlier.
I DON'T UNDERSTAND, FATHER.
WHY ARE WE STOPPING TO CLEAN OUR SWORDS? THERE ARE SERVANTS AT THE PALACE WHO CAN DO THAT FOR US.
A GOOD SWORD IS LIKE A FINE HORSE. THE MAN WHO TREATS HIS WITH CARE...
...WILL OUTLIVE THE FOOL WHO DOESN'T. REMEMBER THAT, CONN.
YES, FATHER.
BE IT THE COLD IRON SWORD OF A BARBARIAN FROM A THOUSAND GENERATIONS OF BARBARIANS.
OR THE FINELY POLISHED STEEL OF AN AQUILONIAN KING.

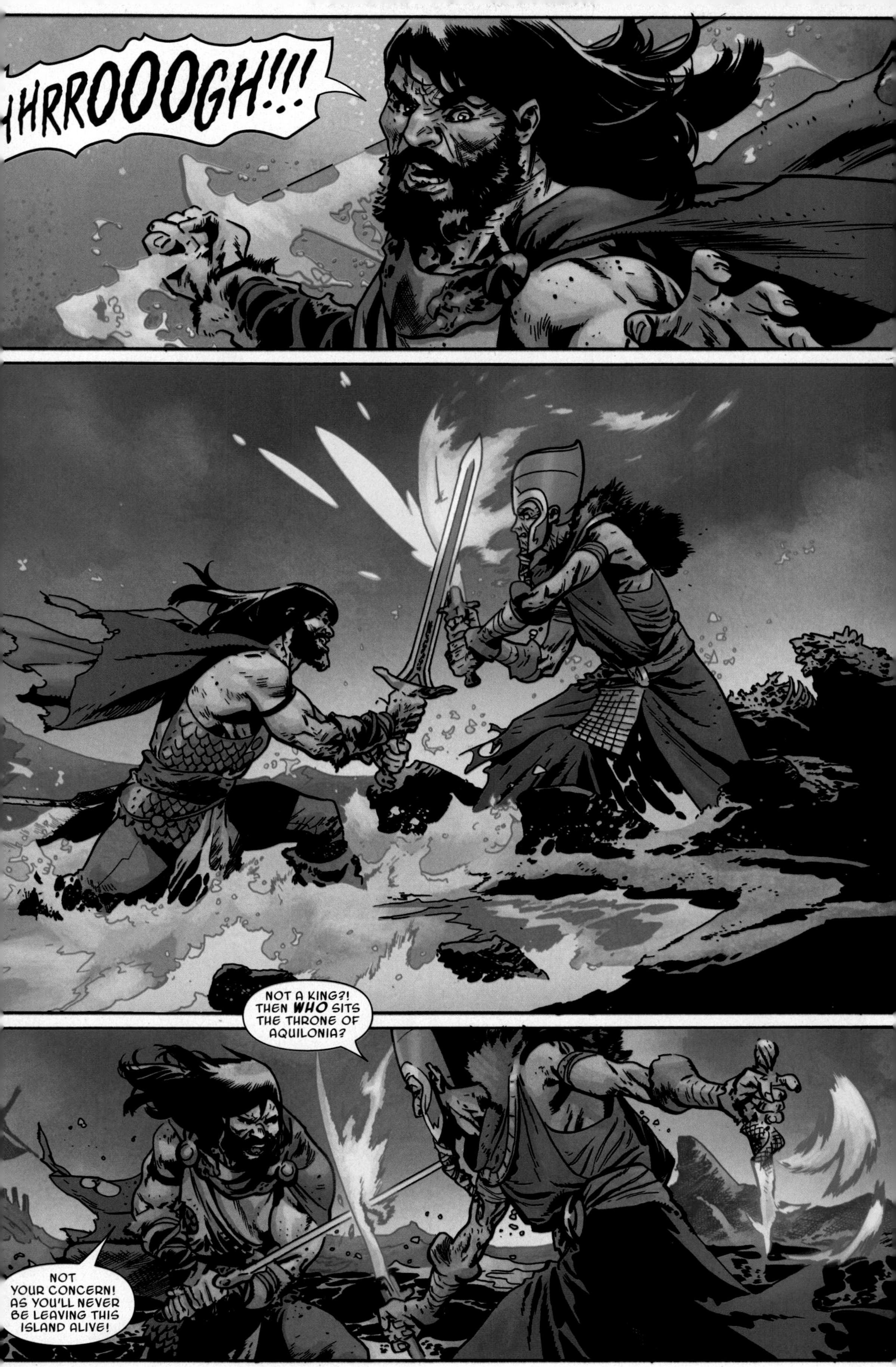
HRROOOGH!!!
NOT A KING?! THEN WHO SITS THE THRONE OF AQUILONIA?
NOT YOUR CONCERN! AS YOU'LL NEVER BE LEAVING THIS ISLAND ALIVE!

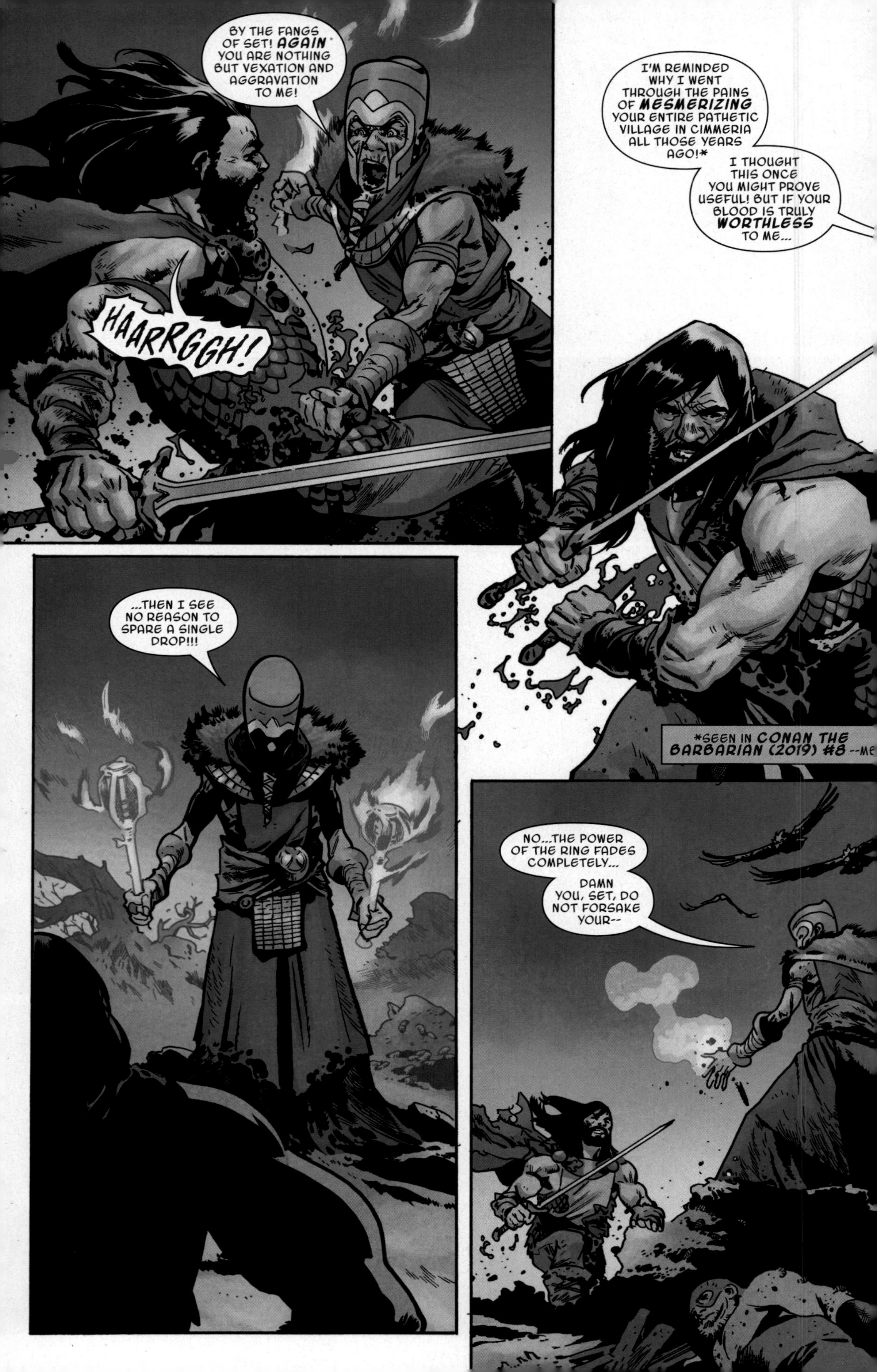
BY THE FANGS OF SET! AGAIN YOU ARE NOTHING BUT VEXATION AND AGGRAVATION TO ME!
HAARRGGH!
I'M REMINDED WHY I WENT THROUGH THE PAINS OF MESMERIZING YOUR ENTIRE PATHETIC VILLAGE IN CIMMERIA ALL THOSE YEARS AGO!*
I THOUGHT THIS ONCE YOU MIGHT PROVE USEFUL! BUT IF YOUR BLOOD IS TRULY WORTHLESS TO ME...
...THEN I SEE NO REASON TO SPARE A SINGLE DROP!!!
*SEEN IN CONAN THE BARBARIAN (2019) #8 --ME
NO...THE POWER OF THE RING FADES COMPLETELY...
DAMN YOU, SET, DO NOT FORSAKE YOUR--

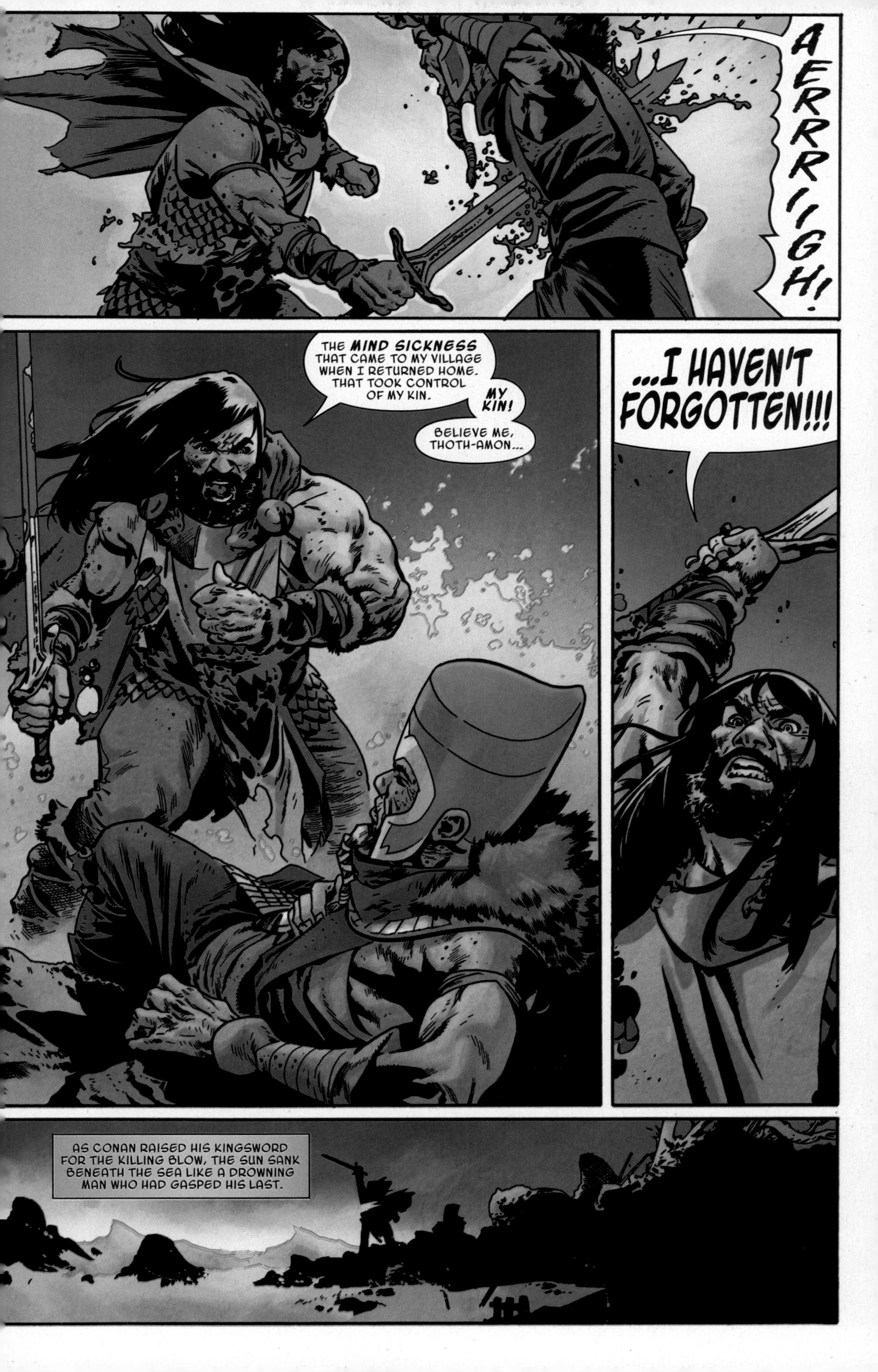
AERRRIIGH!
THE MIND SICKNESS THAT CAME TO MY VILLAGE WHEN I RETURNED HOME. THAT TOOK CONTROL OF MY KIN.
MY KIN!
BELIEVE ME, THOTH-AMON...
...I HAVEN'T FORGOTTEN!!!
AS CONAN RAISED HIS KINGSWORD FOR THE KILLING BLOW, THE SUN SANK BENEATH THE SEA LIKE A DROWNING MAN WHO HAD GASPED HIS LAST.

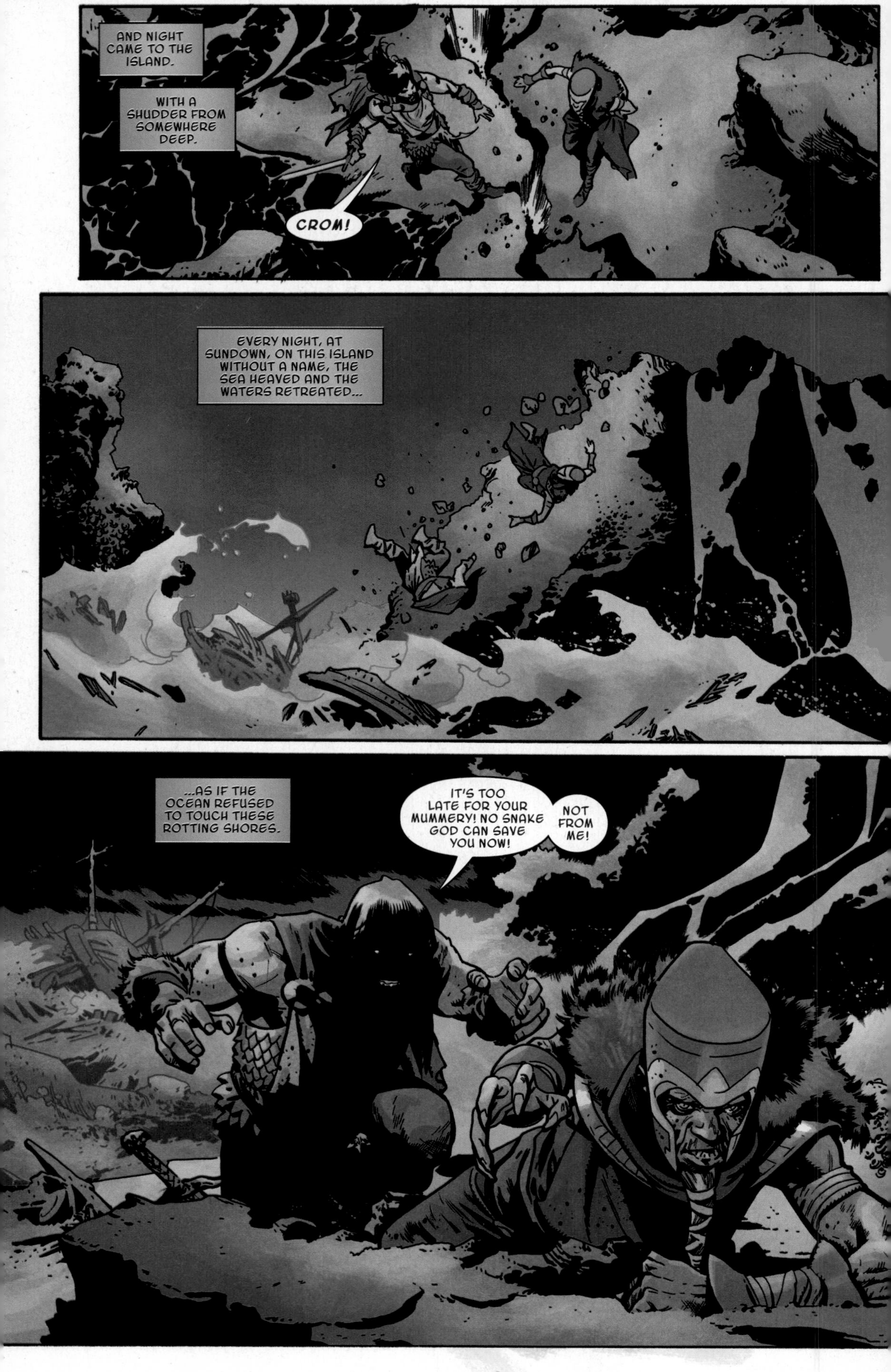
AND NIGHT CAME TO THE ISLAND.
WITH A SHUDDER FROM SOMEWHERE DEEP.
CROM!
EVERY NIGHT, AT SUNDOWN, ON THIS ISLAND WITHOUT A NAME, THE SEA HEAVED AND THE WATERS RETREATED...
...AS IF THE OCEAN REFUSED TO TOUCH THESE ROTTING SHORES.
IT'S TOO LATE FOR YOUR MUMMERY! NO SNAKE GOD CAN SAVE YOU NOW!
NOT FROM ME!

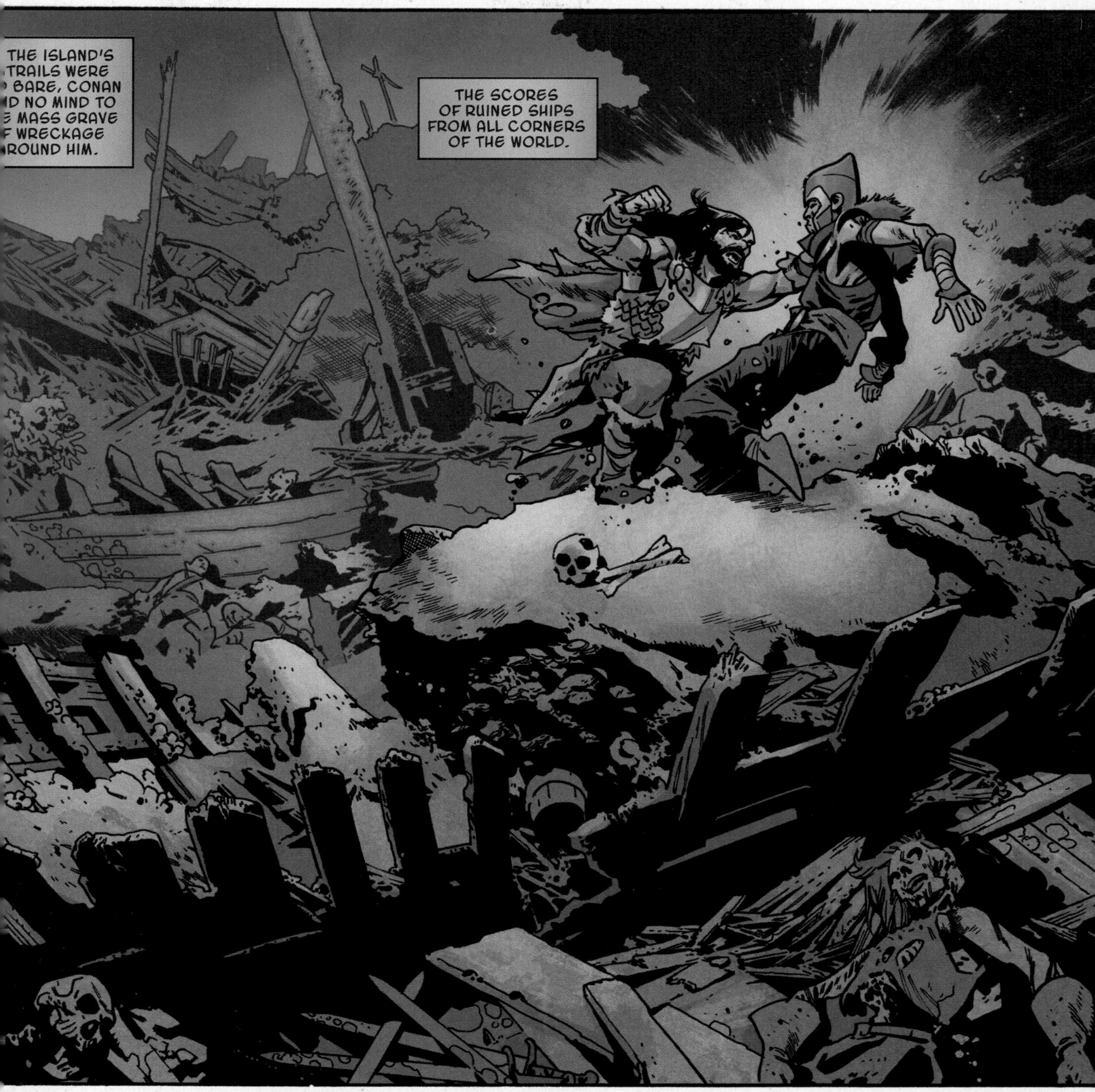
THE ISLAND'S TRAILS WERE SO BARE, CONAN PAID NO MIND TO THE MASS GRAVE OF WRECKAGE AROUND HIM.
THE SCORES OF RUINED SHIPS FROM ALL CORNERS OF THE WORLD.

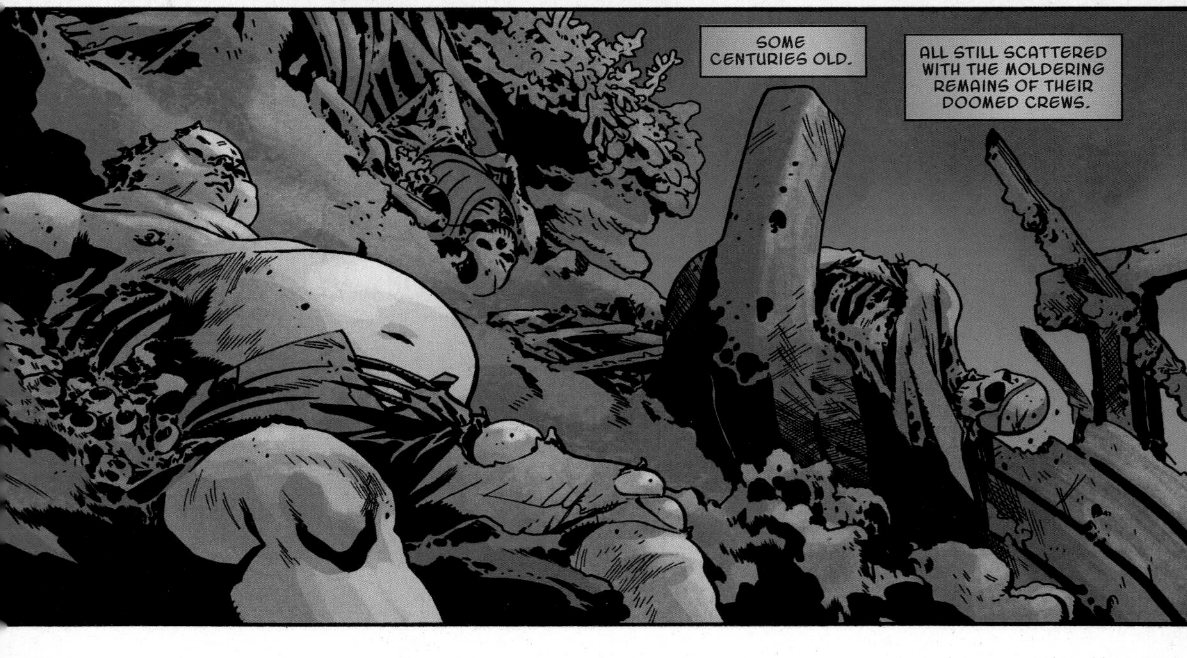
SOME CENTURIES OLD.
ALL STILL SCATTERED WITH THE MOLDERING REMAINS OF THEIR DOOMED CREWS.

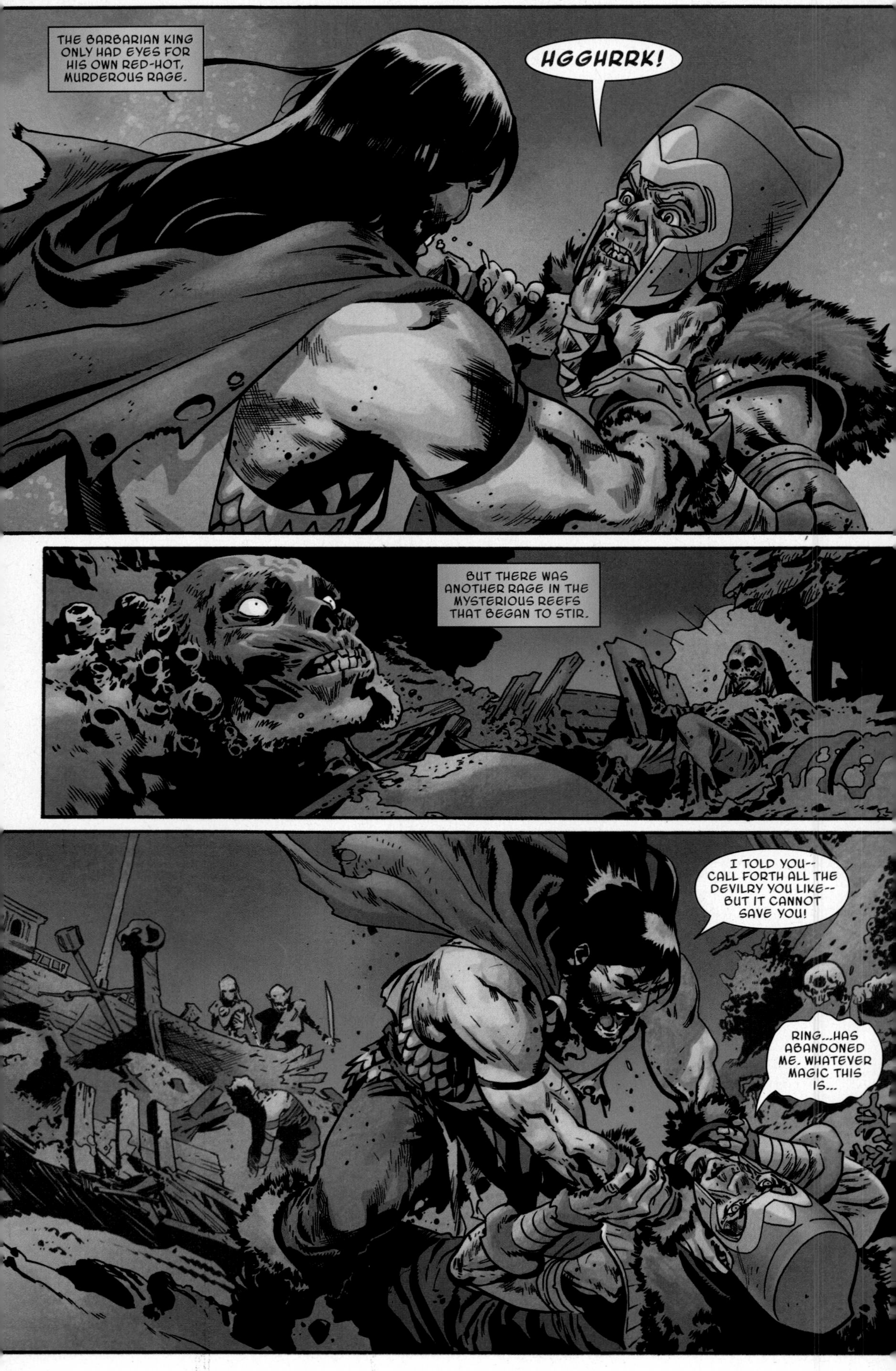
THE BARBARIAN KING ONLY HAD EYES FOR HIS OWN RED-HOT, MURDEROUS RAGE.
HGGHRRK!
BUT THERE WAS ANOTHER RAGE IN THE MYSTERIOUS REEFS THAT BEGAN TO STIR.
I TOLD YOU-- CALL FORTH ALL THE DEVILRY YOU LIKE-- BUT IT CANNOT SAVE YOU!
RING...HAS ABANDONED ME. WHATEVER MAGIC THIS IS...

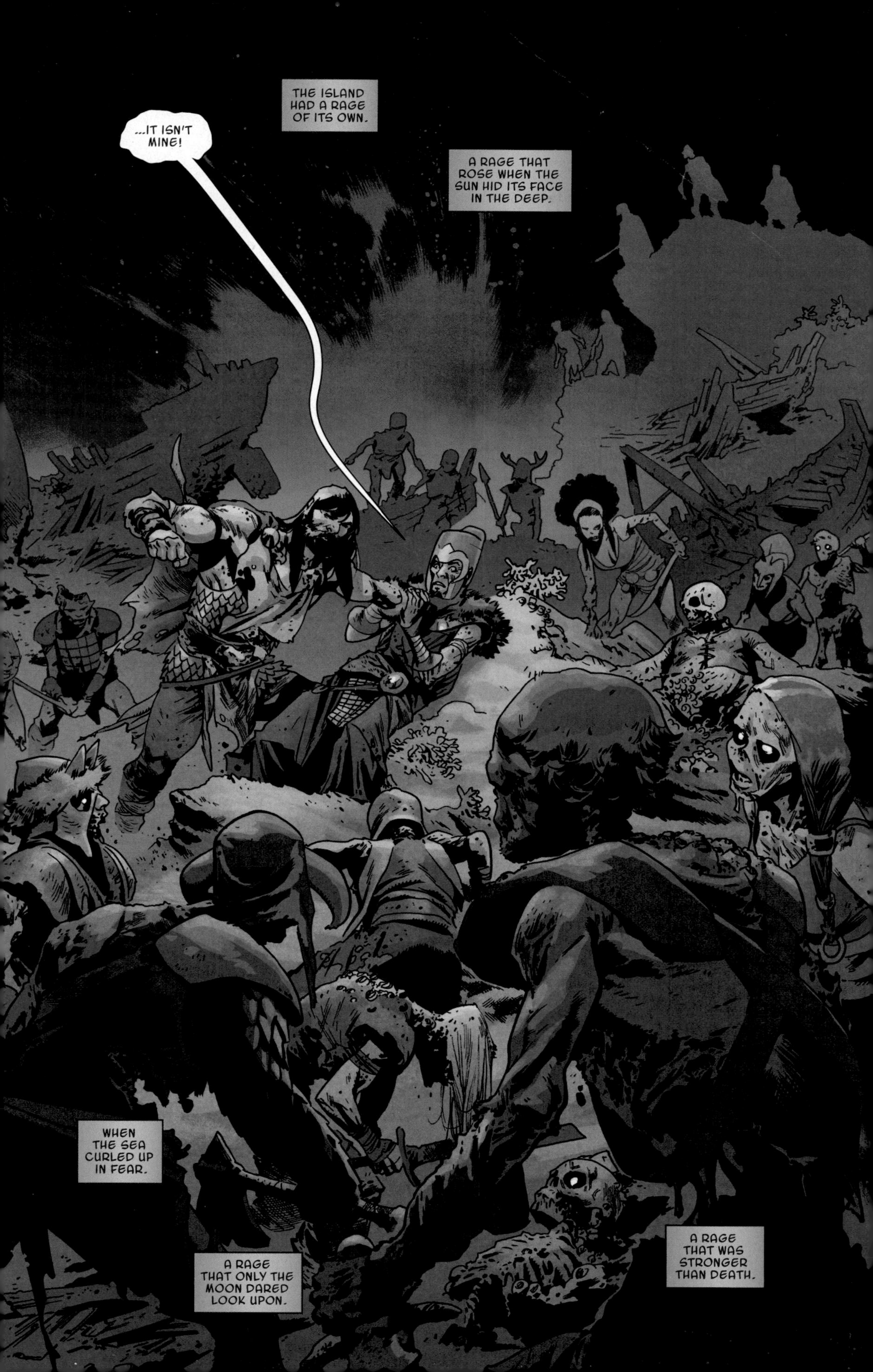
...IT ISN'T MINE!
THE ISLAND HAD A RAGE OF ITS OWN.
A RAGE THAT ROSE WHEN THE SUN HID ITS FACE IN THE DEEP.
WHEN THE SEA CURLED UP IN FEAR.
A RAGE THAT ONLY THE MOON DARED LOOK UPON.
A RAGE THAT WAS STRONGER THAN DEATH.

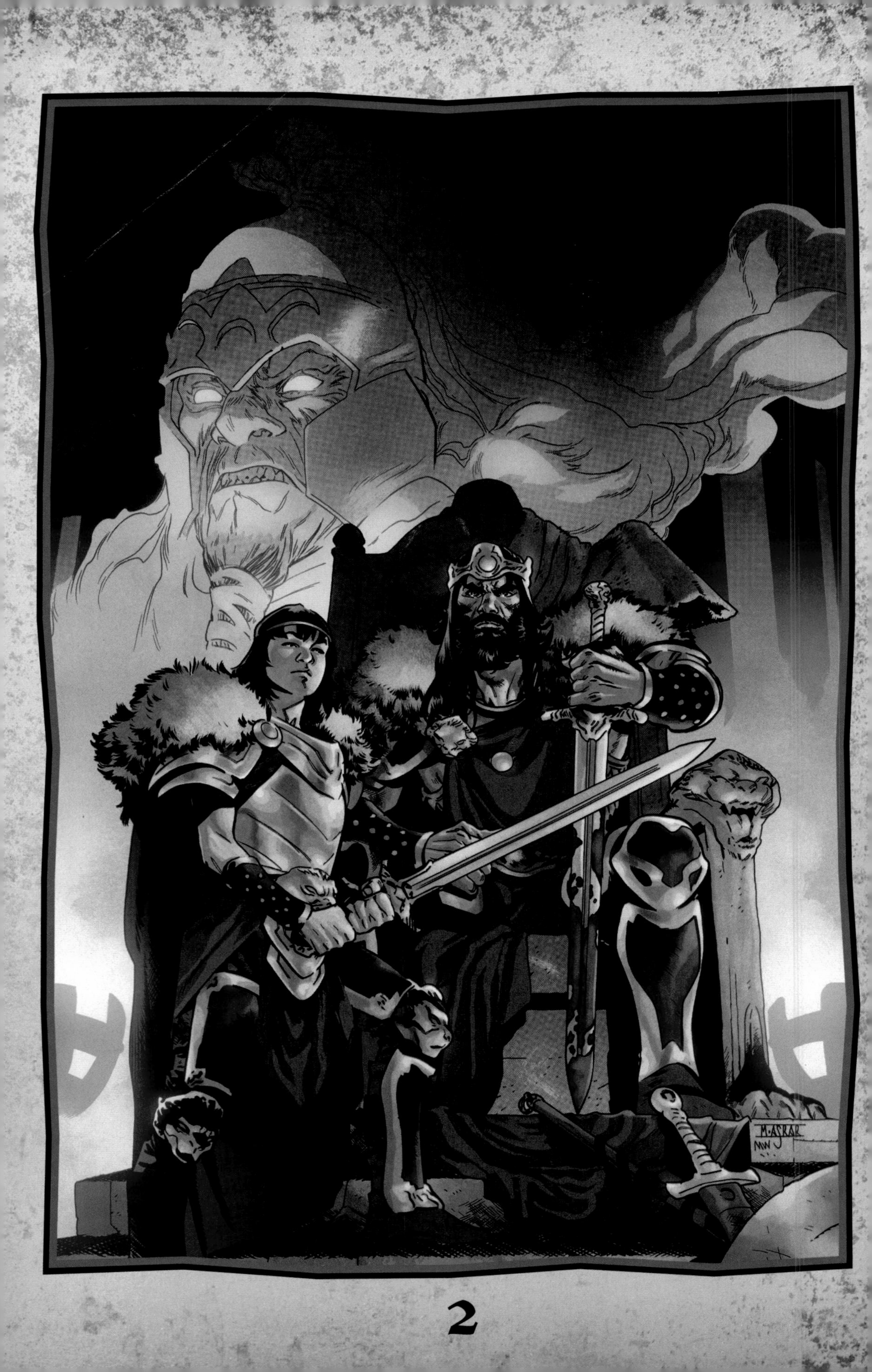
M.ASRAR
MW

2

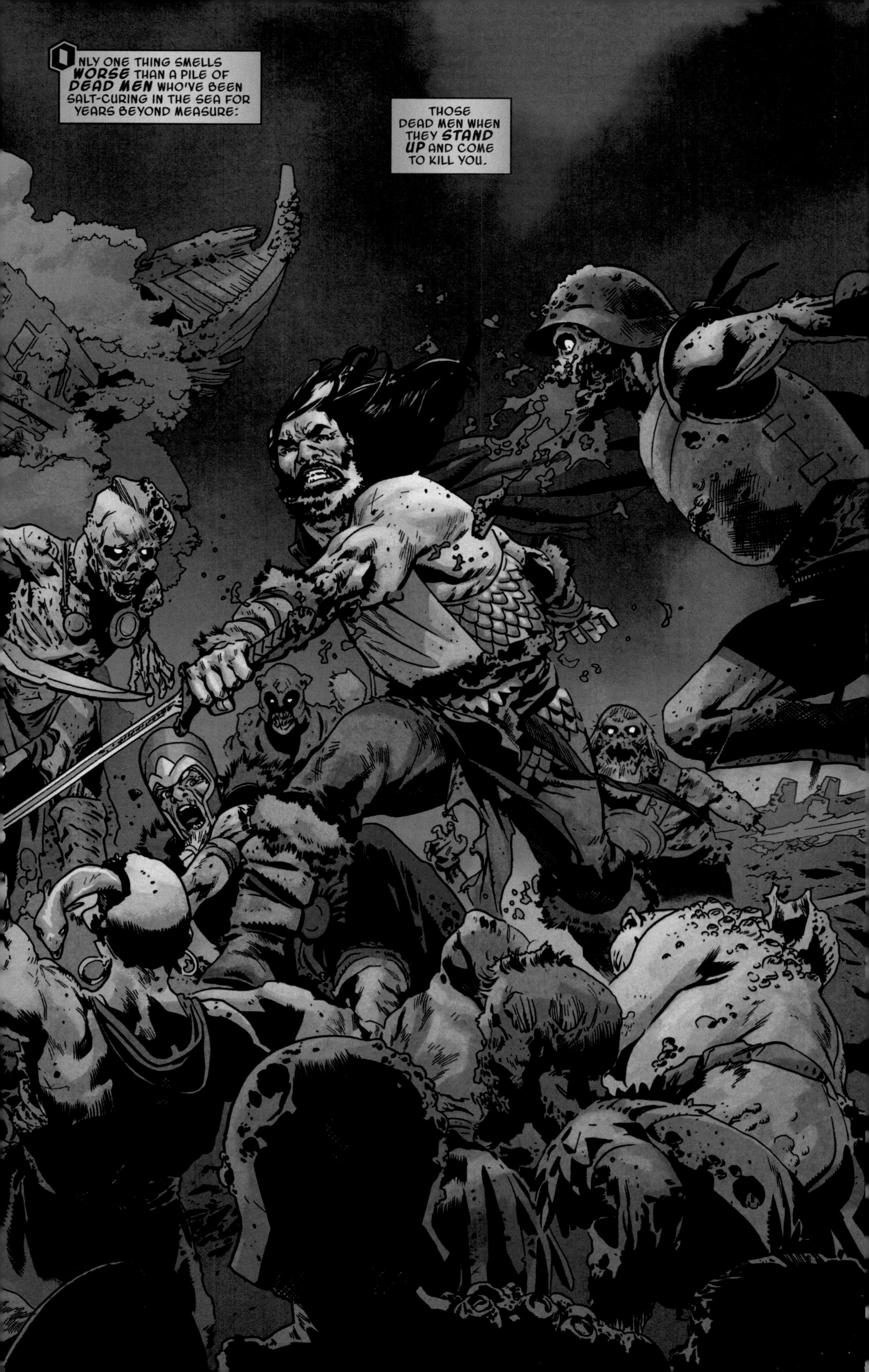
ONLY ONE THING SMELLS WORSE THAN A PILE OF DEAD MEN WHO'VE BEEN SALT-CURING IN THE SEA FOR YEARS BEYOND MEASURE:
THOSE DEAD MEN WHEN THEY STAND UP AND COME TO KILL YOU.

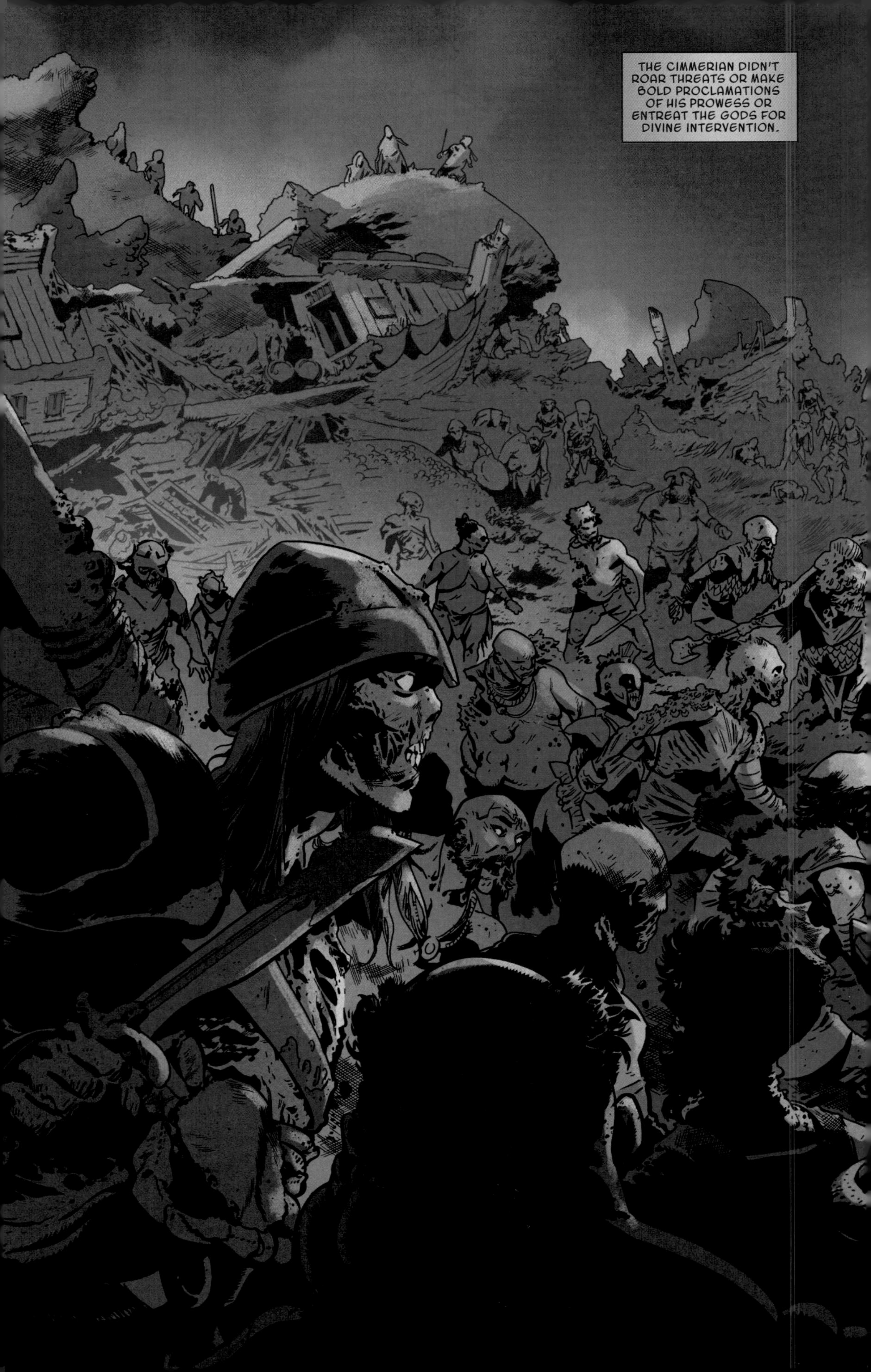
THE CIMMERIAN DIDN'T ROAR THREATS OR MAKE BOLD PROCLAMATIONS OF HIS PROWESS OR ENTREAT THE GODS FOR DIVINE INTERVENTION.

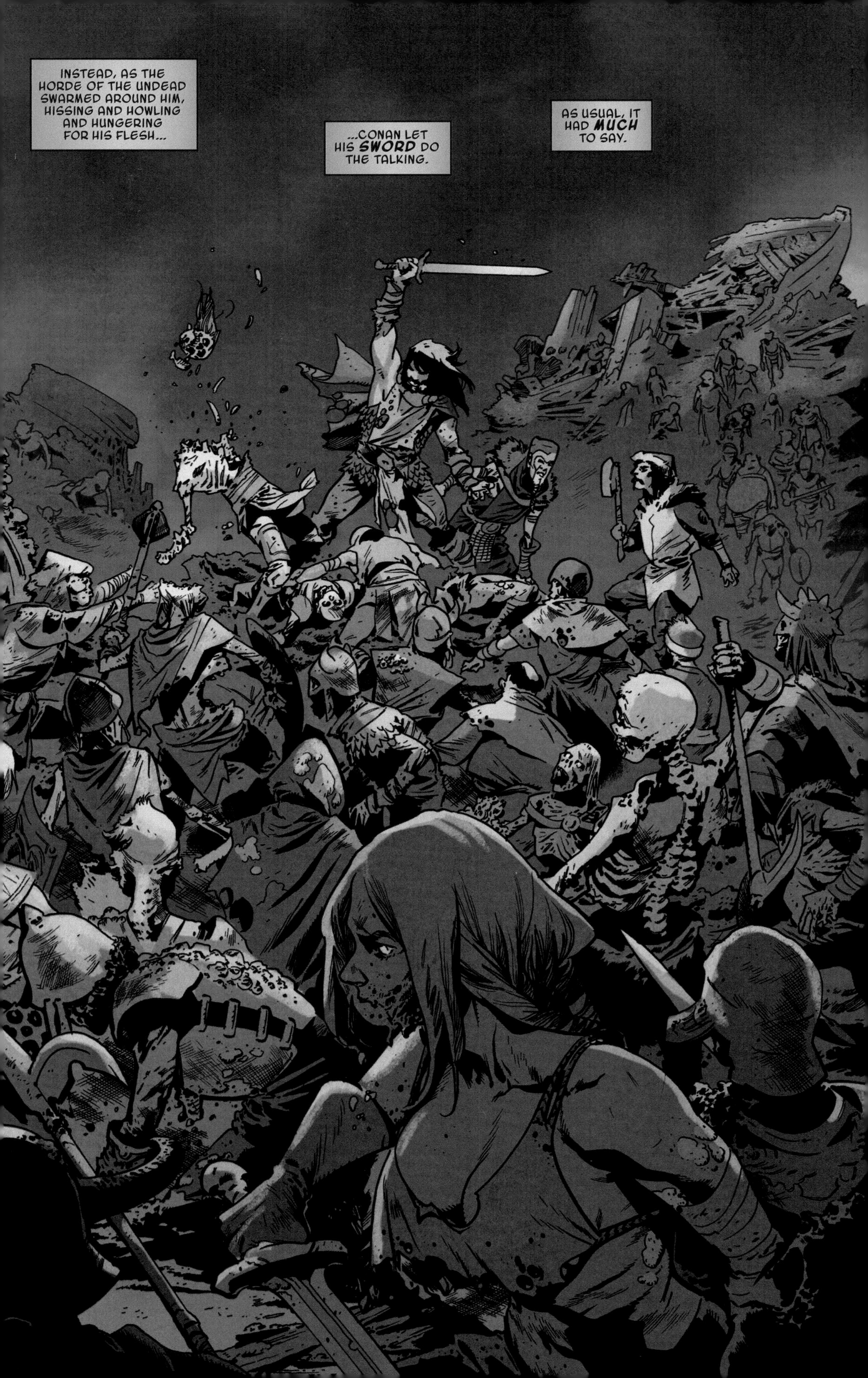
INSTEAD, AS THE HORDE OF THE UNDEAD SWARMED AROUND HIM, HISSING AND HOWLING AND HUNGERING FOR HIS FLESH...
...CONAN LET HIS SWORD DO THE TALKING.
AS USUAL, IT HAD MUCH TO SAY.

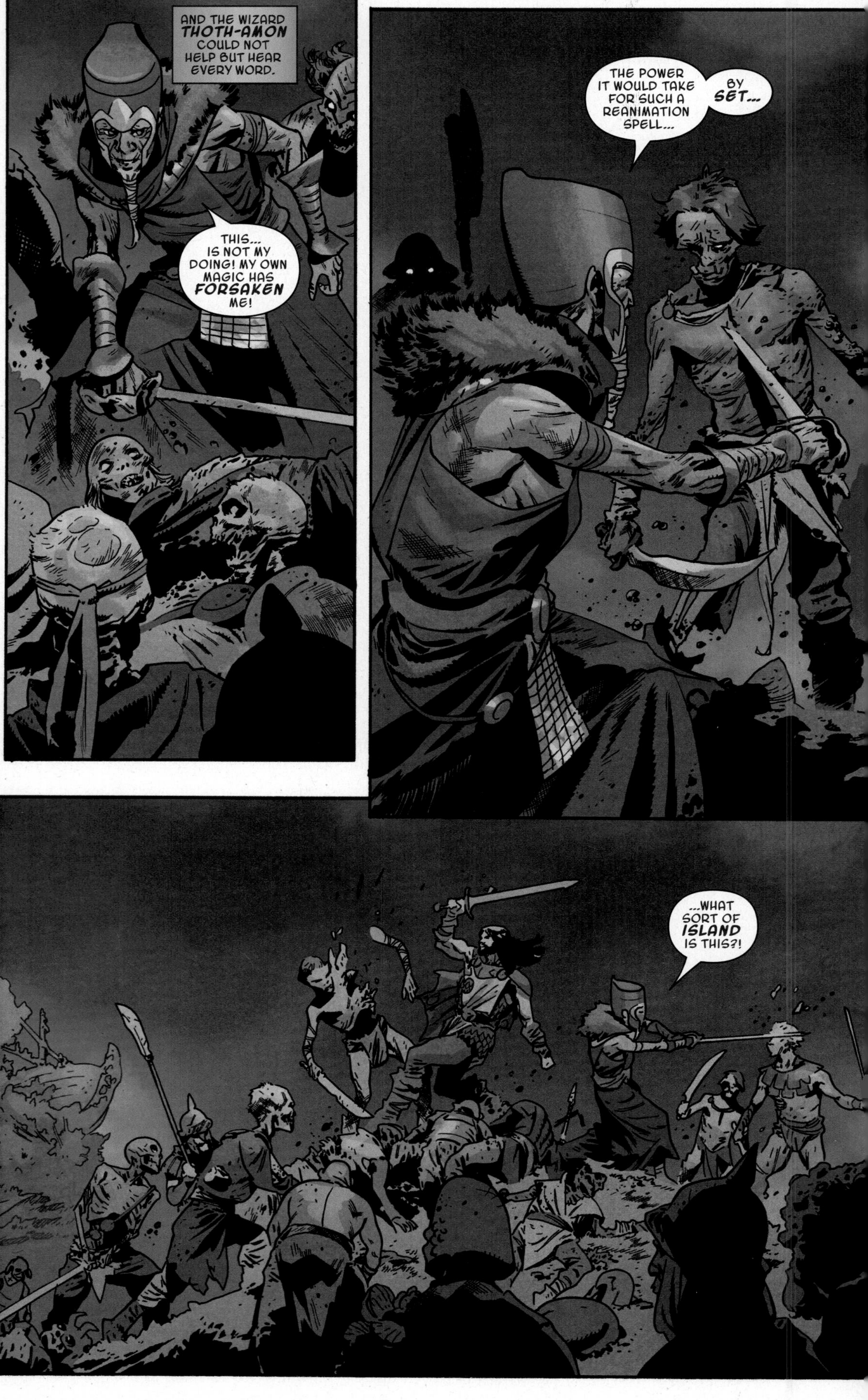
AND THE WIZARD THOTH-AMON COULD NOT HELP BUT HEAR EVERY WORD.
THIS... IS NOT MY DOING! MY OWN MAGIC HAS FORSAKEN ME!
THE POWER IT WOULD TAKE FOR SUCH A REANIMATION SPELL...
BY SET...
...WHAT SORT OF ISLAND IS THIS?!

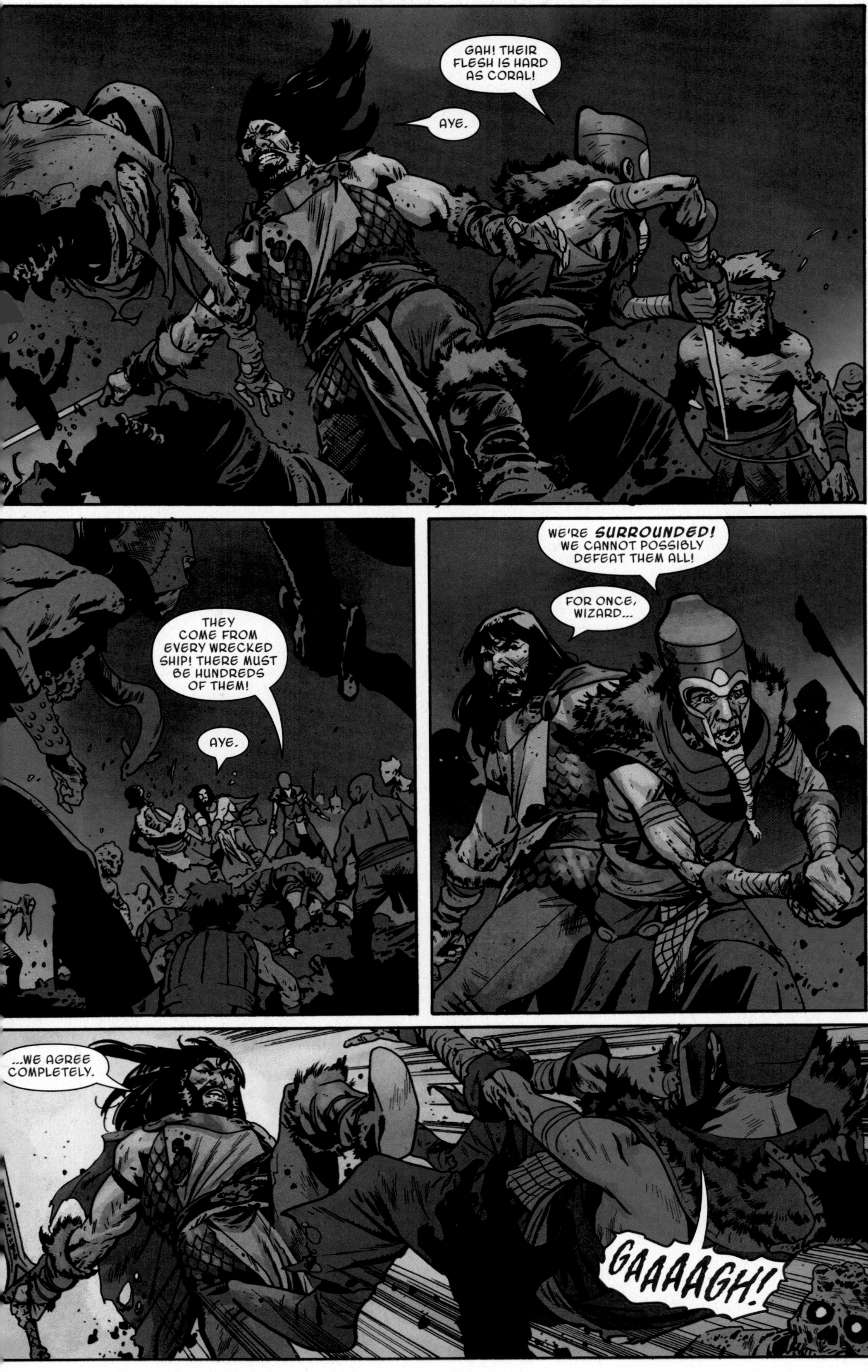
GAH! THEIR FLESH IS HARD AS CORAL!
AYE.
THEY COME FROM EVERY WRECKED SHIP! THERE MUST BE HUNDREDS OF THEM!
AYE.
WE'RE **SURROUNDED!** WE CANNOT POSSIBLY DEFEAT THEM ALL!
FOR ONCE, WIZARD...
...WE AGREE COMPLETELY.
GAAAAGH!

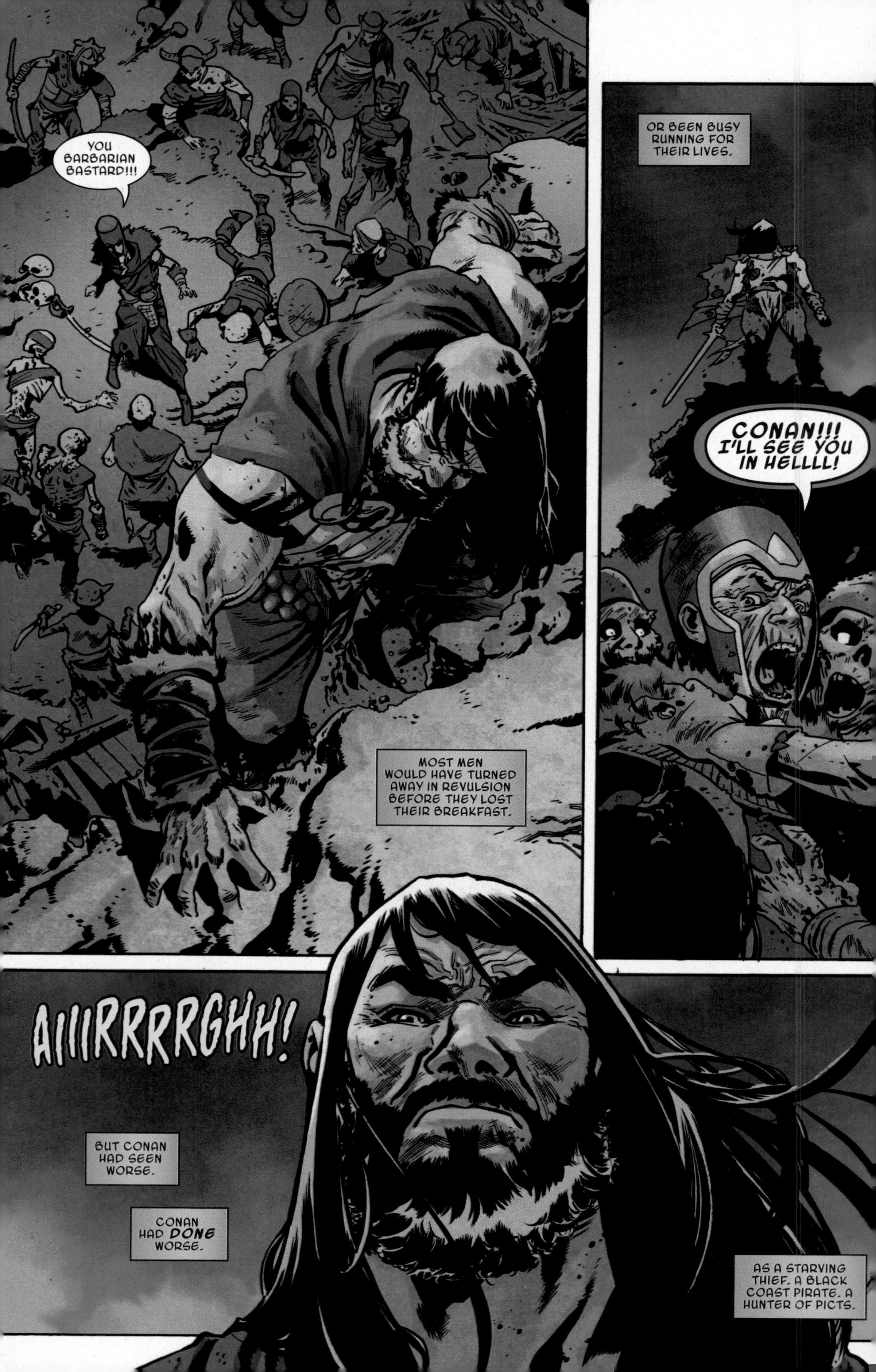
YOU BARBARIAN BASTARD!!!
MOST MEN WOULD HAVE TURNED AWAY IN REVULSION BEFORE THEY LOST THEIR BREAKFAST.
OR BEEN BUSY RUNNING FOR THEIR LIVES.
CONAN!!! I'LL SEE YOU IN HELLLL!
AIIIRRRRGHH!
BUT CONAN HAD SEEN WORSE.
CONAN HAD DONE WORSE.
AS A STARVING THIEF. A BLACK COAST PIRATE. A HUNTER OF PICTS.

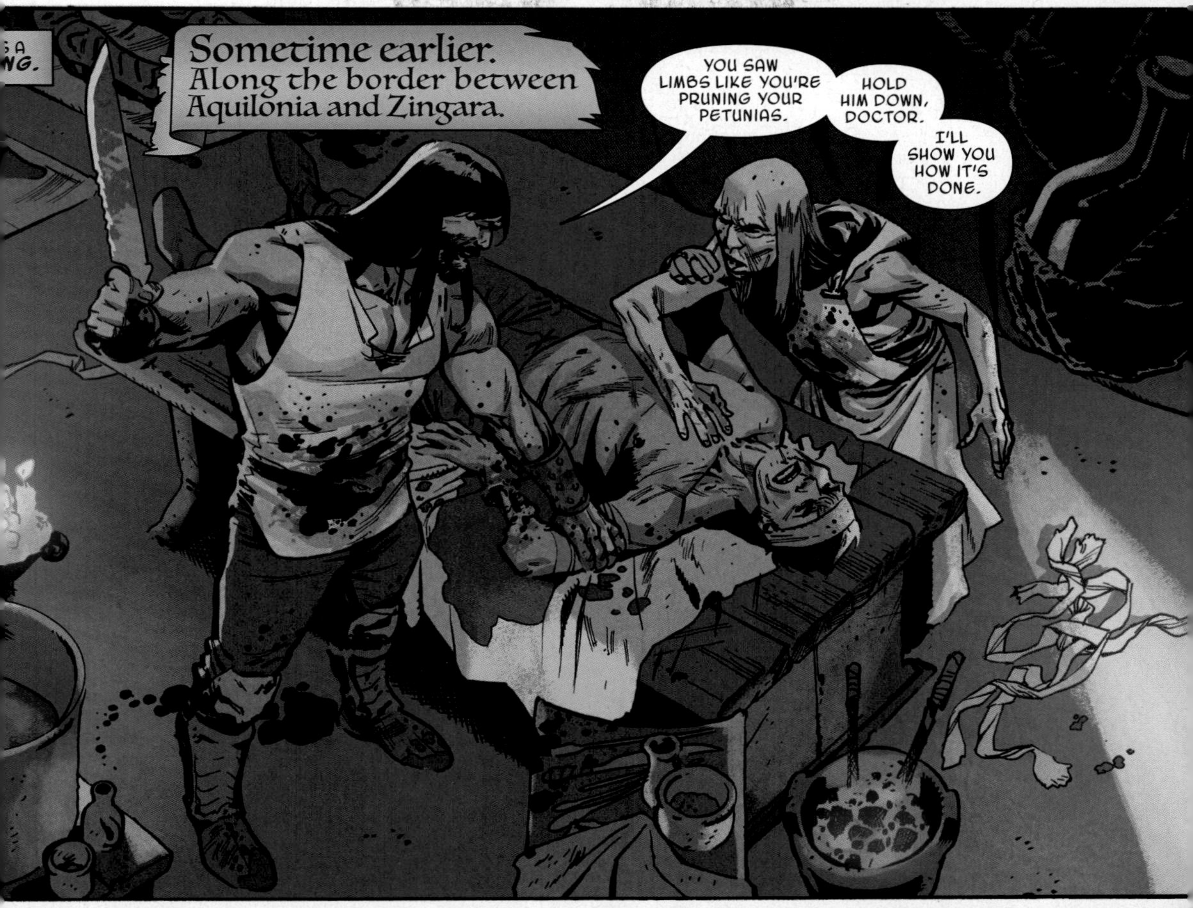
Sometime earlier.
Along the border between Aquilonia and Zingara.
YOU SAW LIMBS LIKE YOU'RE PRUNING YOUR PETUNIAS.
HOLD HIM DOWN, DOCTOR.
I'LL SHOW YOU HOW IT'S DONE.

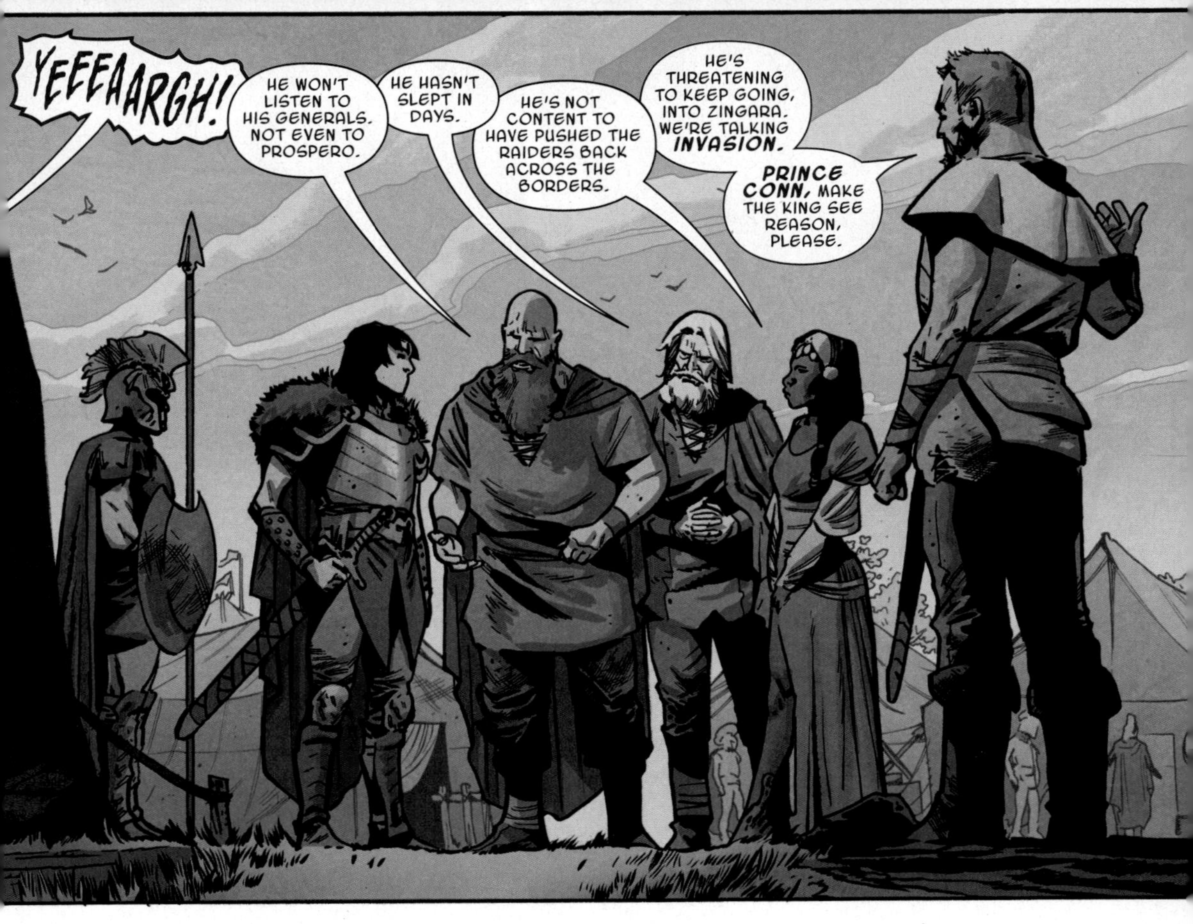
YEEEAARGH!
HE WON'T LISTEN TO HIS GENERALS. NOT EVEN TO PROSPERO.
HE HASN'T SLEPT IN DAYS.
HE'S NOT CONTENT TO HAVE PUSHED THE RAIDERS BACK ACROSS THE BORDERS.
HE'S THREATENING TO KEEP GOING, INTO ZINGARA. WE'RE TALKING INVASION.
PRINCE CONN, MAKE THE KING SEE REASON, PLEASE.

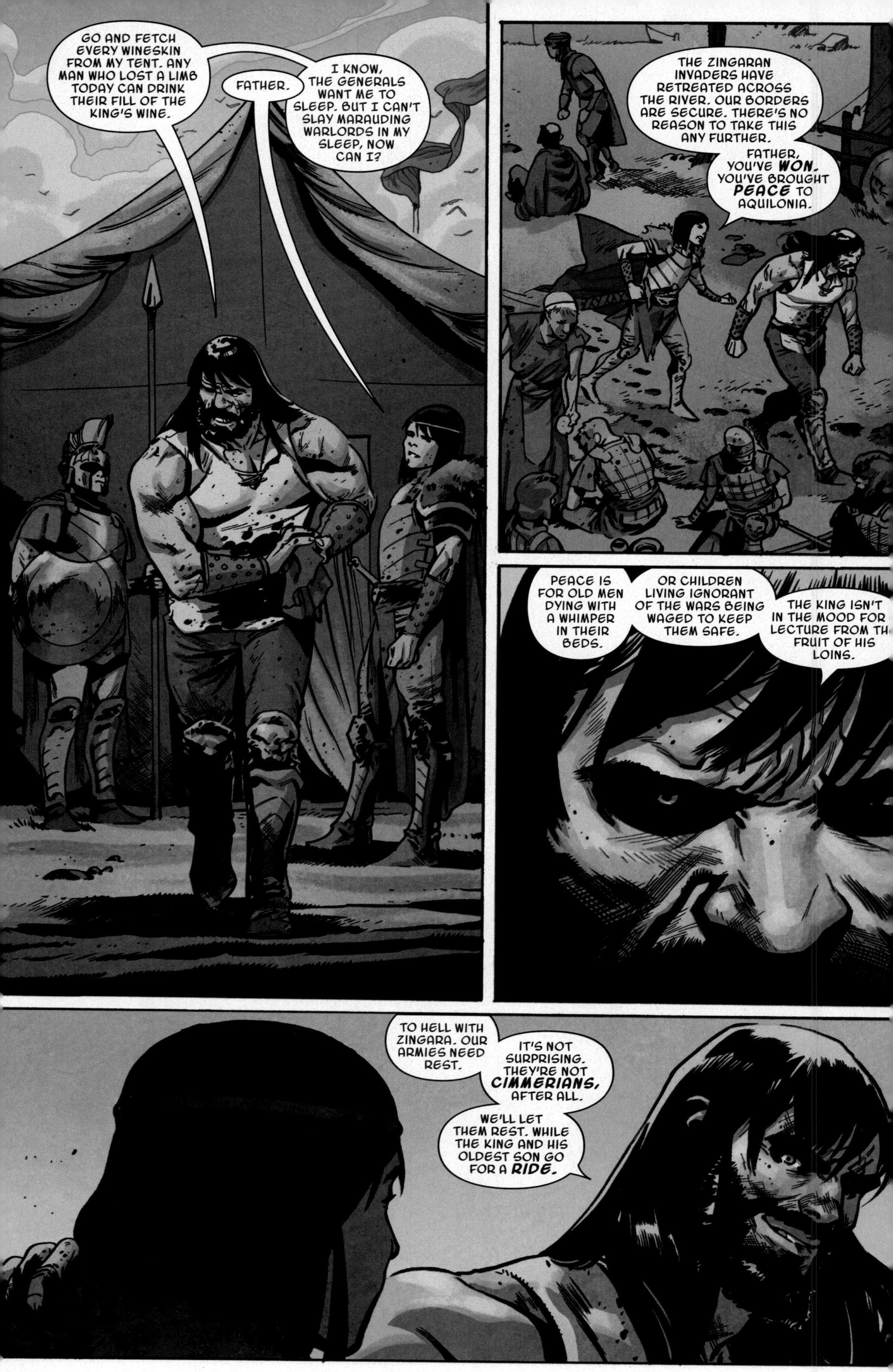
GO AND FETCH EVERY WINESKIN FROM MY TENT. ANY MAN WHO LOST A LIMB TODAY CAN DRINK THEIR FILL OF THE KING'S WINE.
FATHER.
I KNOW, THE GENERALS WANT ME TO SLEEP. BUT I CAN'T SLAY MARAUDING WARLORDS IN MY SLEEP, NOW CAN I?
THE ZINGARAN INVADERS HAVE RETREATED ACROSS THE RIVER. OUR BORDERS ARE SECURE. THERE'S NO REASON TO TAKE THIS ANY FURTHER.
FATHER, YOU'VE WON. YOU'VE BROUGHT PEACE TO AQUILONIA.
PEACE IS FOR OLD MEN DYING WITH A WHIMPER IN THEIR BEDS.
OR CHILDREN LIVING IGNORANT OF THE WARS BEING WAGED TO KEEP THEM SAFE.
THE KING ISN'T IN THE MOOD FOR LECTURE FROM TH FRUIT OF HIS LOINS.
TO HELL WITH ZINGARA. OUR ARMIES NEED REST.
IT'S NOT SURPRISING. THEY'RE NOT CIMMERIANS, AFTER ALL.
WE'LL LET THEM REST. WHILE THE KING AND HIS OLDEST SON GO FOR A RIDE.

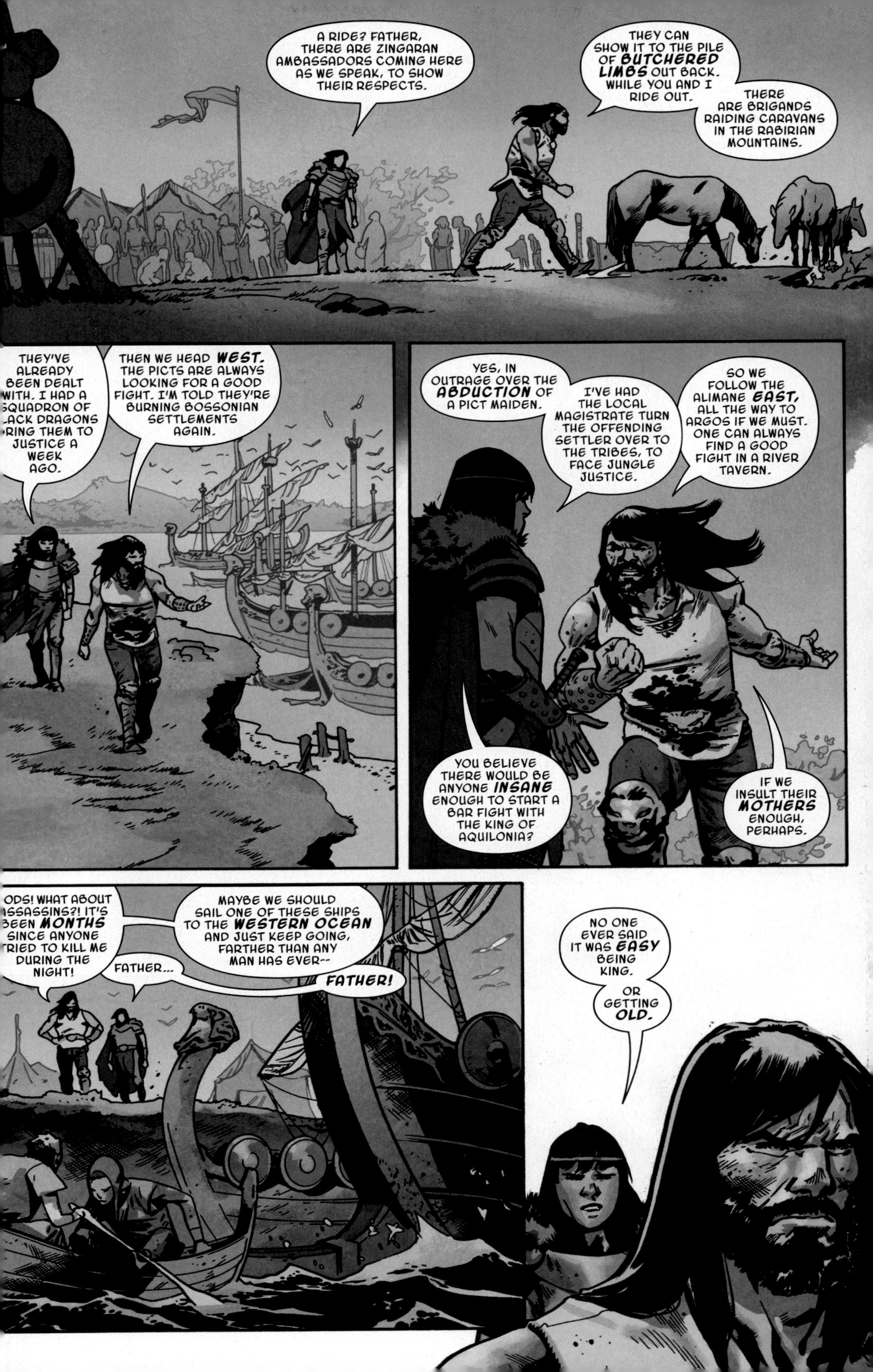
A RIDE? FATHER, THERE ARE ZINGARAN AMBASSADORS COMING HERE AS WE SPEAK, TO SHOW THEIR RESPECTS.
THEY CAN SHOW IT TO THE PILE OF BUTCHERED LIMBS OUT BACK. WHILE YOU AND I RIDE OUT.
THERE ARE BRIGANDS RAIDING CARAVANS IN THE RABIRIAN MOUNTAINS.
THEY'VE ALREADY BEEN DEALT WITH. I HAD A SQUADRON OF LACK DRAGONS RING THEM TO JUSTICE A WEEK AGO.
THEN WE HEAD WEST. THE PICTS ARE ALWAYS LOOKING FOR A GOOD FIGHT. I'M TOLD THEY'RE BURNING BOSSONIAN SETTLEMENTS AGAIN.
YES, IN OUTRAGE OVER THE ABDUCTION OF A PICT MAIDEN.
I'VE HAD THE LOCAL MAGISTRATE TURN THE OFFENDING SETTLER OVER TO THE TRIBES, TO FACE JUNGLE JUSTICE.
SO WE FOLLOW THE ALIMANE EAST, ALL THE WAY TO ARGOS IF WE MUST. ONE CAN ALWAYS FIND A GOOD FIGHT IN A RIVER TAVERN.
YOU BELIEVE THERE WOULD BE ANYONE INSANE ENOUGH TO START A BAR FIGHT WITH THE KING OF AQUILONIA?
IF WE INSULT THEIR MOTHERS ENOUGH, PERHAPS.
ODS! WHAT ABOUT ASSASSINS?! IT'S BEEN MONTHS SINCE ANYONE TRIED TO KILL ME DURING THE NIGHT!
MAYBE WE SHOULD SAIL ONE OF THESE SHIPS TO THE WESTERN OCEAN AND JUST KEEP GOING, FARTHER THAN ANY MAN HAS EVER--
FATHER...
FATHER!
NO ONE EVER SAID IT WAS EASY BEING KING.
OR GETTING OLD.

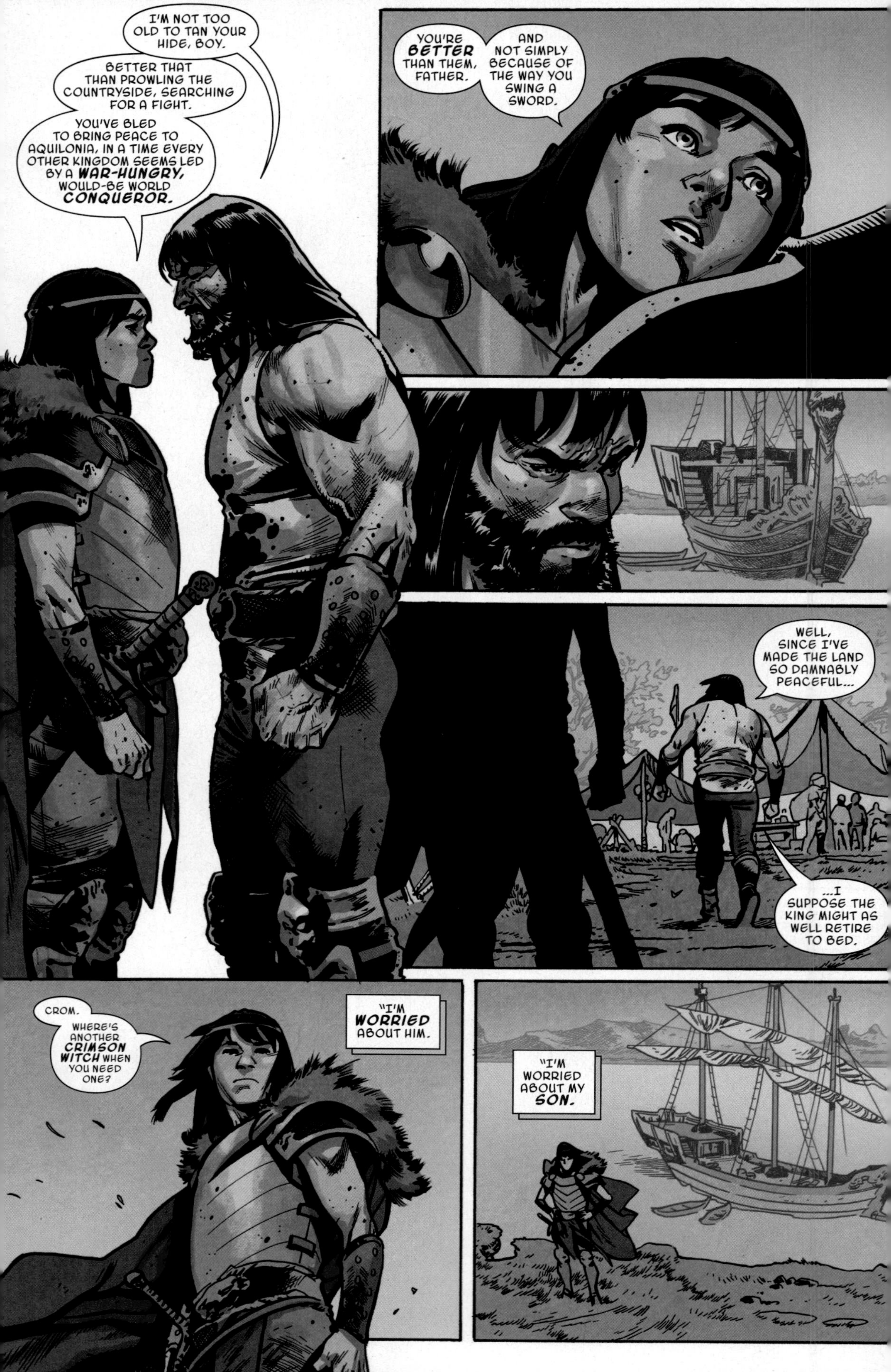
I'M NOT TOO OLD TO TAN YOUR HIDE, BOY.
BETTER THAT THAN PROWLING THE COUNTRYSIDE, SEARCHING FOR A FIGHT.
YOU'VE BLED TO BRING PEACE TO AQUILONIA, IN A TIME EVERY OTHER KINGDOM SEEMS LED BY A WAR-HUNGRY, WOULD-BE WORLD CONQUEROR.
YOU'RE BETTER THAN THEM, FATHER.
AND NOT SIMPLY BECAUSE OF THE WAY YOU SWING A SWORD.
WELL, SINCE I'VE MADE THE LAND SO DAMNABLY PEACEFUL...
...I SUPPOSE THE KING MIGHT AS WELL RETIRE TO BED.
CROM.
WHERE'S ANOTHER CRIMSON WITCH WHEN YOU NEED ONE?
"I'M WORRIED ABOUT HIM.
"I'M WORRIED ABOUT MY SON.

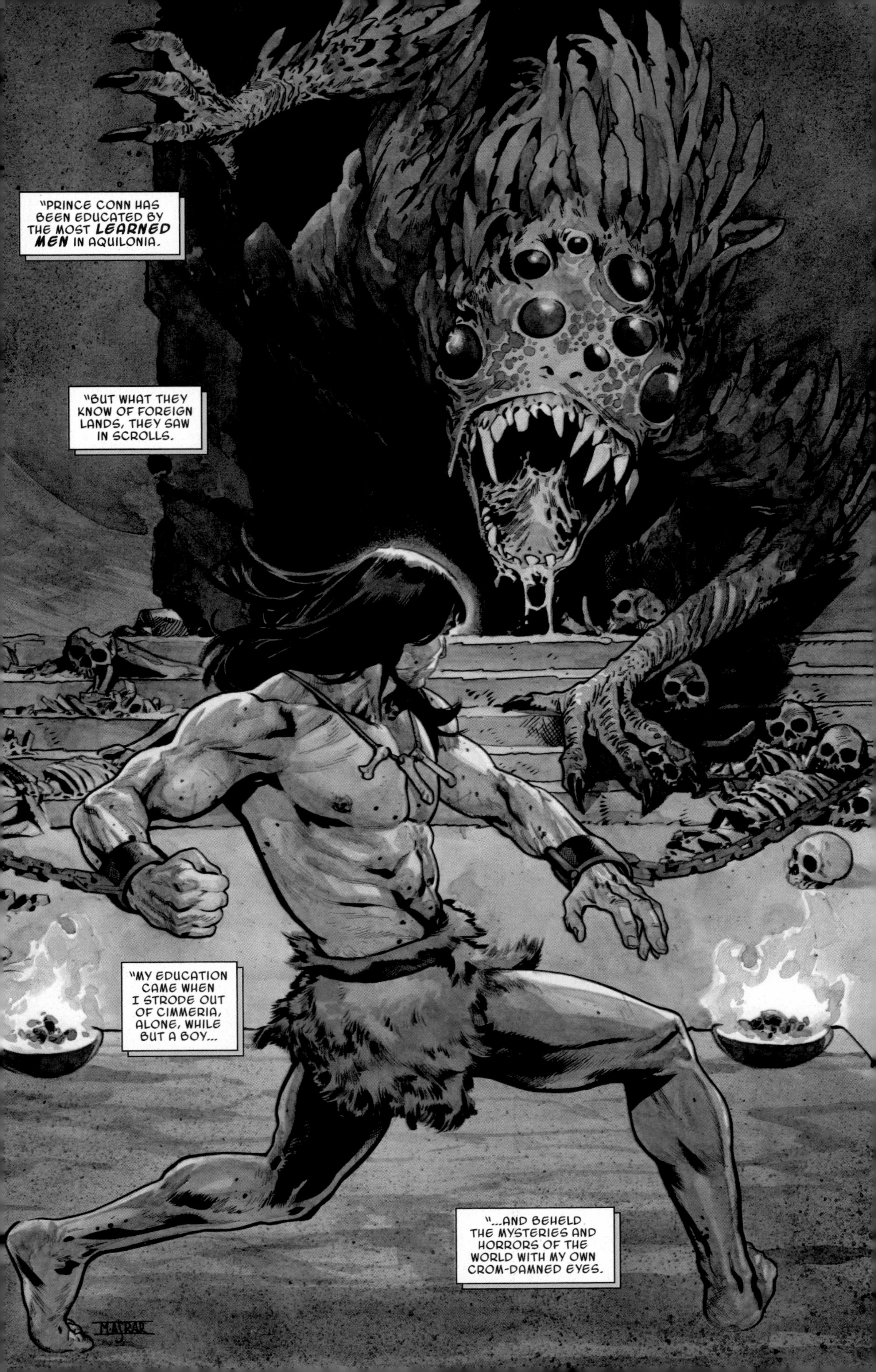
"PRINCE CONN HAS BEEN EDUCATED BY THE MOST LEARNED MEN IN AQUILONIA.
"BUT WHAT THEY KNOW OF FOREIGN LANDS, THEY SAW IN SCROLLS.
"MY EDUCATION CAME WHEN I STRODE OUT OF CIMMERIA, ALONE, WHILE BUT A BOY...
"...AND BEHELD THE MYSTERIES AND HORRORS OF THE WORLD WITH MY OWN CROM-DAMNED EYES.
MASRAR

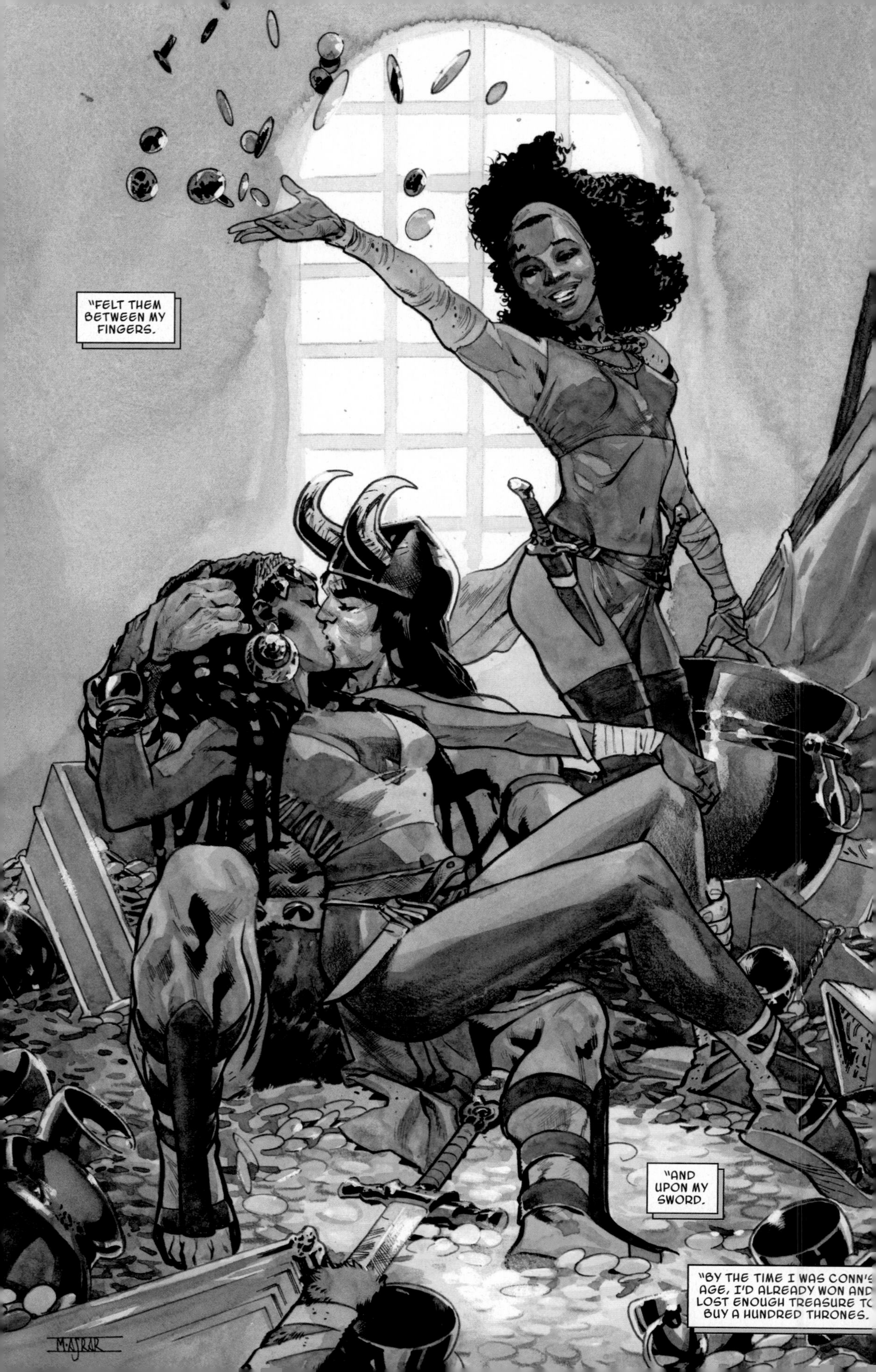
"FELT THEM BETWEEN MY FINGERS.
"AND UPON MY SWORD.
"BY THE TIME I WAS CONN'S AGE, I'D ALREADY WON AND LOST ENOUGH TREASURE TO BUY A HUNDRED THRONES.
M.AJRAR

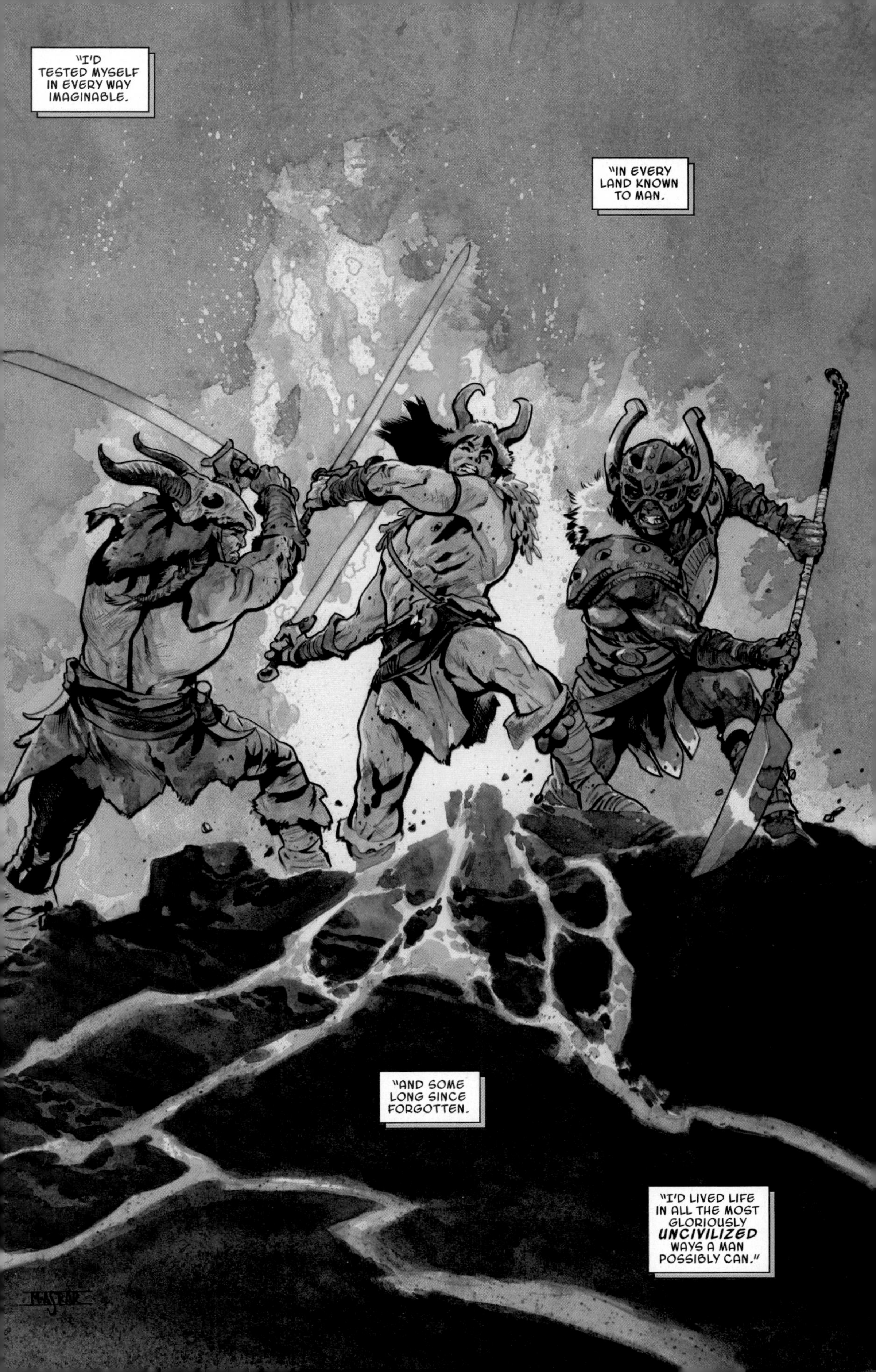
"I'D TESTED MYSELF IN EVERY WAY IMAGINABLE.
"IN EVERY LAND KNOWN TO MAN.
"AND SOME LONG SINCE FORGOTTEN.
"I'D LIVED LIFE IN ALL THE MOST GLORIOUSLY ***UNCIVILIZED*** WAYS A MAN POSSIBLY CAN."

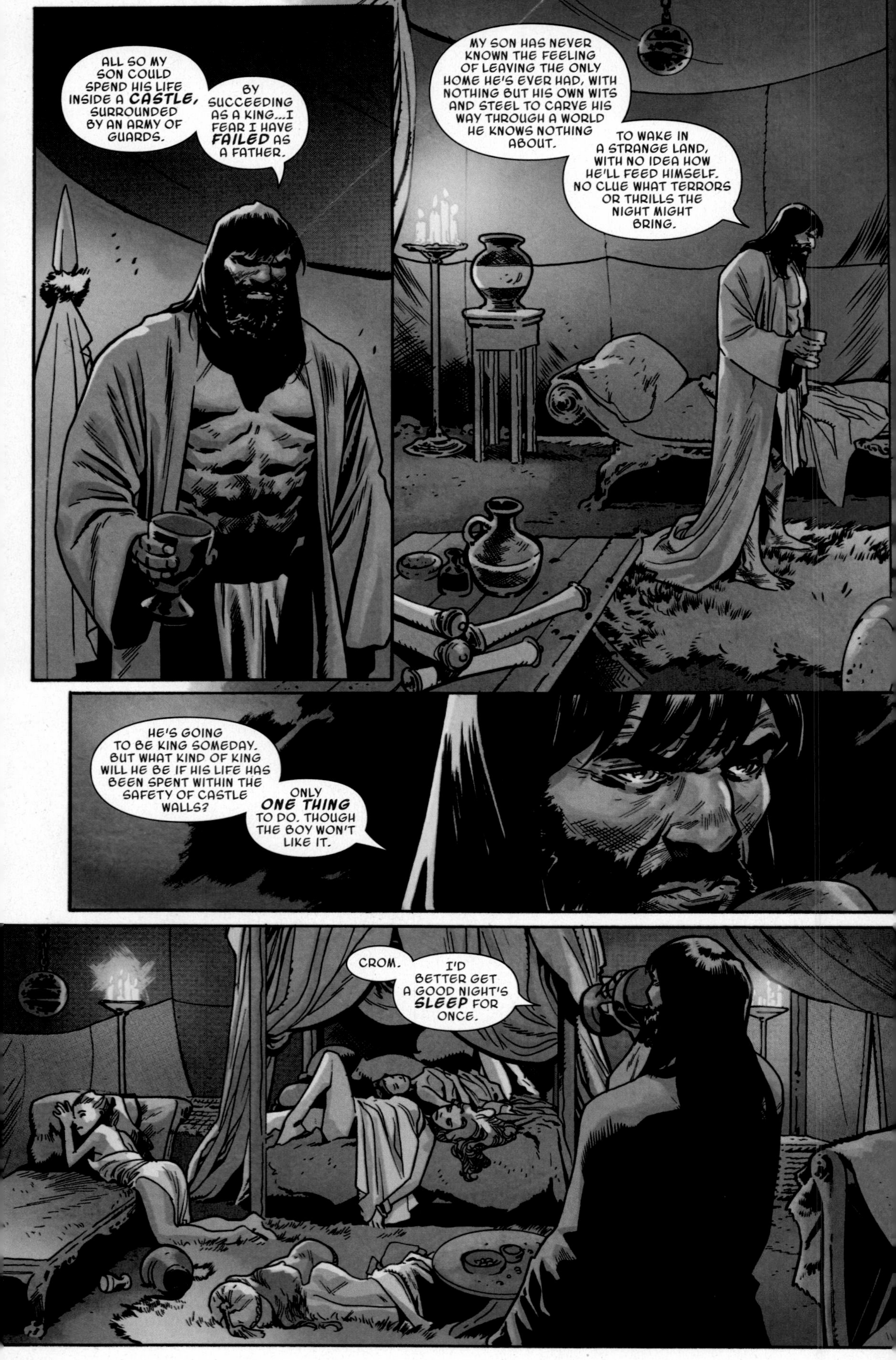
ALL SO MY SON COULD SPEND HIS LIFE INSIDE A CASTLE, SURROUNDED BY AN ARMY OF GUARDS.
BY SUCCEEDING AS A KING...I FEAR I HAVE FAILED AS A FATHER.
MY SON HAS NEVER KNOWN THE FEELING OF LEAVING THE ONLY HOME HE'S EVER HAD, WITH NOTHING BUT HIS OWN WITS AND STEEL TO CARVE HIS WAY THROUGH A WORLD HE KNOWS NOTHING ABOUT.
TO WAKE IN A STRANGE LAND, WITH NO IDEA HOW HE'LL FEED HIMSELF. NO CLUE WHAT TERRORS OR THRILLS THE NIGHT MIGHT BRING.
HE'S GOING TO BE KING SOMEDAY. BUT WHAT KIND OF KING WILL HE BE IF HIS LIFE HAS BEEN SPENT WITHIN THE SAFETY OF CASTLE WALLS?
ONLY ONE THING TO DO. THOUGH THE BOY WON'T LIKE IT.
CROM.
I'D BETTER GET A GOOD NIGHT'S SLEEP FOR ONCE.

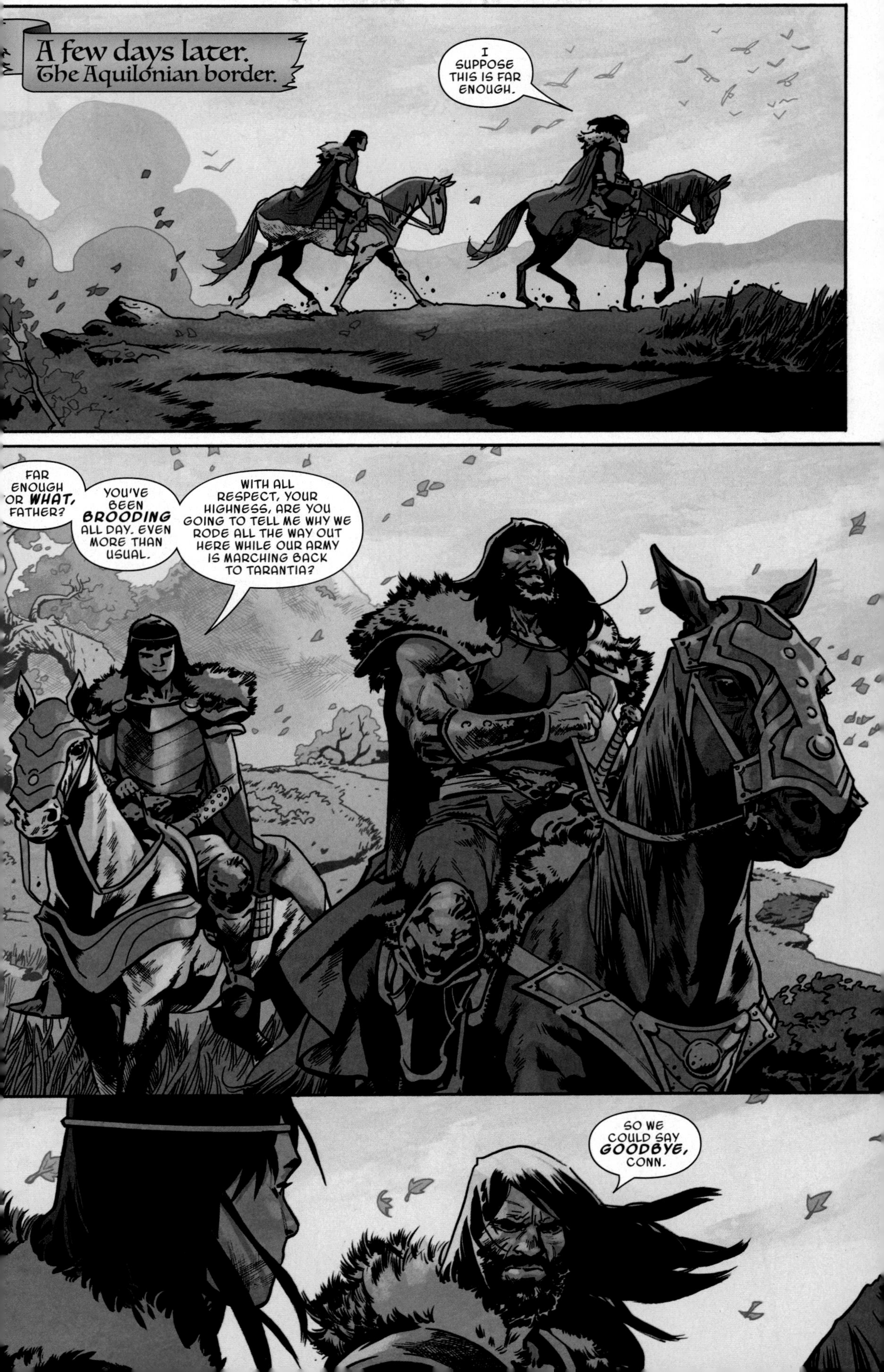
A few days later. The Aquilonian border.
I SUPPOSE THIS IS FAR ENOUGH.
FAR ENOUGH FOR WHAT, FATHER?
YOU'VE BEEN BROODING ALL DAY. EVEN MORE THAN USUAL.
WITH ALL RESPECT, YOUR HIGHNESS, ARE YOU GOING TO TELL ME WHY WE RODE ALL THE WAY OUT HERE WHILE OUR ARMY IS MARCHING BACK TO TARANTIA?
SO WE COULD SAY GOODBYE, CONN.

WHAT? WHERE ARE YOU *GOING?*

DON'T TELL ME YOU'RE ABOUT TO START A *WAR* WITH--

I'M NOT GOING ANYWHERE.

YOU ARE.

FATHER...IF YOU'VE ARRANGED A *MARRIAGE* FOR ME...

I'VE ARRANGED NOTHING.

WHATEVER YOU HAVE ON YOU IS ALL YOU'LL LEAVE WITH. AND UNTIL YOU CAN BRING ME A TALE FROM EVERY LAND ON THE MAP...

...YOU WON'T BE ALLOWED BACK ACROSS THE BORDER.

WHAT ARE YOU TALKING ABOUT?

UNTIL THAT DAY...YOU WON'T BE THE SON OF THE KING. YOU'LL JUST BE CONN.

A BOY WHO'S HEREBY *EXILED* FROM AQUILONIA.

YOU'VE LOST YOUR MIND.

NO, SON.

I'M HELPING YOU FIND *YOURS.*

NOW GO.

AND LET NO ONE BA YOUR JOURN BACK HOME. THEY MAN OR GOD...

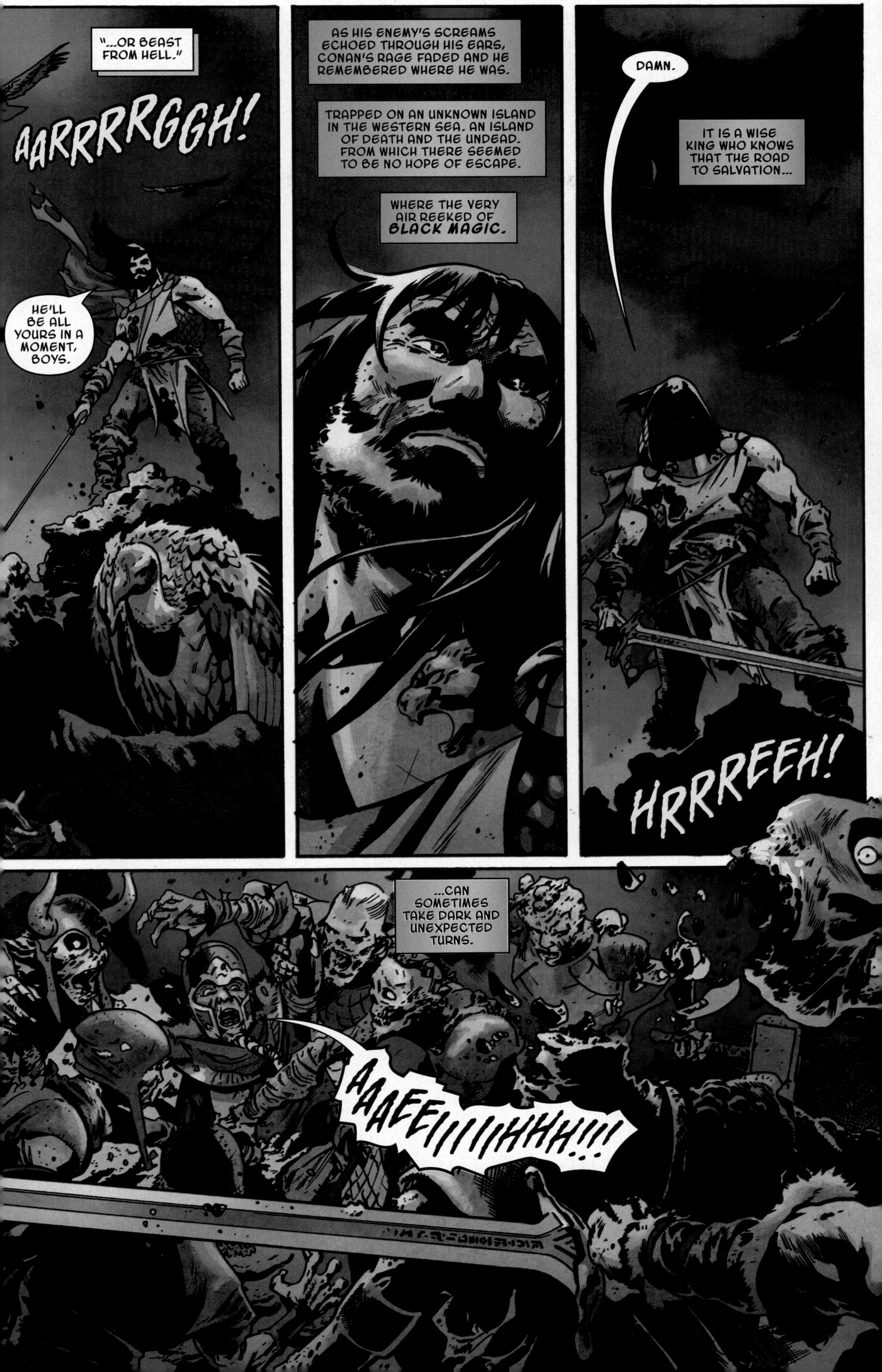
"...OR BEAST FROM HELL."
AARRRRGGH!
HE'LL BE ALL YOURS IN A MOMENT, BOYS.
AS HIS ENEMY'S SCREAMS ECHOED THROUGH HIS EARS, CONAN'S RAGE FADED AND HE REMEMBERED WHERE HE WAS.
TRAPPED ON AN UNKNOWN ISLAND IN THE WESTERN SEA. AN ISLAND OF DEATH AND THE UNDEAD. FROM WHICH THERE SEEMED TO BE NO HOPE OF ESCAPE.
WHERE THE VERY AIR REEKED OF BLACK MAGIC.
DAMN.
IT IS A WISE KING WHO KNOWS THAT THE ROAD TO SALVATION...
HRRREEH!
...CAN SOMETIMES TAKE DARK AND UNEXPECTED TURNS.
AAAEEIIIIIIKKKK!!!

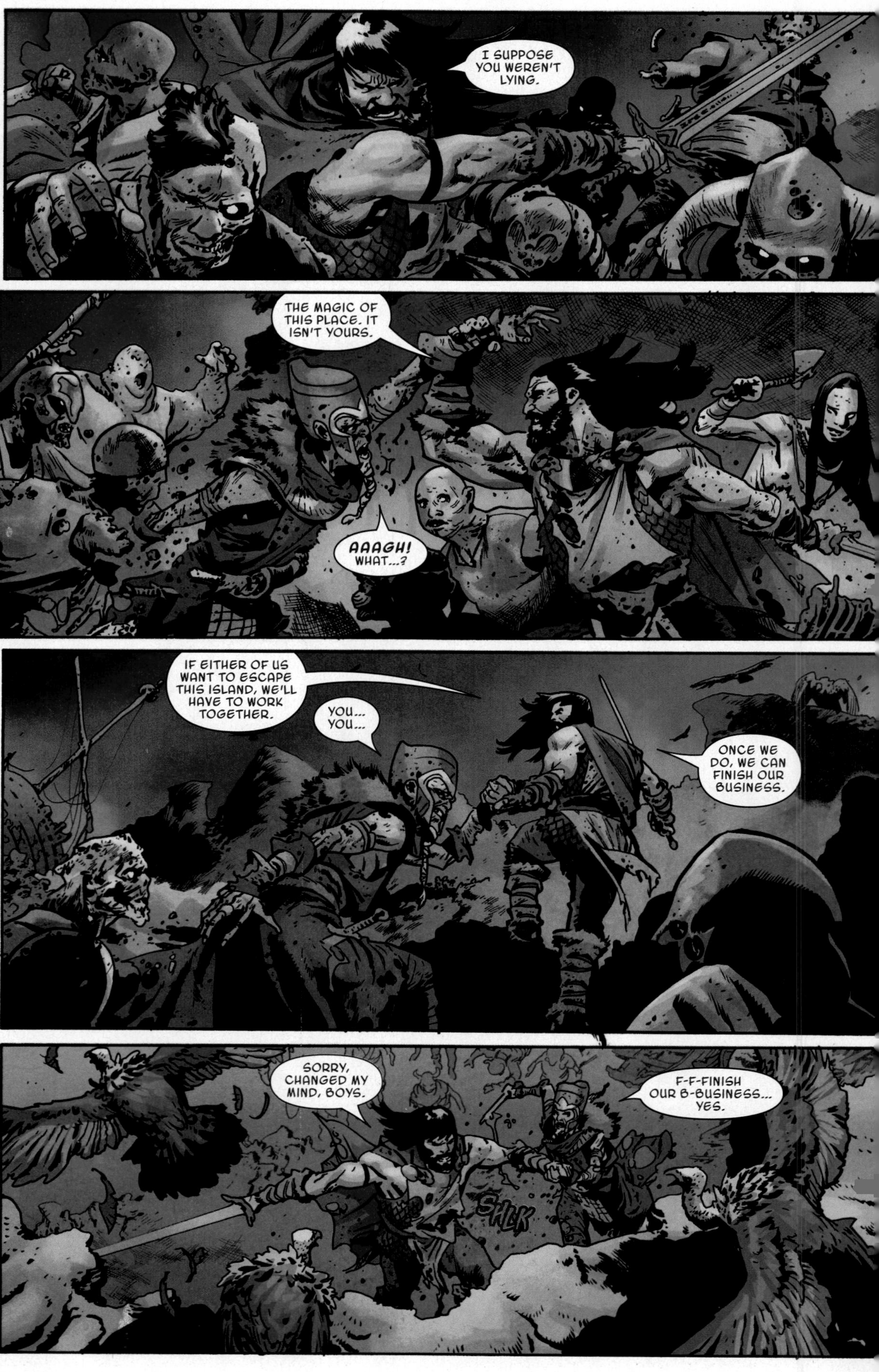
I SUPPOSE YOU WEREN'T LYING.
THE MAGIC OF THIS PLACE. IT ISN'T YOURS.
AAAGH! WHAT...?
IF EITHER OF US WANT TO ESCAPE THIS ISLAND, WE'LL HAVE TO WORK TOGETHER.
YOU... YOU...
ONCE WE DO, WE CAN FINISH OUR BUSINESS.
SORRY, CHANGED MY MIND, BOYS.
F-F-FINISH OUR B-BUSINESS... YES.
SHLK

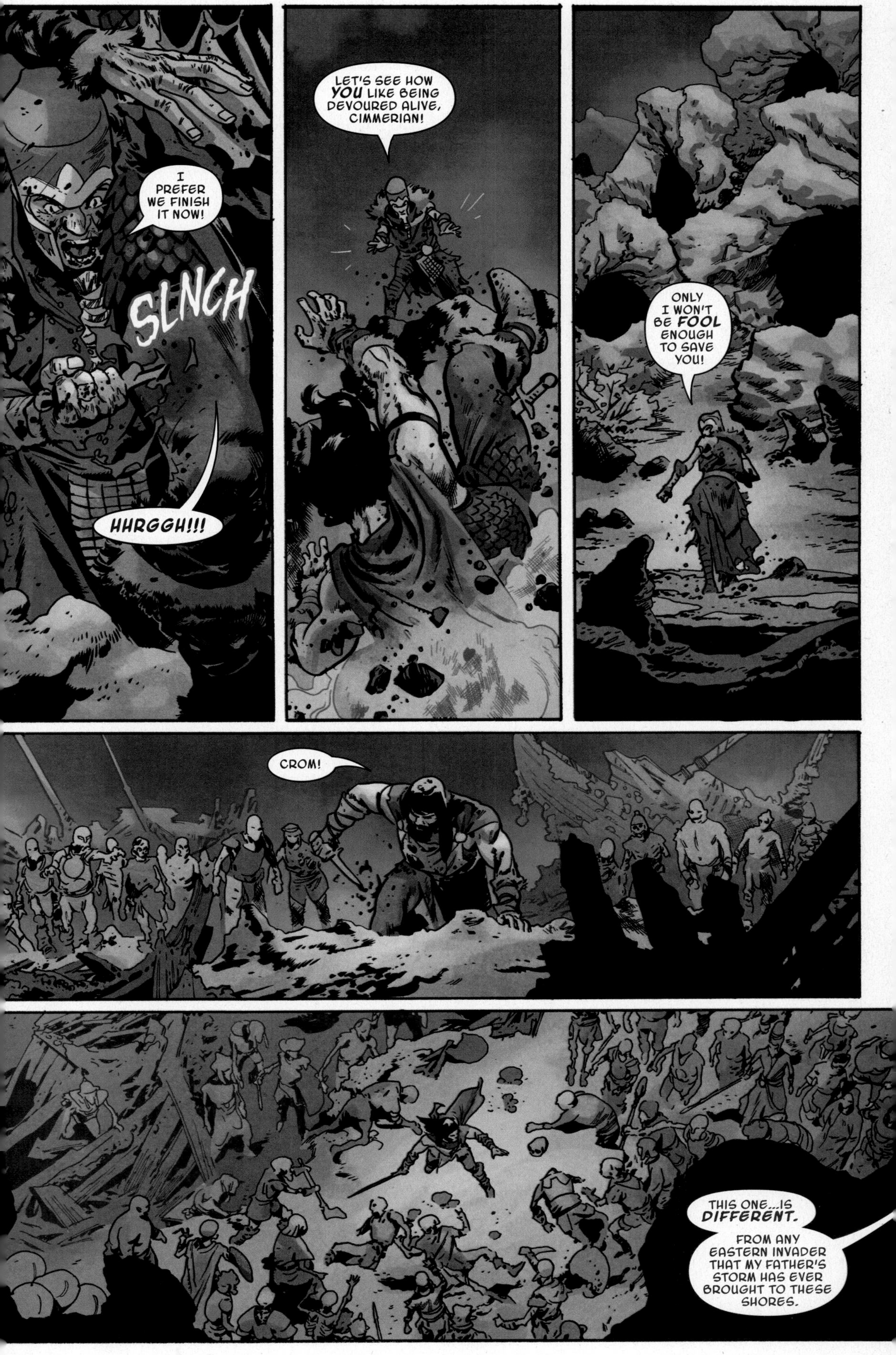
I PREFER WE FINISH IT NOW!
SLNCH
HHRGGH!!!
LET'S SEE HOW YOU LIKE BEING DEVOURED ALIVE, CIMMERIAN!
ONLY I WON'T BE FOOL ENOUGH TO SAVE YOU!
CROM!
THIS ONE...IS DIFFERENT.
FROM ANY EASTERN INVADER THAT MY FATHER'S STORM HAS EVER BROUGHT TO THESE SHORES.

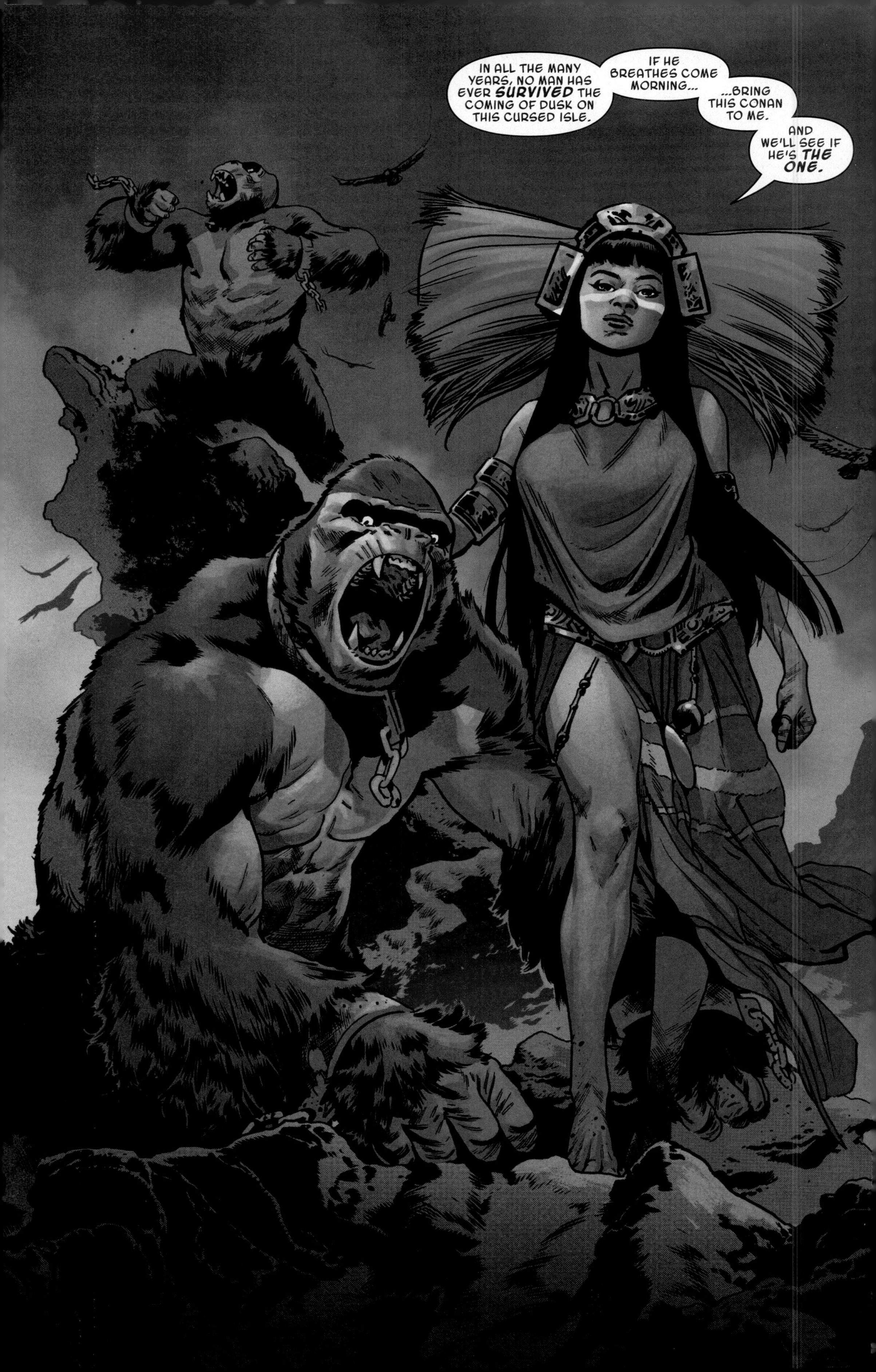
IN ALL THE MANY YEARS, NO MAN HAS EVER SURVIVED THE COMING OF DUSK ON THIS CURSED ISLE.
IF HE BREATHES COME MORNING...
...BRING THIS CONAN TO ME.
AND WE'LL SEE IF HE'S THE ONE.

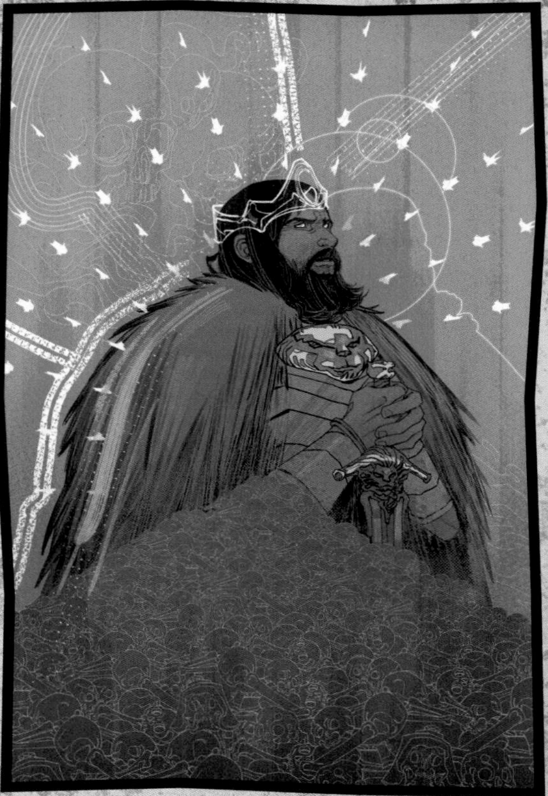

#1 VARIANT BY **MARGUERITE SAUVAGE**

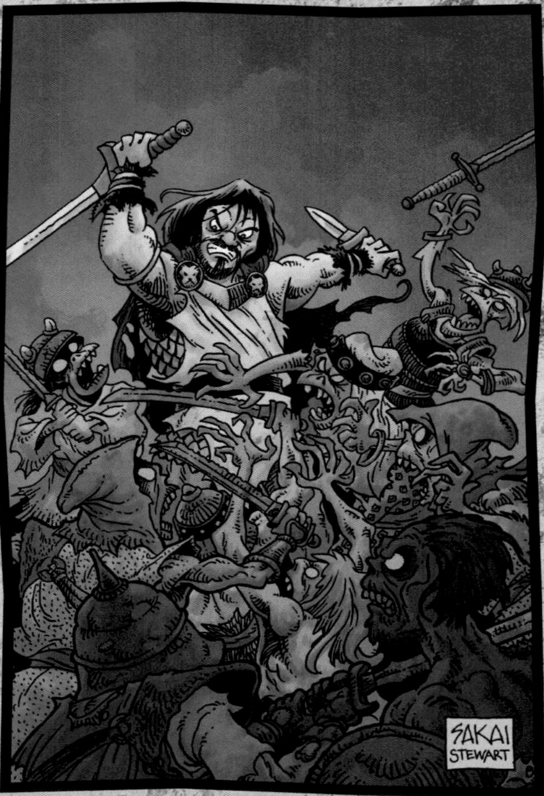
SAKAI
STEWART

#1 VARIANT BY **STAN SAKAI & DAVE STEWART**

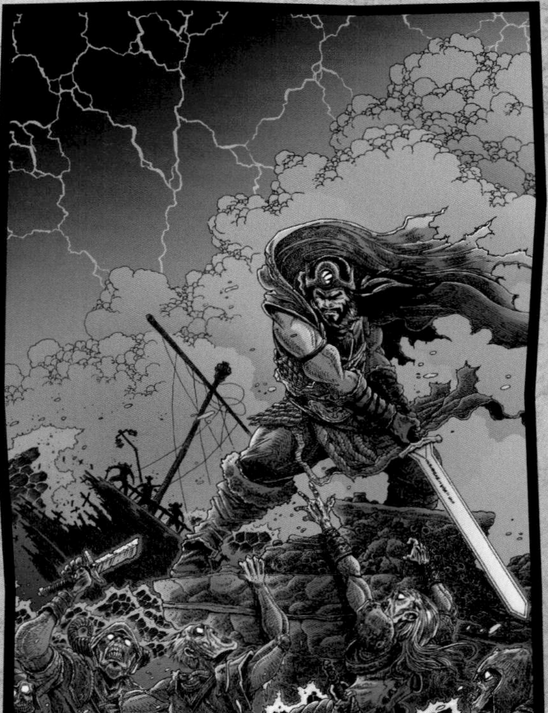

#1 VARIANT BY **JAMES STOKOE**

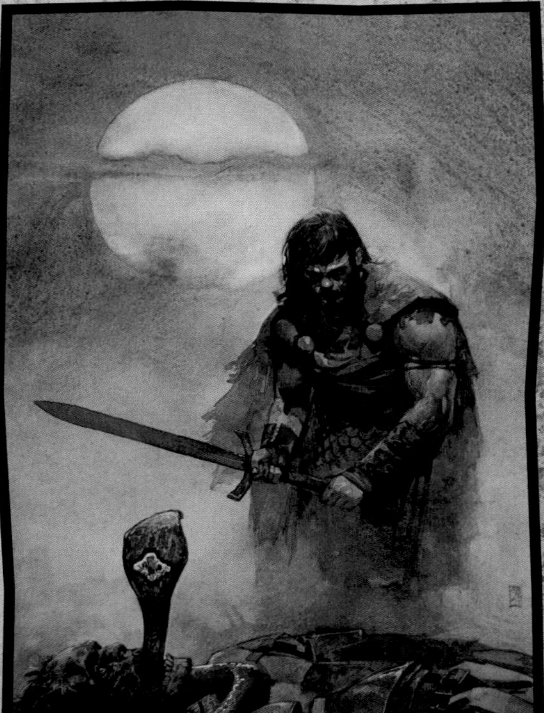

#1 VARIANT BY **ALEX MALEEV**

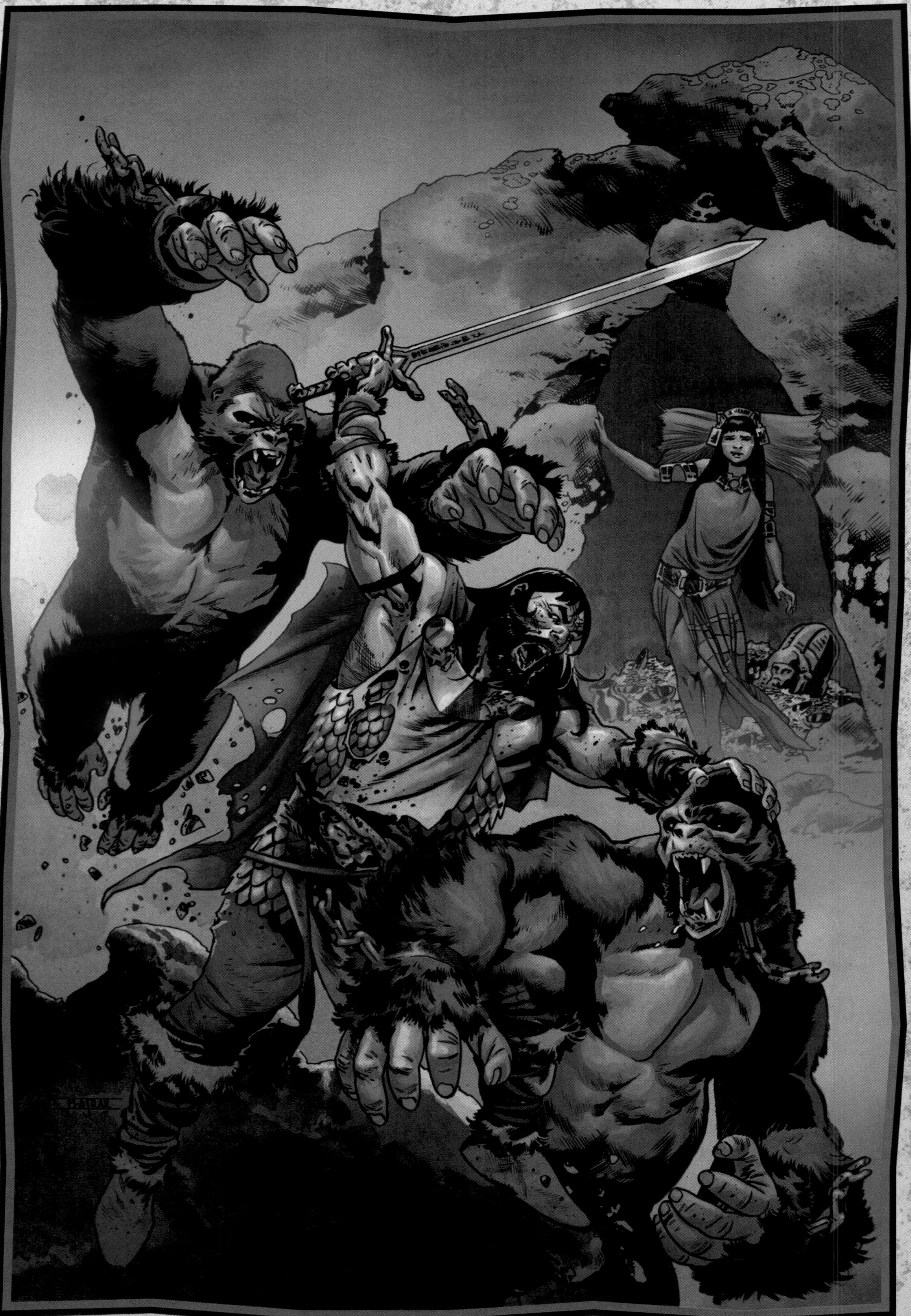

3

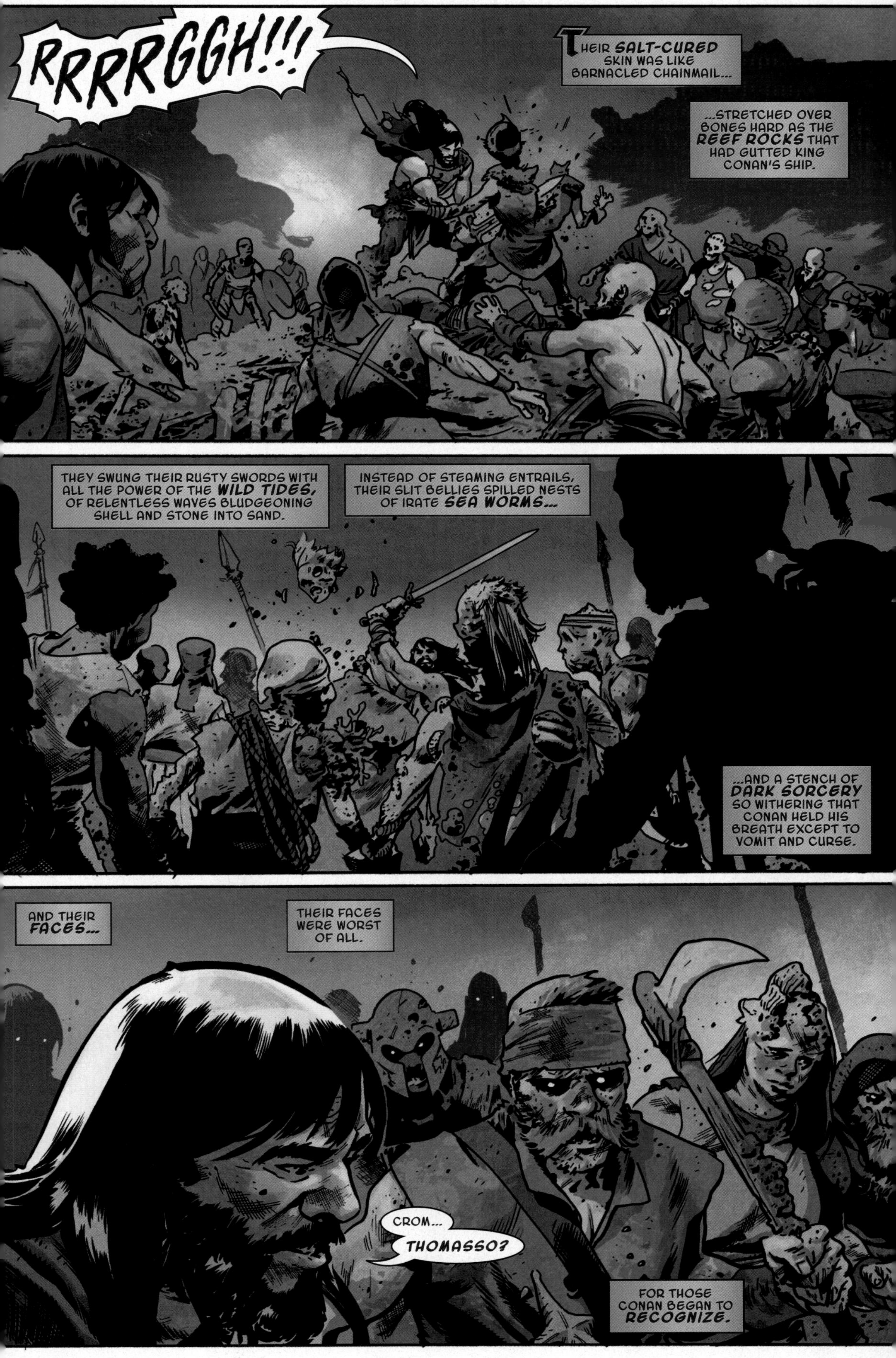

RRRRGGH!!!
THEIR SALT-CURED SKIN WAS LIKE BARNACLED CHAINMAIL...
...STRETCHED OVER BONES HARD AS THE REEF ROCKS THAT HAD GUTTED KING CONAN'S SHIP.
THEY SWUNG THEIR RUSTY SWORDS WITH ALL THE POWER OF THE WILD TIDES, OF RELENTLESS WAVES BLUDGEONING SHELL AND STONE INTO SAND.
INSTEAD OF STEAMING ENTRAILS, THEIR SLIT BELLIES SPILLED NESTS OF IRATE SEA WORMS...
...AND A STENCH OF DARK SORCERY SO WITHERING THAT CONAN HELD HIS BREATH EXCEPT TO VOMIT AND CURSE.
AND THEIR FACES...
THEIR FACES WERE WORST OF ALL.
CROM... THOMASSO?
FOR THOSE CONAN BEGAN TO RECOGNIZE.

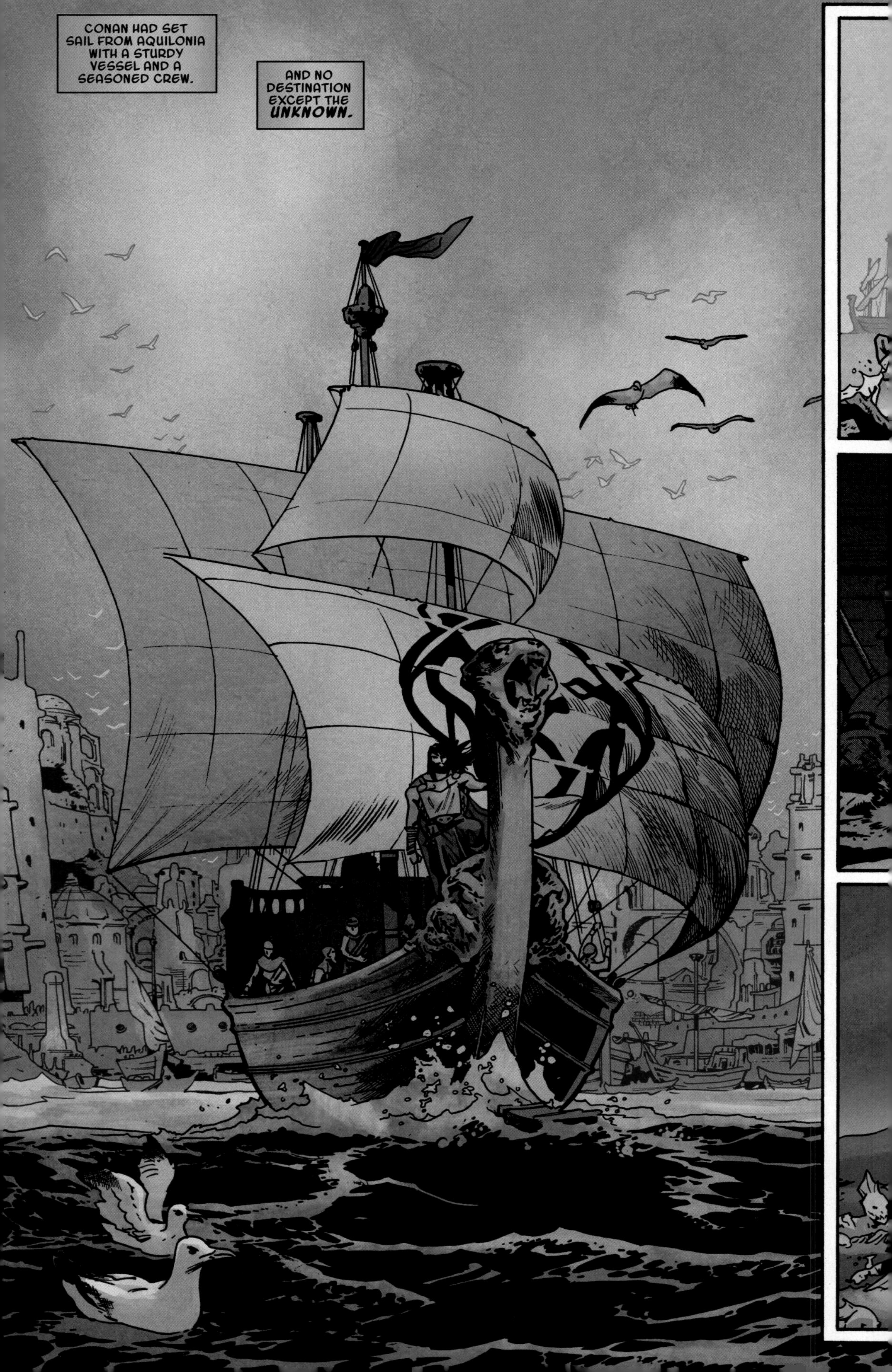
CONAN HAD SET SAIL FROM AQUILONIA WITH A STURDY VESSEL AND A SEASONED CREW.
AND NO DESTINATION EXCEPT THE *UNKNOWN.*

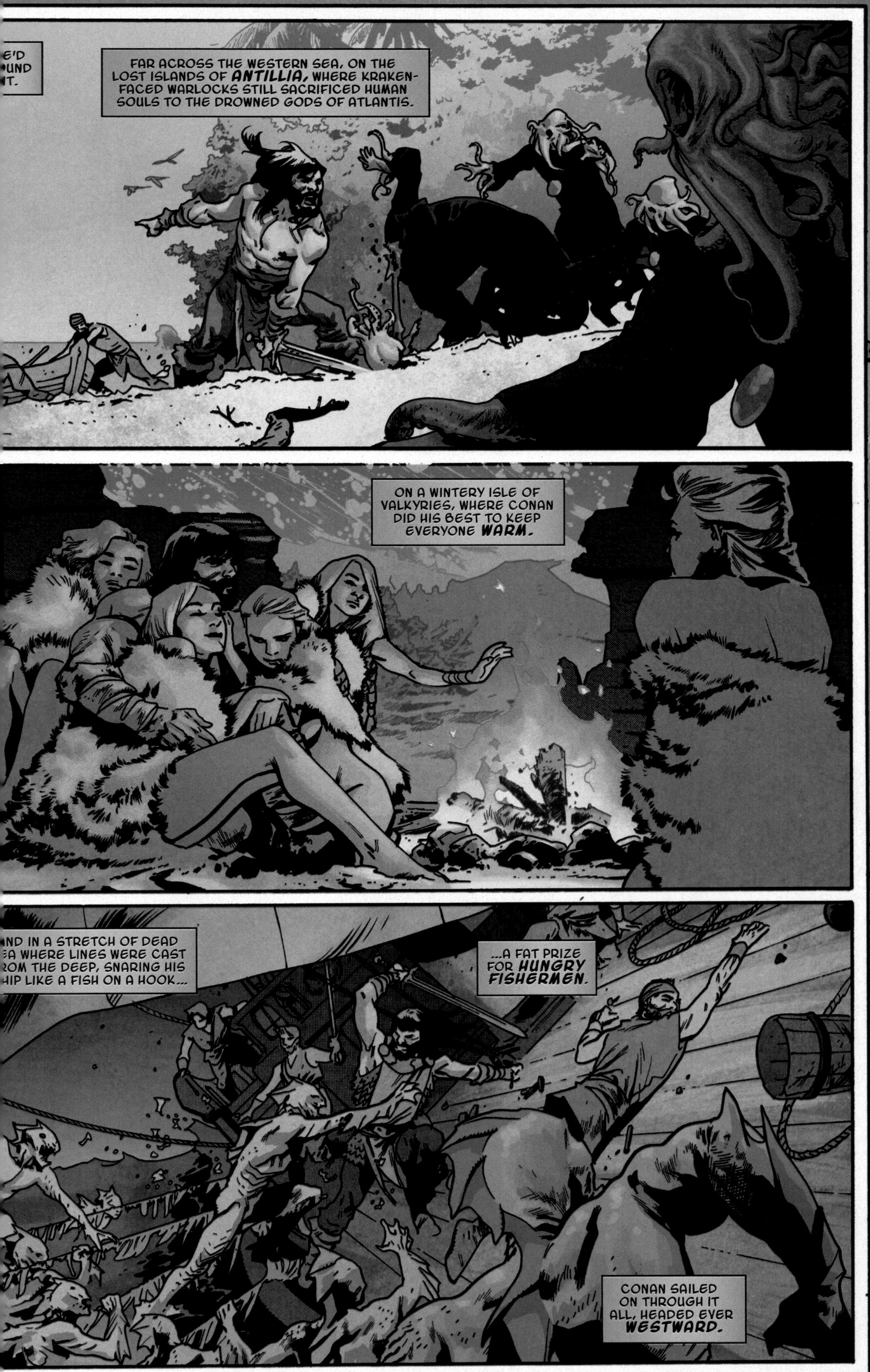
FAR ACROSS THE WESTERN SEA, ON THE LOST ISLANDS OF ANTILLIA, WHERE KRAKEN-FACED WARLOCKS STILL SACRIFICED HUMAN SOULS TO THE DROWNED GODS OF ATLANTIS.
ON A WINTERY ISLE OF VALKYRIES, WHERE CONAN DID HIS BEST TO KEEP EVERYONE WARM.
ND IN A STRETCH OF DEAD EA WHERE LINES WERE CAST ROM THE DEEP, SNARING HIS HIP LIKE A FISH ON A HOOK...
...A FAT PRIZE FOR HUNGRY FISHERMEN.
CONAN SAILED ON THROUGH IT ALL, HEADED EVER WESTWARD.

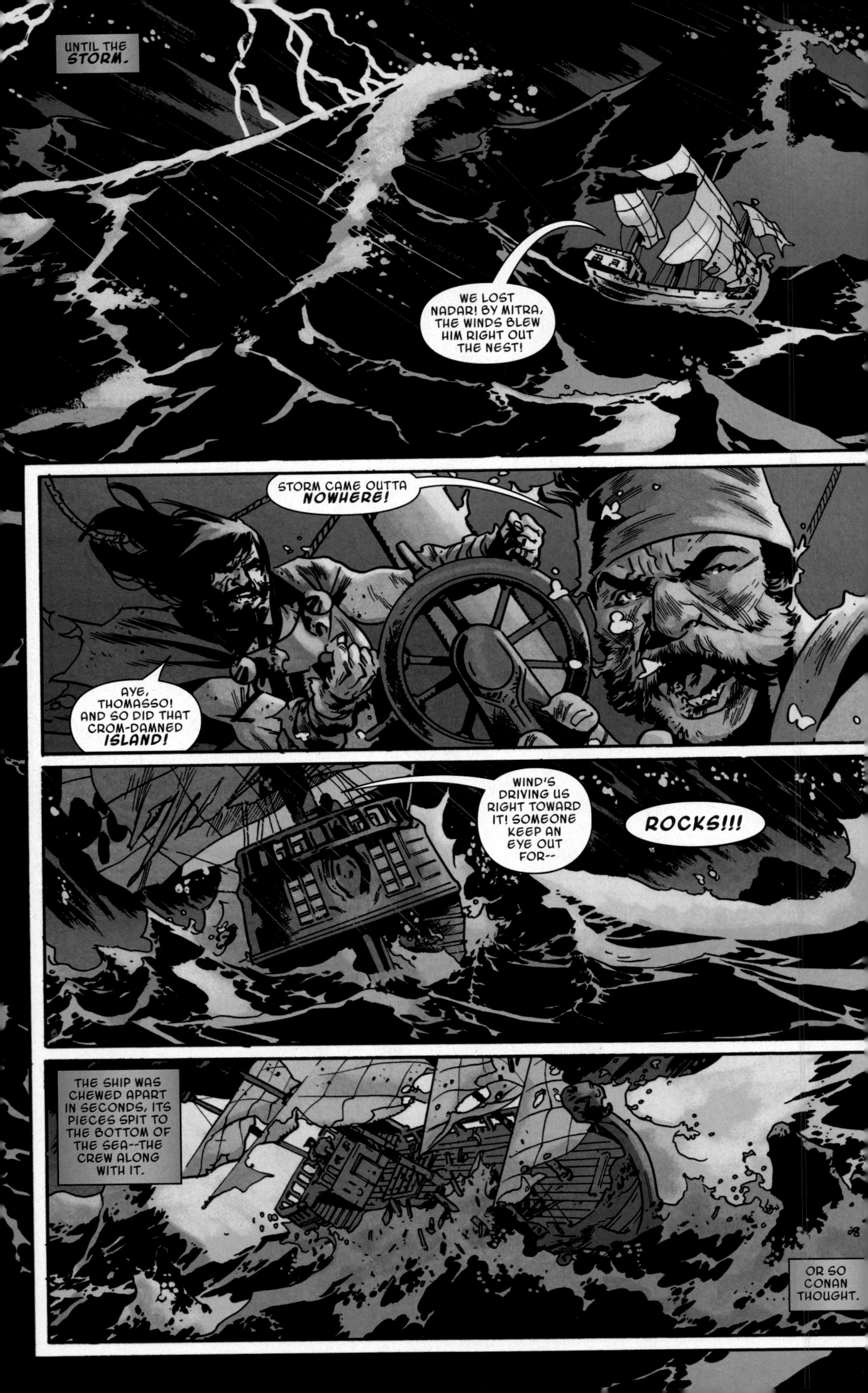

UNTIL THE STORM.
WE LOST NADAR! BY MITRA, THE WINDS BLEW HIM RIGHT OUT THE NEST!
STORM CAME OUTTA NOWHERE!
AYE, THOMASSO! AND SO DID THAT CROM-DAMNED ISLAND!
WIND'S DRIVING US RIGHT TOWARD IT! SOMEONE KEEP AN EYE OUT FOR--
ROCKS!!!
THE SHIP WAS CHEWED APART IN SECONDS, ITS PIECES SPIT TO THE BOTTOM OF THE SEA--THE CREW ALONG WITH IT.
OR SO CONAN THOUGHT.

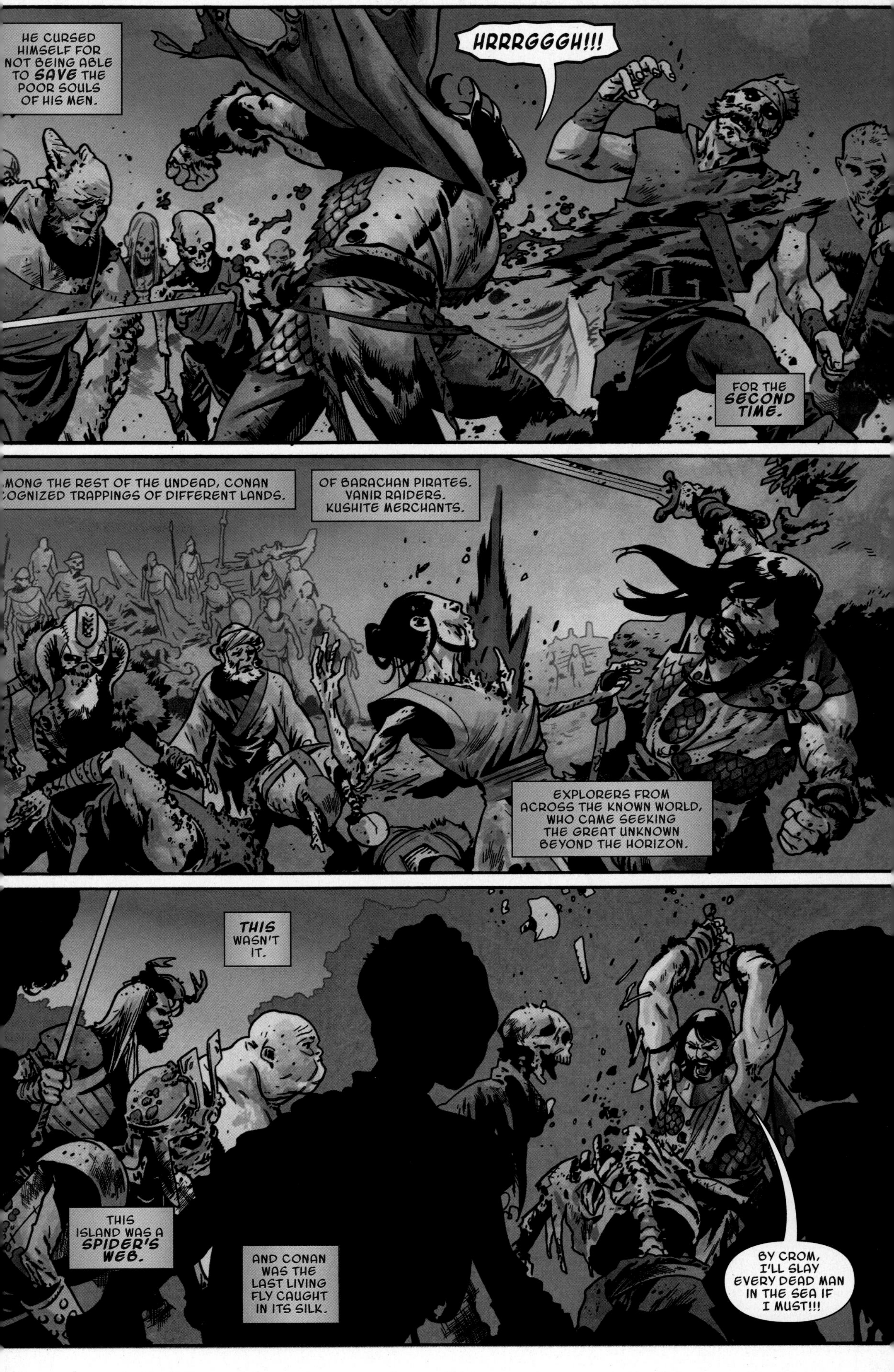
HE CURSED HIMSELF FOR NOT BEING ABLE TO SAVE THE POOR SOULS OF HIS MEN.
HRRRGGGH!!!
FOR THE SECOND TIME.
MONG THE REST OF THE UNDEAD, CONAN COGNIZED TRAPPINGS OF DIFFERENT LANDS.
OF BARACHAN PIRATES. VANIR RAIDERS. KUSHITE MERCHANTS.
EXPLORERS FROM ACROSS THE KNOWN WORLD, WHO CAME SEEKING THE GREAT UNKNOWN BEYOND THE HORIZON.
THIS WASN'T IT.
THIS ISLAND WAS A SPIDER'S WEB.
AND CONAN WAS THE LAST LIVING FLY CAUGHT IN ITS SILK.
BY CROM, I'LL SLAY EVERY DEAD MAN IN THE SEA IF I MUST!!!

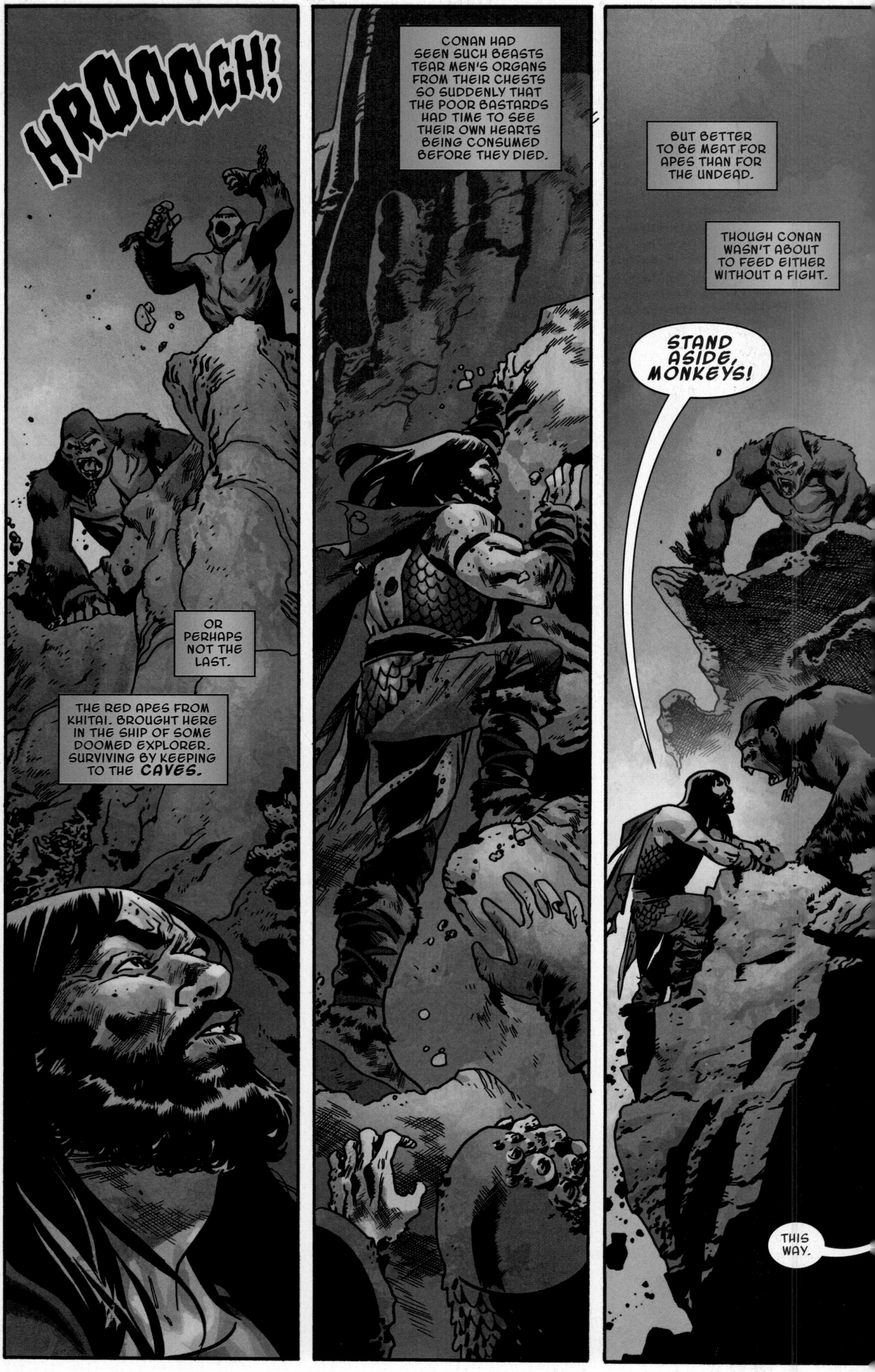
HROOOGH!
OR PERHAPS NOT THE LAST.
THE RED APES FROM KHITAI. BROUGHT HERE IN THE SHIP OF SOME DOOMED EXPLORER. SURVIVING BY KEEPING TO THE CAVES.
CONAN HAD SEEN SUCH BEASTS TEAR MEN'S ORGANS FROM THEIR CHESTS SO SUDDENLY THAT THE POOR BASTARDS HAD TIME TO SEE THEIR OWN HEARTS BEING CONSUMED BEFORE THEY DIED.
BUT BETTER TO BE MEAT FOR APES THAN FOR THE UNDEAD.
THOUGH CONAN WASN'T ABOUT TO FEED EITHER WITHOUT A FIGHT.
STAND ASIDE, MONKEYS!
THIS WAY.

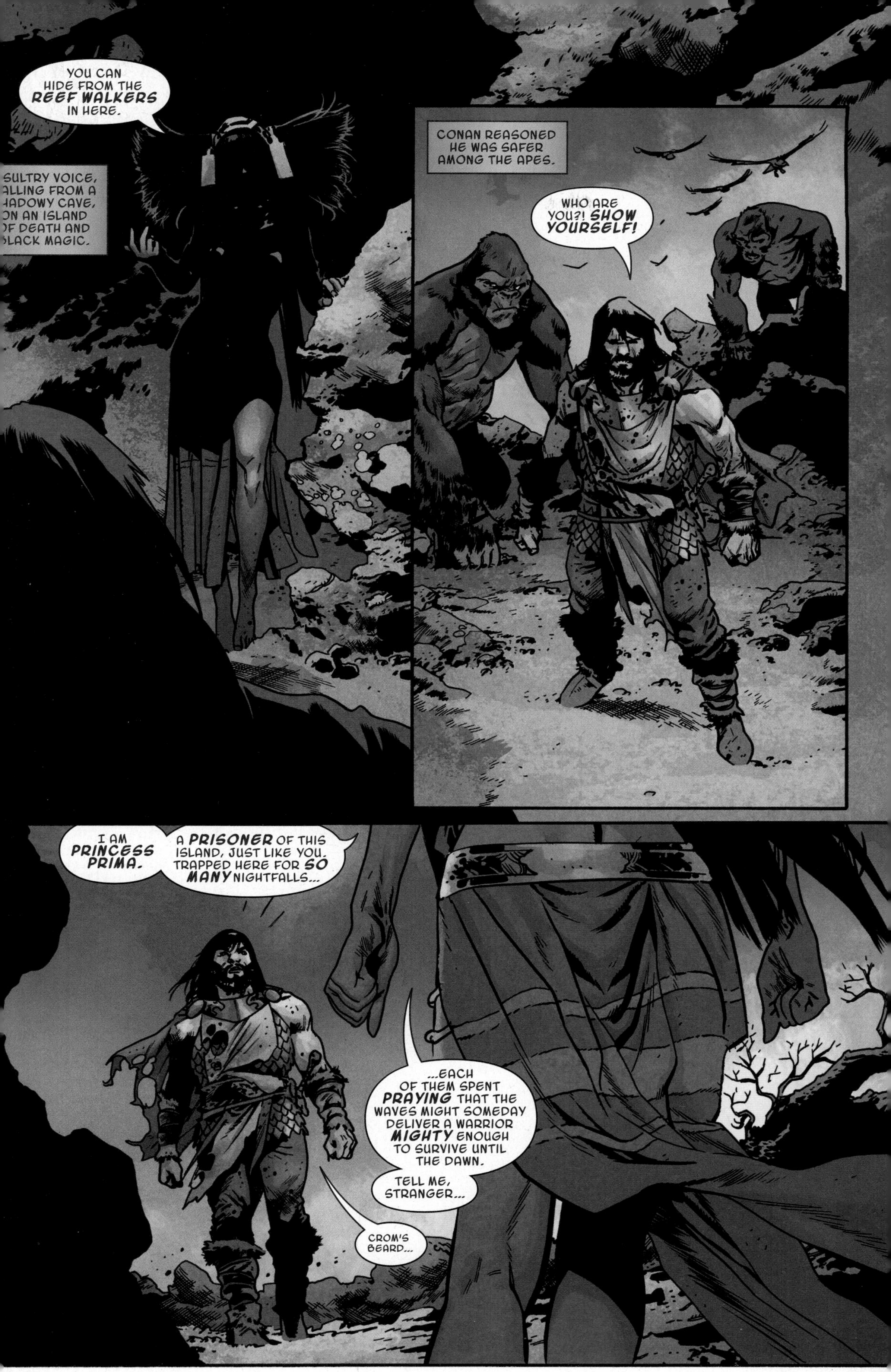

YOU CAN HIDE FROM THE REEF WALKERS IN HERE.
SULTRY VOICE, ALLING FROM A HADOWY CAVE, ON AN ISLAND OF DEATH AND BLACK MAGIC.
CONAN REASONED HE WAS SAFER AMONG THE APES.
WHO ARE YOU?! SHOW YOURSELF!
I AM PRINCESS PRIMA.
A PRISONER OF THIS ISLAND, JUST LIKE YOU. TRAPPED HERE FOR SO MANY NIGHTFALLS...
...EACH OF THEM SPENT PRAYING THAT THE WAVES MIGHT SOMEDAY DELIVER A WARRIOR MIGHTY ENOUGH TO SURVIVE UNTIL THE DAWN.
TELL ME, STRANGER...
CROM'S BEARD...

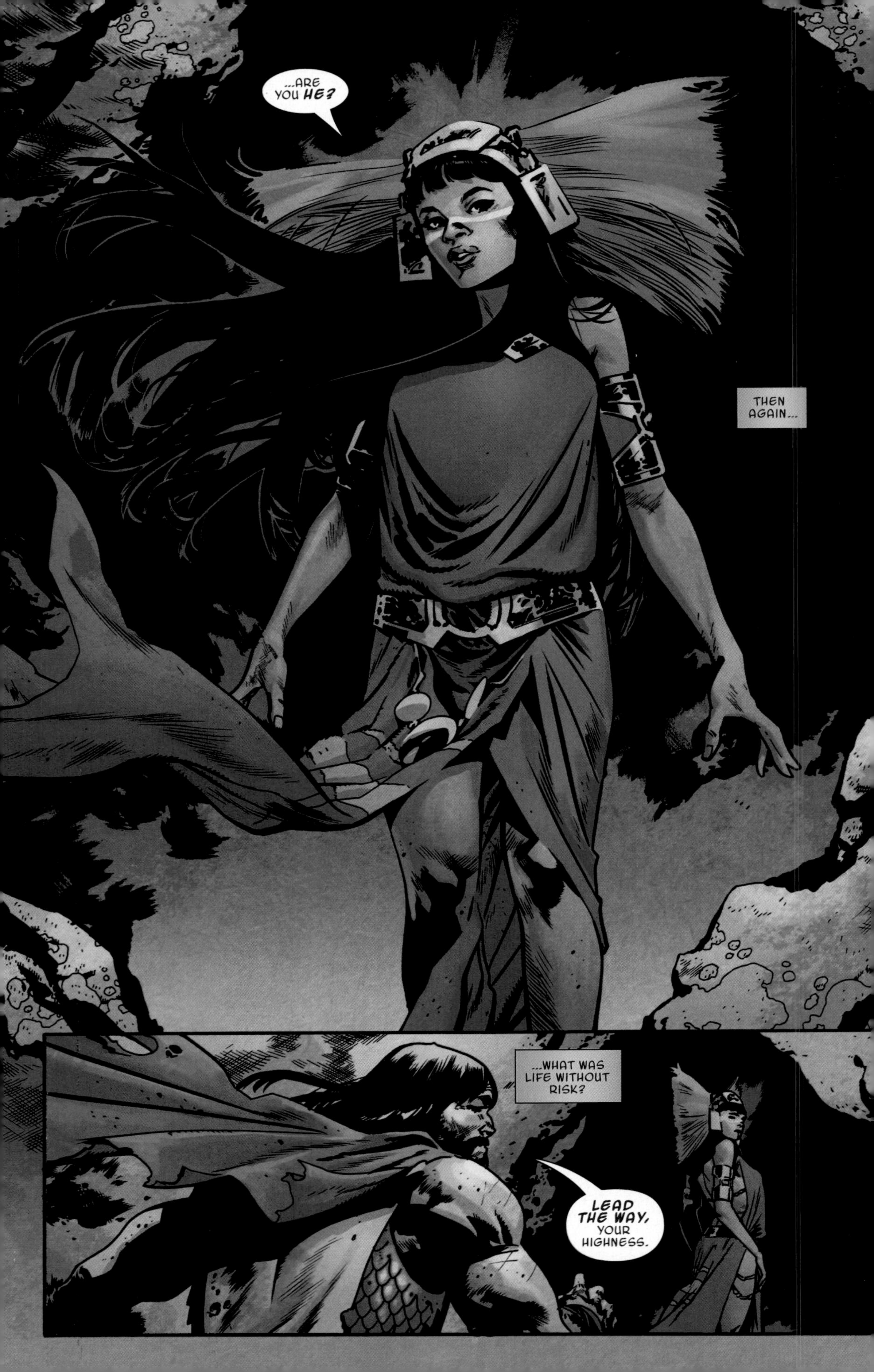
...ARE YOU HE?
THEN AGAIN...
...WHAT WAS LIFE WITHOUT RISK?
LEAD THE WAY, YOUR HIGHNESS.

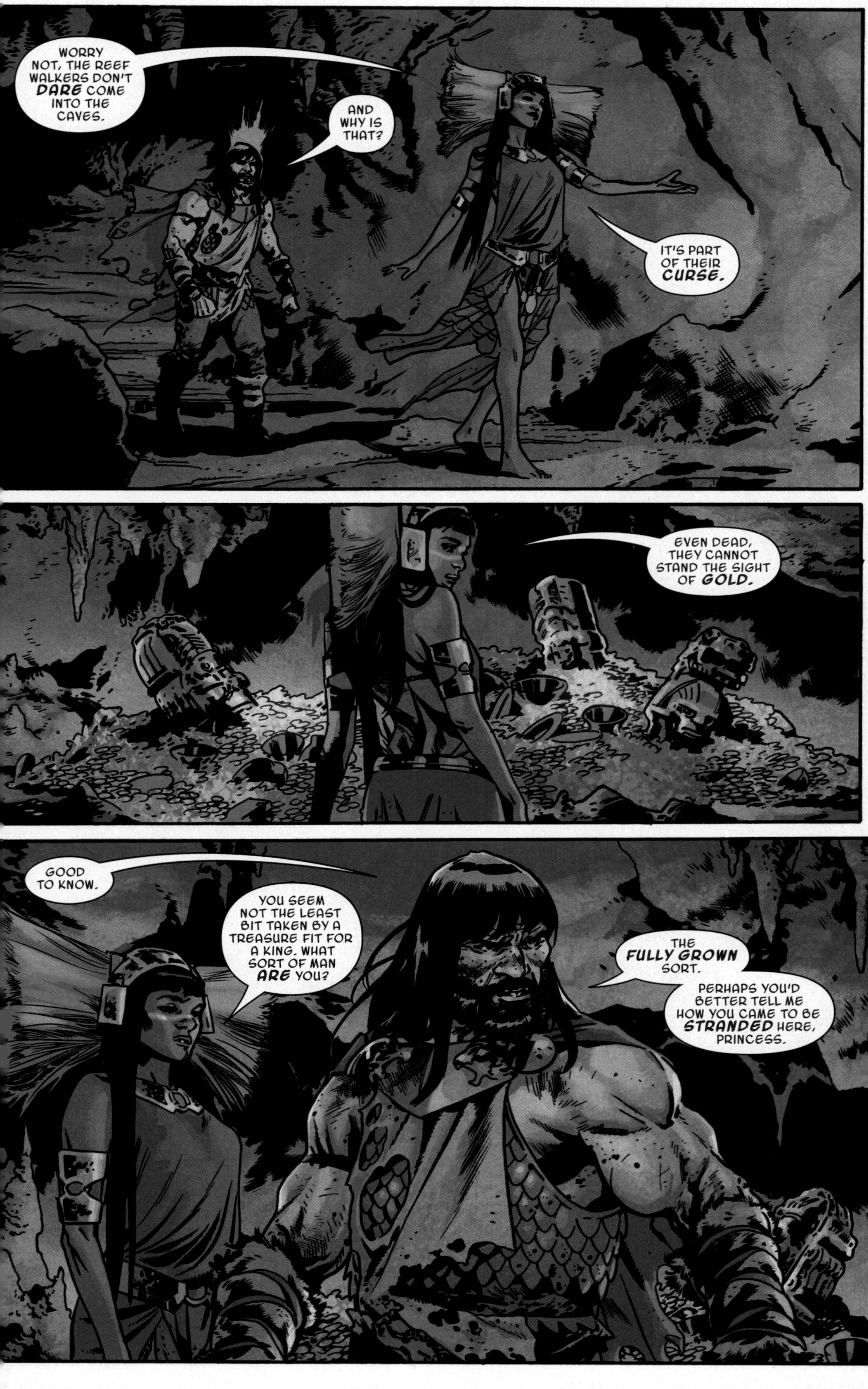
WORRY NOT, THE REEF WALKERS DON'T DARE COME INTO THE CAVES.
AND WHY IS THAT?
IT'S PART OF THEIR CURSE.
EVEN DEAD, THEY CANNOT STAND THE SIGHT OF GOLD.
GOOD TO KNOW.
YOU SEEM NOT THE LEAST BIT TAKEN BY A TREASURE FIT FOR A KING. WHAT SORT OF MAN ARE YOU?
THE FULLY GROWN SORT.
PERHAPS YOU'D BETTER TELL ME HOW YOU CAME TO BE STRANDED HERE, PRINCESS.

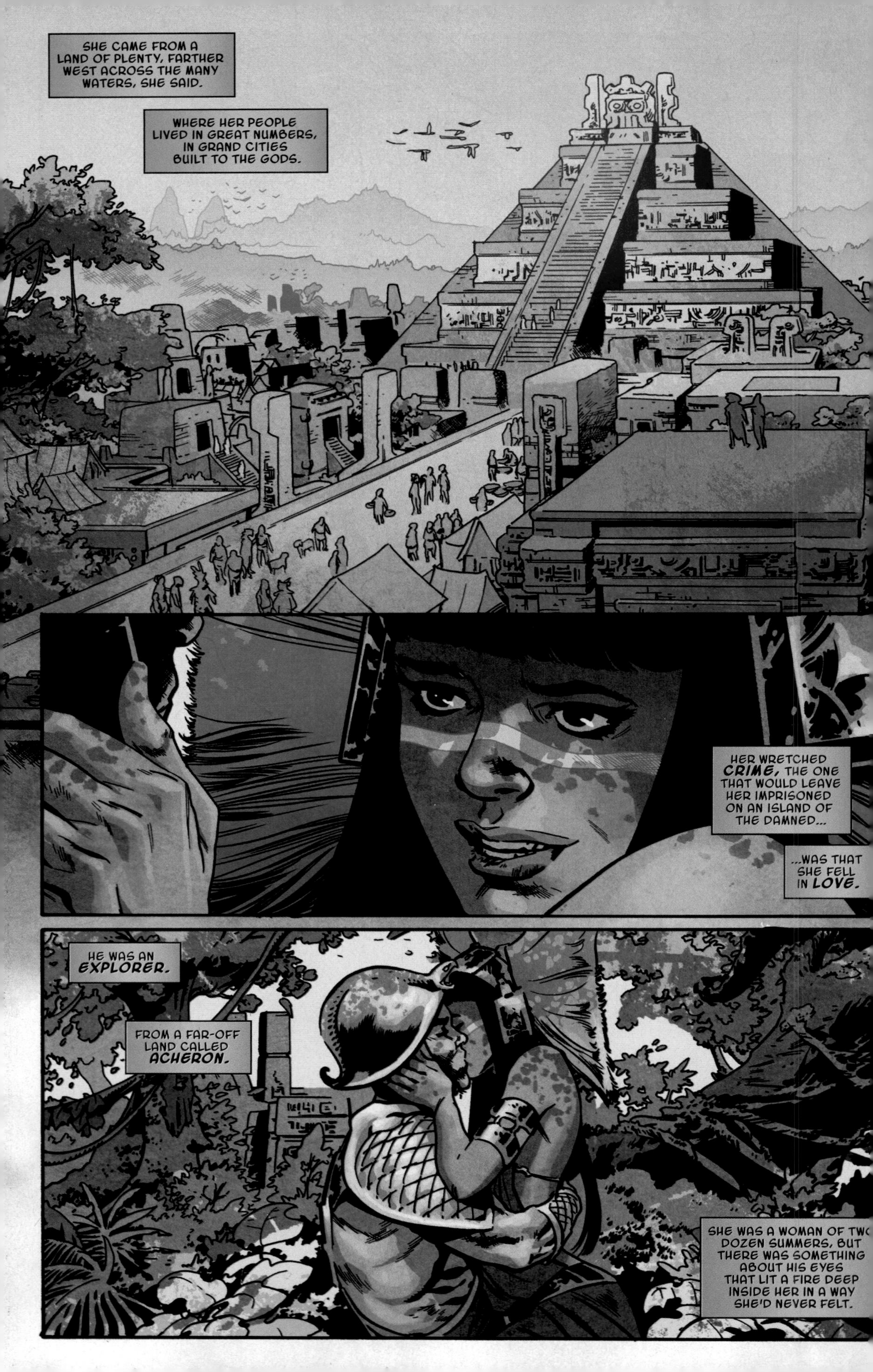
SHE CAME FROM A LAND OF PLENTY, FARTHER WEST ACROSS THE MANY WATERS, SHE SAID.
WHERE HER PEOPLE LIVED IN GREAT NUMBERS, IN GRAND CITIES BUILT TO THE GODS.
HER WRETCHED CRIME, THE ONE THAT WOULD LEAVE HER IMPRISONED ON AN ISLAND OF THE DAMNED...
...WAS THAT SHE FELL IN LOVE.
HE WAS AN EXPLORER.
FROM A FAR-OFF LAND CALLED ACHERON.
SHE WAS A WOMAN OF TWO DOZEN SUMMERS, BUT THERE WAS SOMETHING ABOUT HIS EYES THAT LIT A FIRE DEEP INSIDE HER IN A WAY SHE'D NEVER FELT.

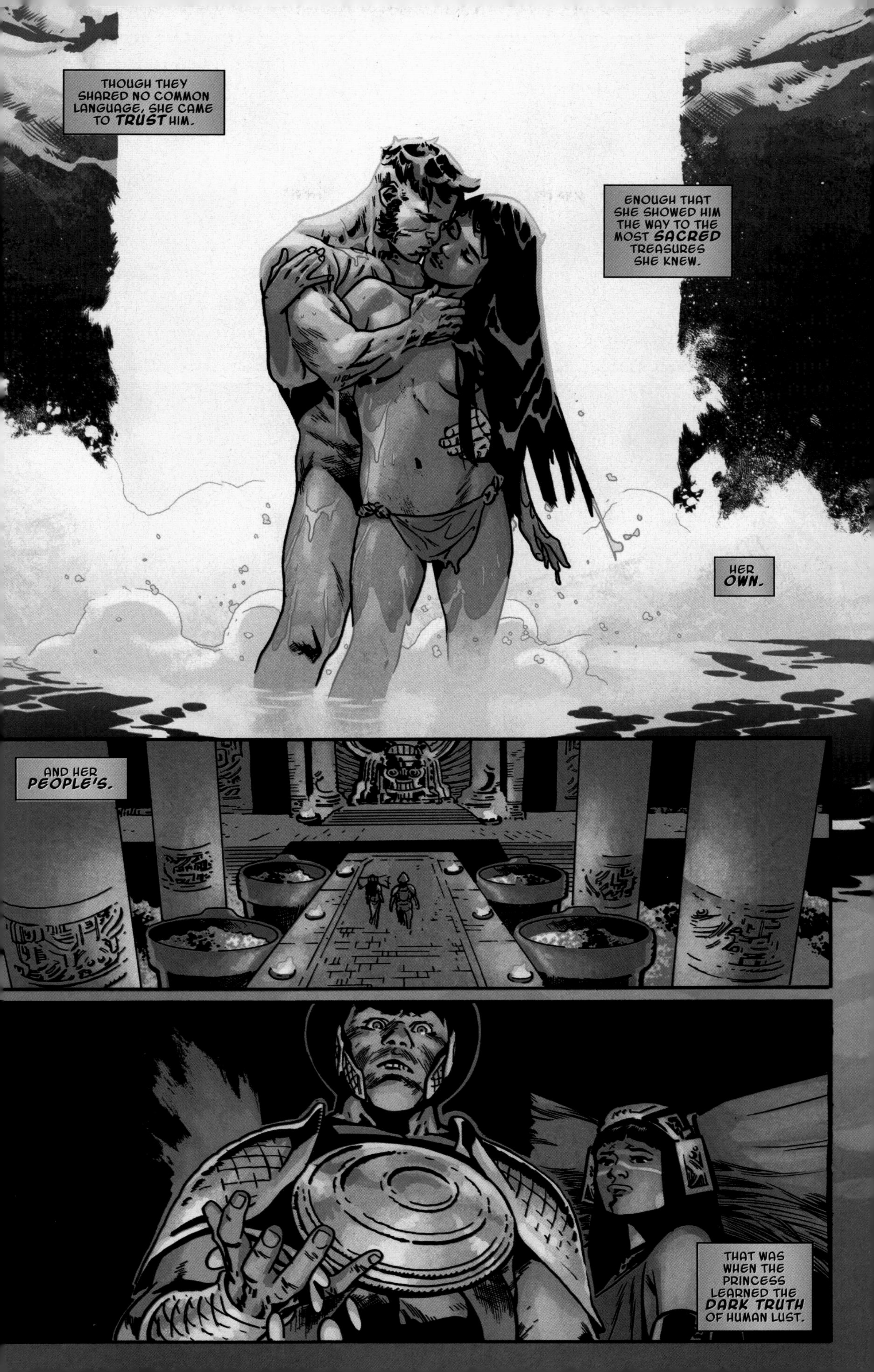
THOUGH THEY SHARED NO COMMON LANGUAGE, SHE CAME TO TRUST HIM.
ENOUGH THAT SHE SHOWED HIM THE WAY TO THE MOST SACRED TREASURES SHE KNEW.
HER OWN.
AND HER PEOPLE'S.
THAT WAS WHEN THE PRINCESS LEARNED THE DARK TRUTH OF HUMAN LUST.

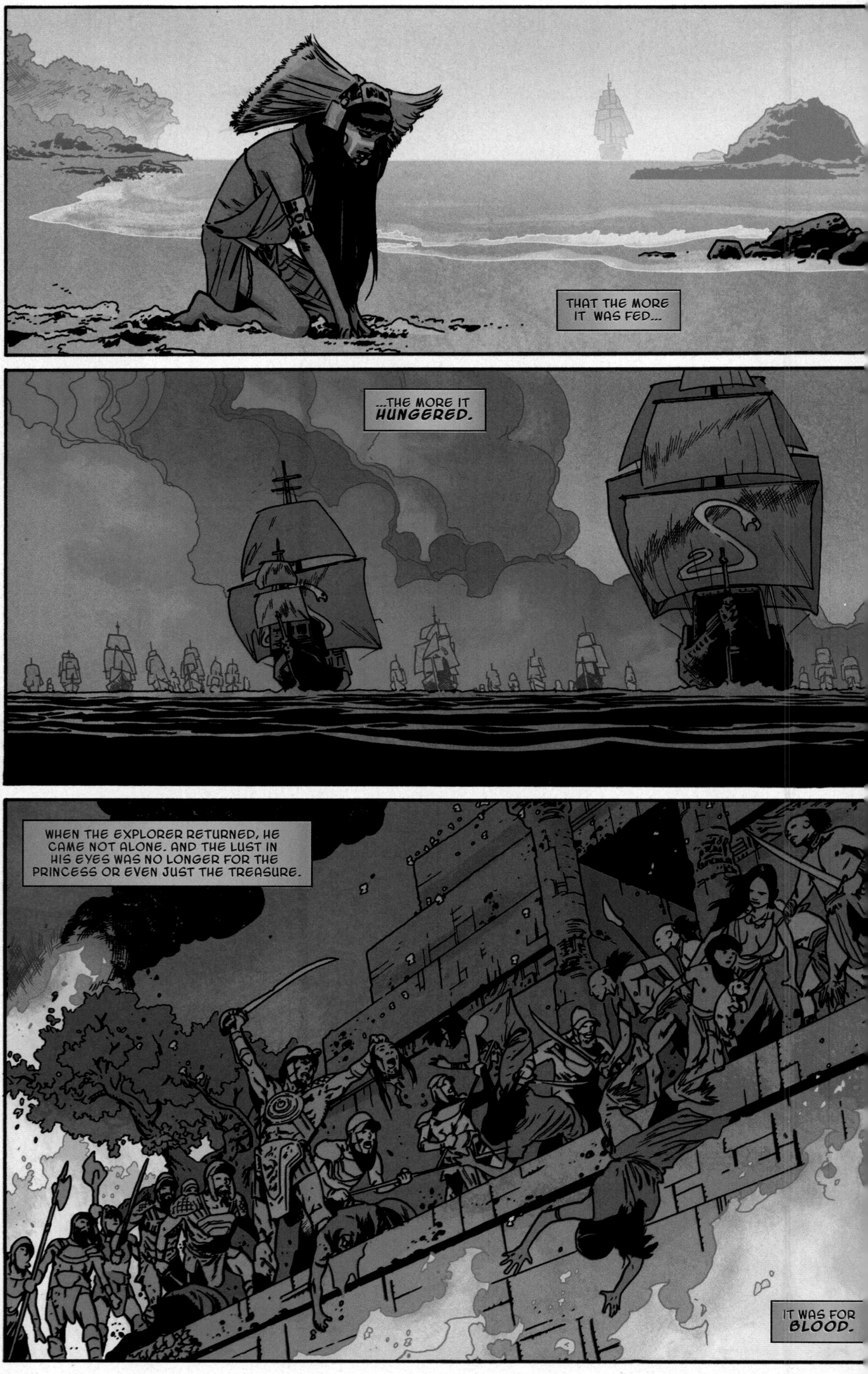
THAT THE MORE IT WAS FED...
...THE MORE IT HUNGERED.
WHEN THE EXPLORER RETURNED, HE CAME NOT ALONE. AND THE LUST IN HIS EYES WAS NO LONGER FOR THE PRINCESS OR EVEN JUST THE TREASURE.
IT WAS FOR BLOOD.

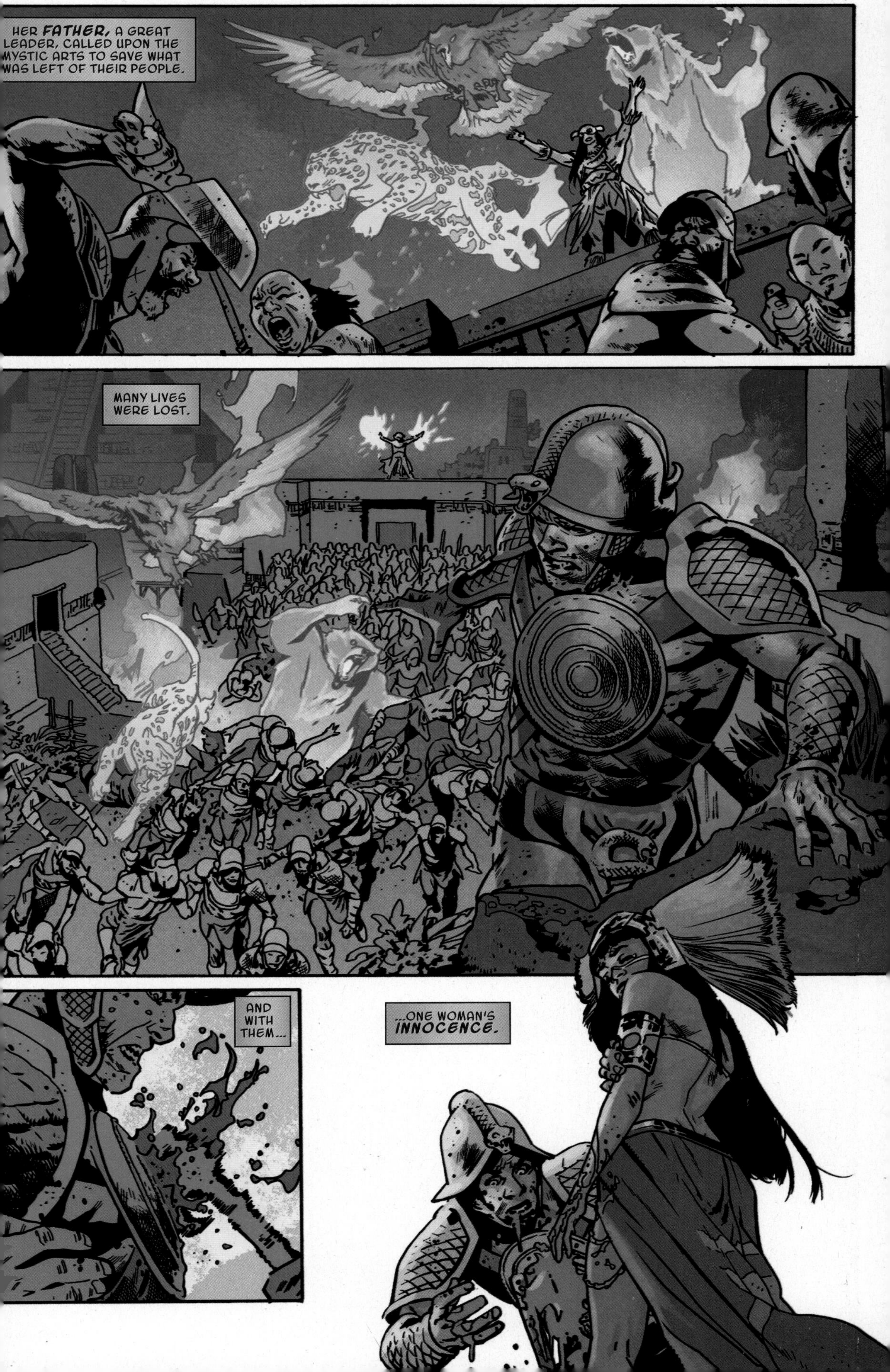
HER FATHER, A GREAT LEADER, CALLED UPON THE MYSTIC ARTS TO SAVE WHAT WAS LEFT OF THEIR PEOPLE.
MANY LIVES WERE LOST.
AND WITH THEM...
...ONE WOMAN'S INNOCENCE.

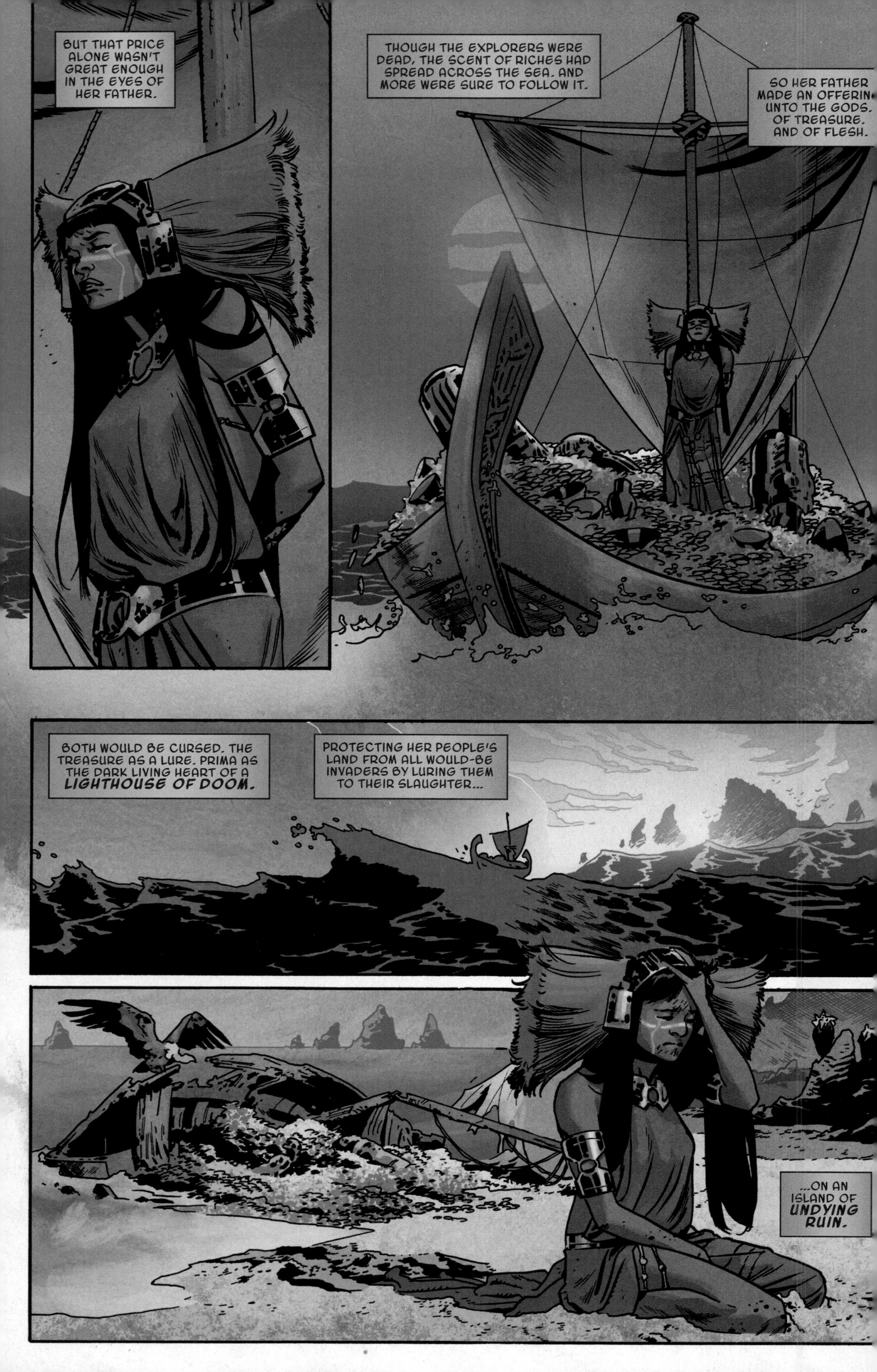
BUT THAT PRICE ALONE WASN'T GREAT ENOUGH IN THE EYES OF HER FATHER.
THOUGH THE EXPLORERS WERE DEAD, THE SCENT OF RICHES HAD SPREAD ACROSS THE SEA. AND MORE WERE SURE TO FOLLOW IT.
SO HER FATHER MADE AN OFFERIN UNTO THE GODS. OF TREASURE. AND OF FLESH.
BOTH WOULD BE CURSED. THE TREASURE AS A LURE. PRIMA AS THE DARK LIVING HEART OF A LIGHTHOUSE OF DOOM.
PROTECTING HER PEOPLE'S LAND FROM ALL WOULD-BE INVADERS BY LURING THEM TO THEIR SLAUGHTER...
...ON AN ISLAND OF UNDYING RUIN.

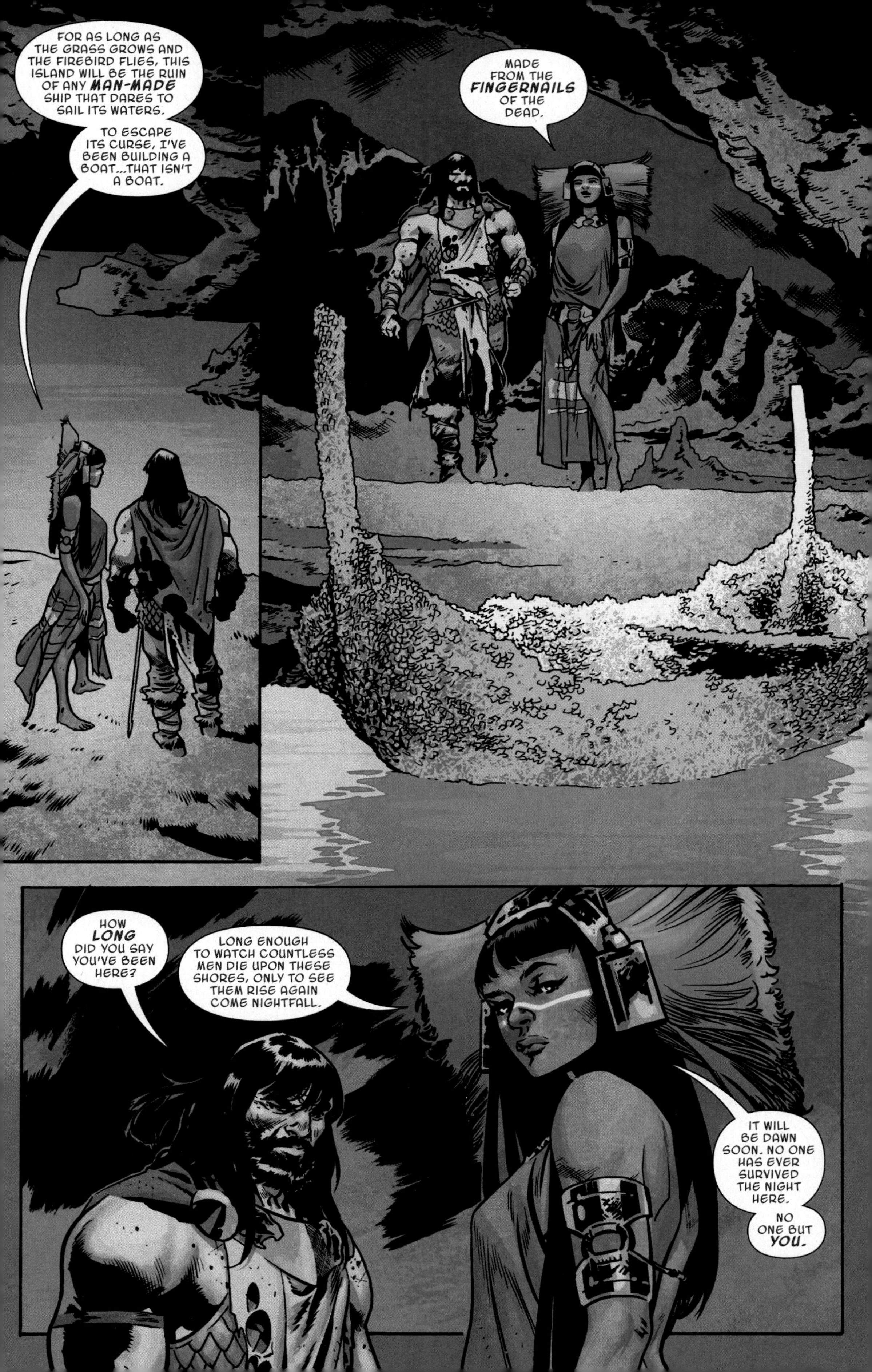
FOR AS LONG AS THE GRASS GROWS AND THE FIREBIRD FLIES, THIS ISLAND WILL BE THE RUIN OF ANY MAN-MADE SHIP THAT DARES TO SAIL ITS WATERS.
TO ESCAPE ITS CURSE, I'VE BEEN BUILDING A BOAT...THAT ISN'T A BOAT.
MADE FROM THE FINGERNAILS OF THE DEAD.
HOW LONG DID YOU SAY YOU'VE BEEN HERE?
LONG ENOUGH TO WATCH COUNTLESS MEN DIE UPON THESE SHORES, ONLY TO SEE THEM RISE AGAIN COME NIGHTFALL.
IT WILL BE DAWN SOON. NO ONE HAS EVER SURVIVED THE NIGHT HERE.
NO ONE BUT YOU.

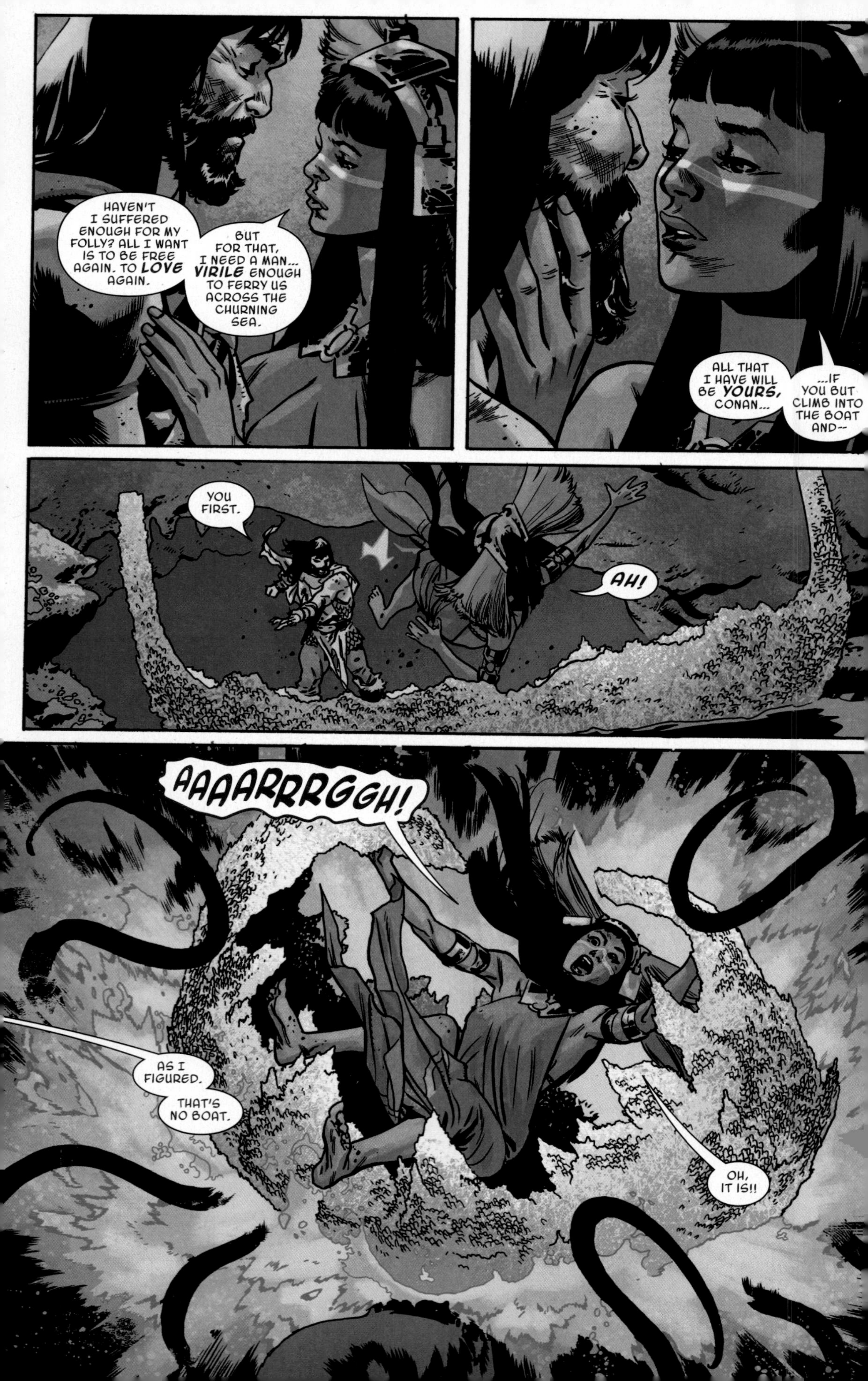
HAVEN'T I SUFFERED ENOUGH FOR MY FOLLY? ALL I WANT IS TO BE FREE AGAIN. TO LOVE AGAIN.
BUT FOR THAT, I NEED A MAN... VIRILE ENOUGH TO FERRY US ACROSS THE CHURNING SEA.
ALL THAT I HAVE WILL BE YOURS, CONAN...
...IF YOU BUT CLIMB INTO THE BOAT AND--
YOU FIRST.
AH!
AAAARRRRGGH!
AS I FIGURED.
THAT'S NO BOAT.
OH, IT IS!!

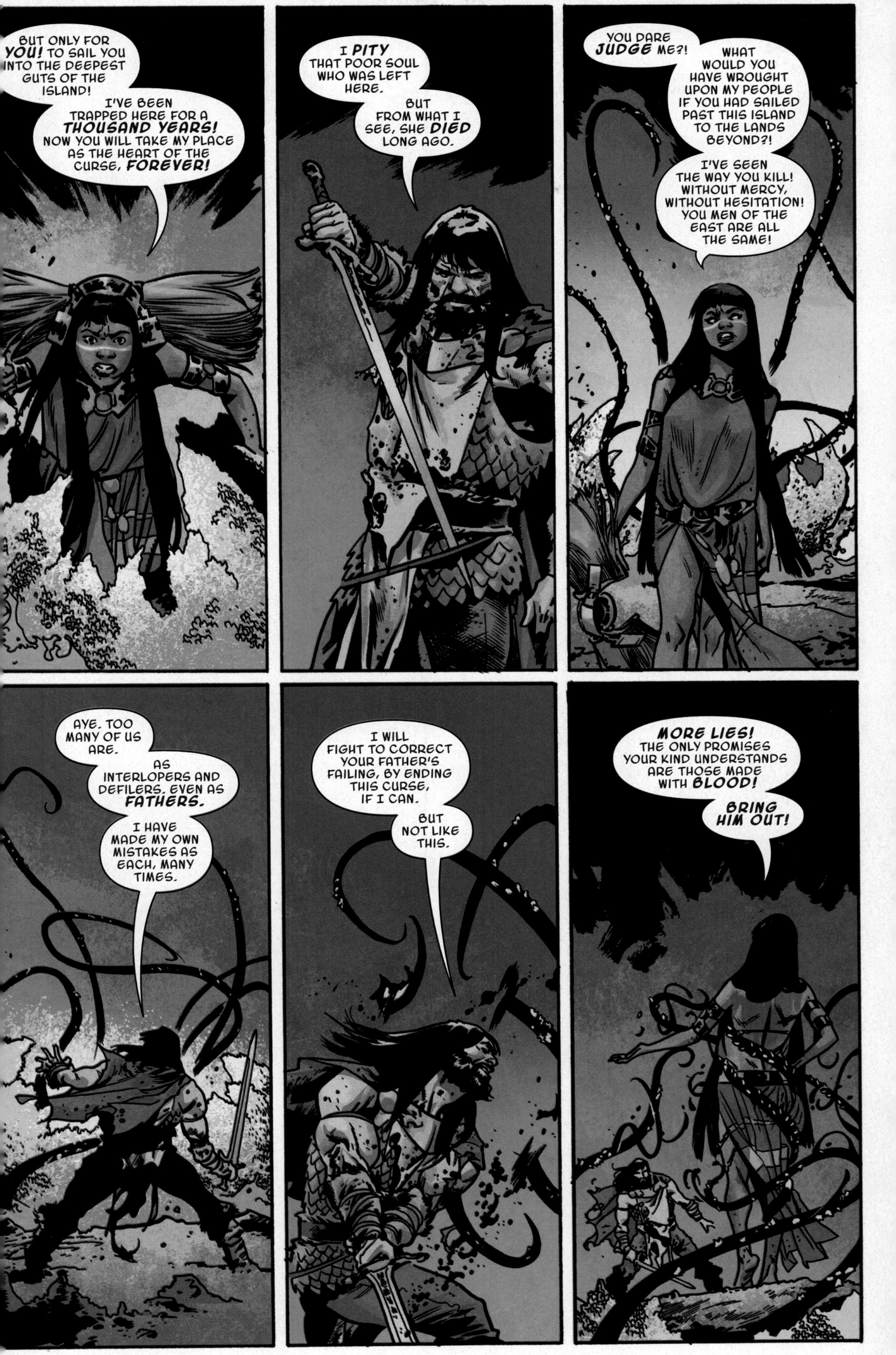
BUT ONLY FOR YOU! TO SAIL YOU INTO THE DEEPEST GUTS OF THE ISLAND!
I'VE BEEN TRAPPED HERE FOR A THOUSAND YEARS! NOW YOU WILL TAKE MY PLACE AS THE HEART OF THE CURSE, FOREVER!
I PITY THAT POOR SOUL WHO WAS LEFT HERE.
BUT FROM WHAT I SEE, SHE DIED LONG AGO.
YOU DARE JUDGE ME?!
WHAT WOULD YOU HAVE WROUGHT UPON MY PEOPLE IF YOU HAD SAILED PAST THIS ISLAND TO THE LANDS BEYOND?!
I'VE SEEN THE WAY YOU KILL! WITHOUT MERCY, WITHOUT HESITATION! YOU MEN OF THE EAST ARE ALL THE SAME!
AYE. TOO MANY OF US ARE.
AS INTERLOPERS AND DEFILERS. EVEN AS FATHERS.
I HAVE MADE MY OWN MISTAKES AS EACH, MANY TIMES.
I WILL FIGHT TO CORRECT YOUR FATHER'S FAILING, BY ENDING THIS CURSE, IF I CAN.
BUT NOT LIKE THIS.
MORE LIES! THE ONLY PROMISES YOUR KIND UNDERSTANDS ARE THOSE MADE WITH BLOOD!
BRING HIM OUT!

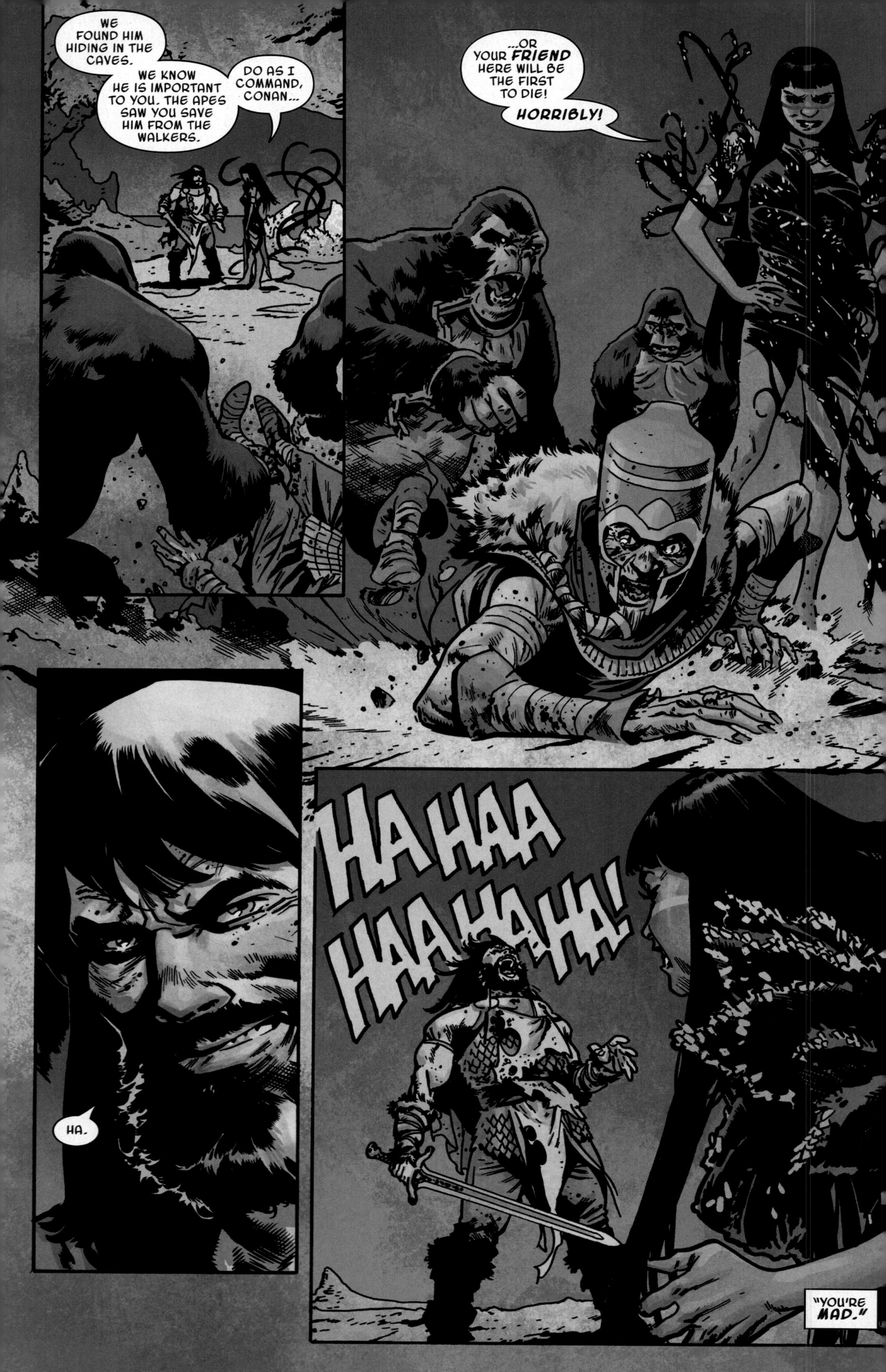
WE FOUND HIM HIDING IN THE CAVES.
WE KNOW HE IS IMPORTANT TO YOU. THE APES SAW YOU SAVE HIM FROM THE WALKERS.
DO AS I COMMAND, CONAN...
...OR YOUR FRIEND HERE WILL BE THE FIRST TO DIE!
HORRIBLY!
HA.
HA HAA HAAHAHA!
"YOU'RE MAD."

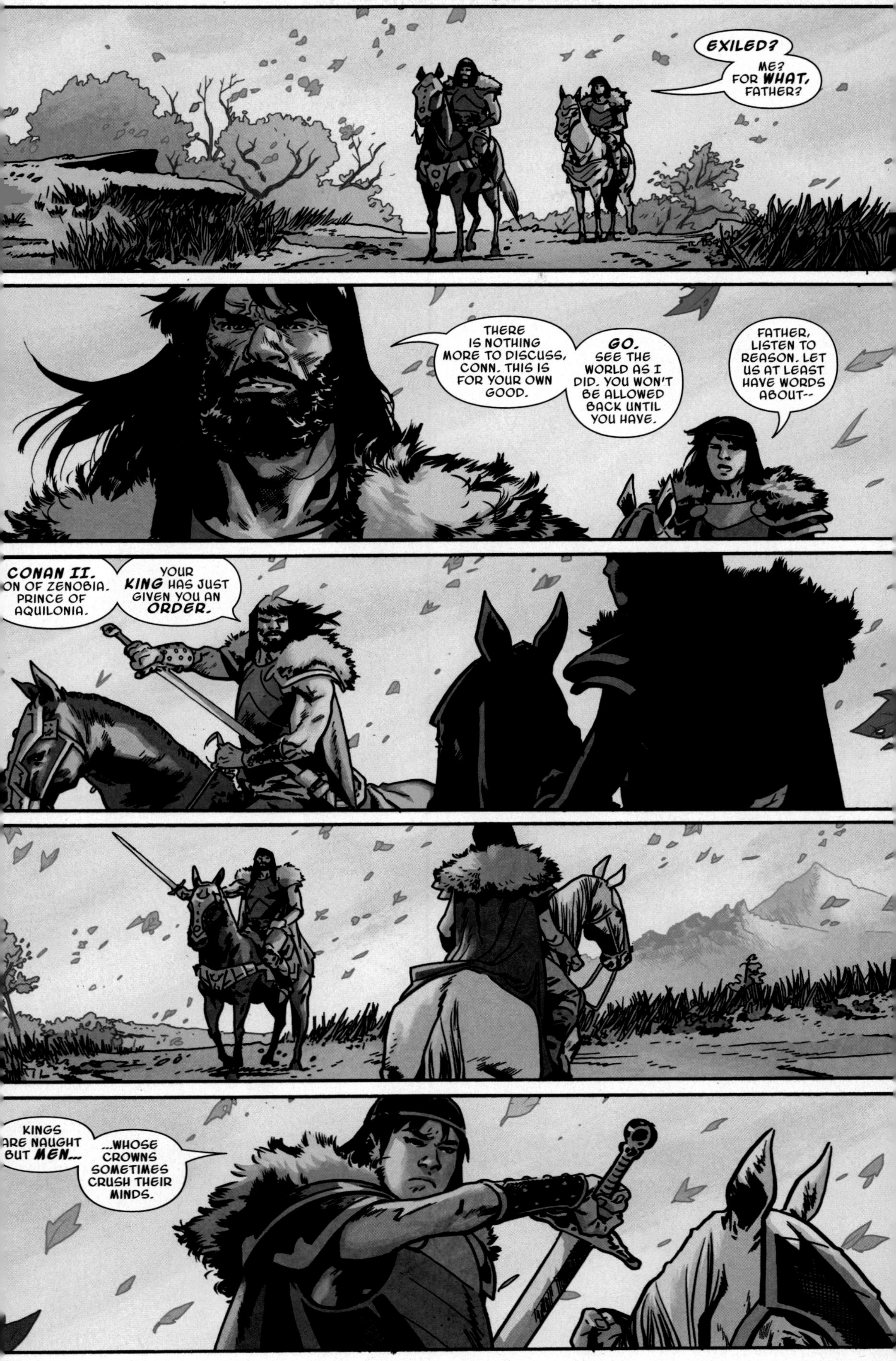
EXILED? ME? FOR WHAT, FATHER?
THERE IS NOTHING MORE TO DISCUSS, CONN. THIS IS FOR YOUR OWN GOOD.
GO. SEE THE WORLD AS I DID. YOU WON'T BE ALLOWED BACK UNTIL YOU HAVE.
FATHER, LISTEN TO REASON. LET US AT LEAST HAVE WORDS ABOUT--
CONAN II. ON OF ZENOBIA. PRINCE OF AQUILONIA.
YOUR KING HAS JUST GIVEN YOU AN ORDER.
KINGS ARE NAUGHT BUT MEN...
...WHOSE CROWNS SOMETIMES CRUSH THEIR MINDS.

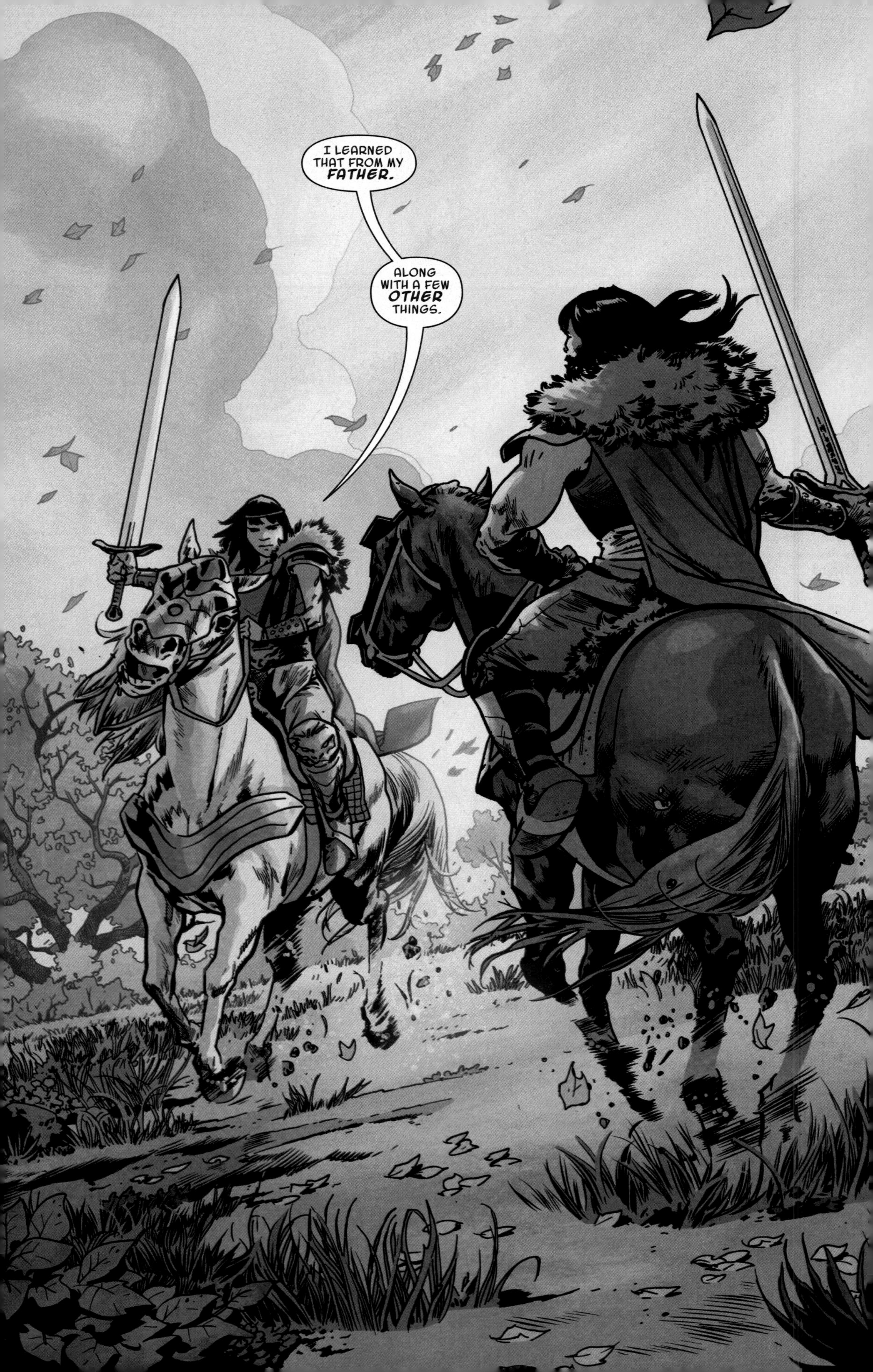

I LEARNED THAT FROM MY FATHER.
ALONG WITH A FEW OTHER THINGS.

#1 VARIANT BY **STEPHANIE HANS**

KING-SIZE CONAN
CONAN
VENGEANCE
CONAN THE KING
CONAN

#1 VARIANT BY **MR GARCIN**

#1 HIDDEN GEM VARIANT BY
JOHN BUSCEMA & RACHELLE ROSENBERG

#2 VARIANT BY
ROBERTO DE LA TORRE & JAVA TARTAGLIA

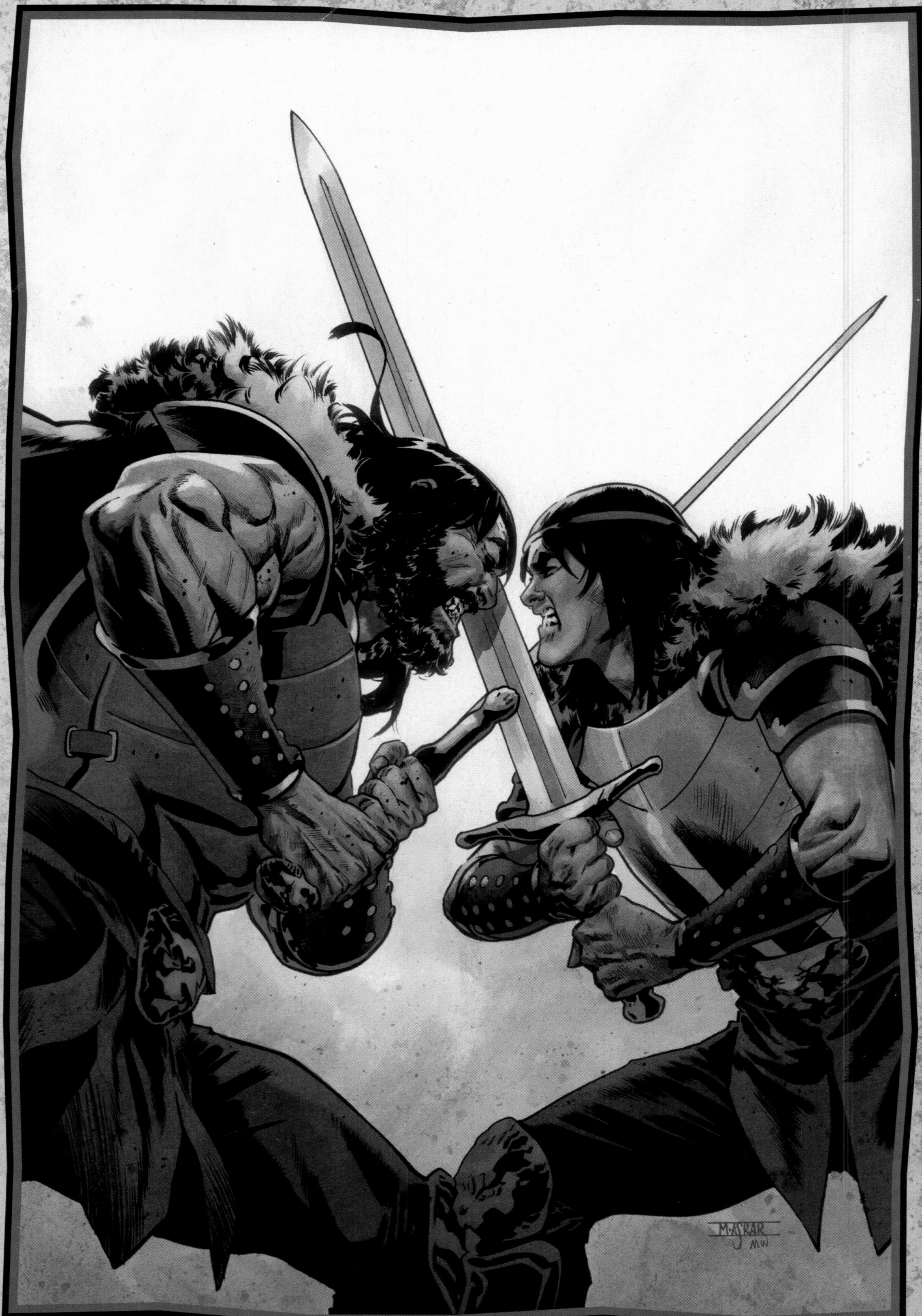

4

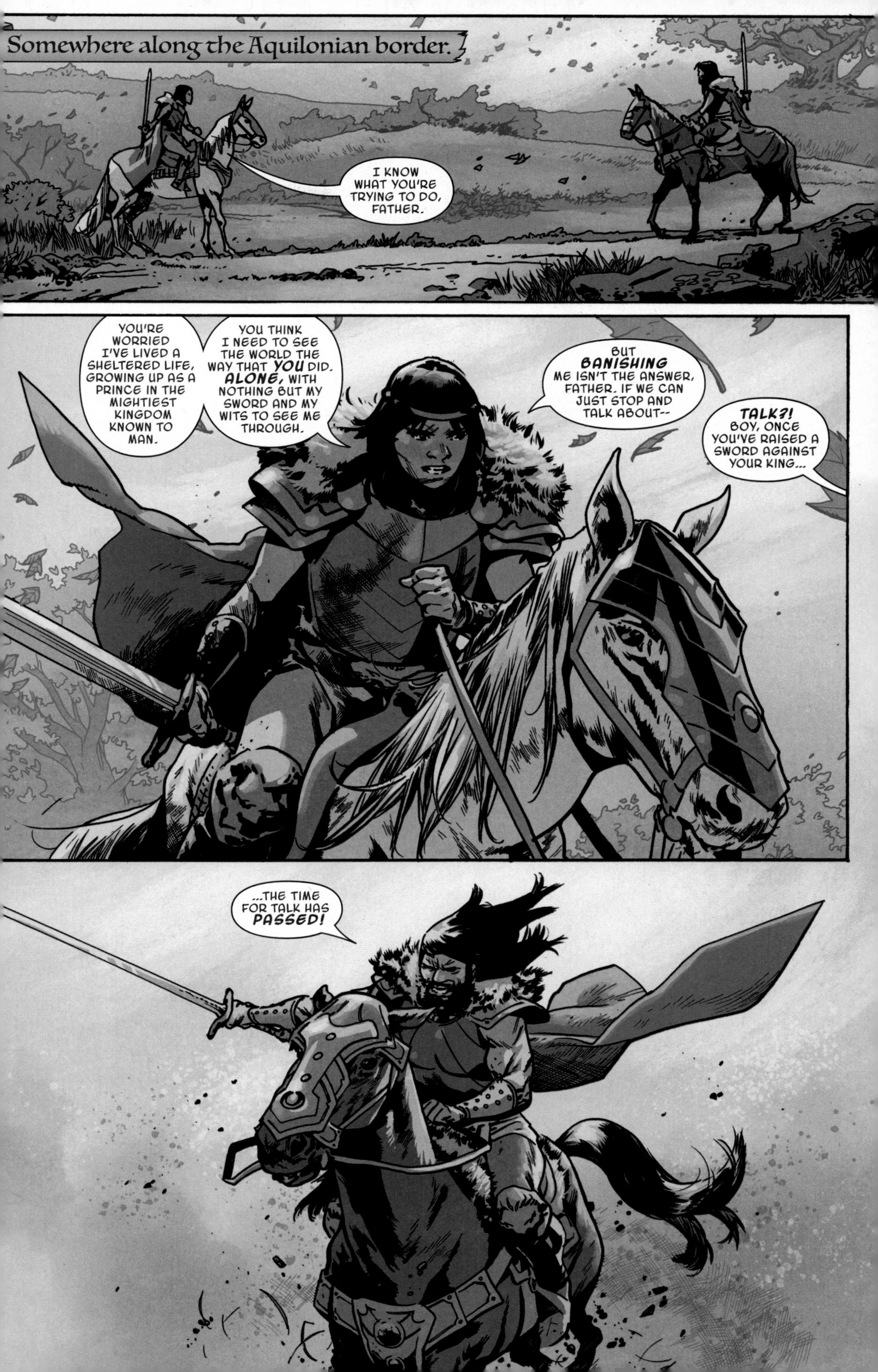
Somewhere along the Aquilonian border.
I KNOW WHAT YOU'RE TRYING TO DO, FATHER.
YOU'RE WORRIED I'VE LIVED A SHELTERED LIFE, GROWING UP AS A PRINCE IN THE MIGHTIEST KINGDOM KNOWN TO MAN.
YOU THINK I NEED TO SEE THE WORLD THE WAY THAT **YOU** DID. ***ALONE,*** WITH NOTHING BUT MY SWORD AND MY WITS TO SEE ME THROUGH.
BUT **BANISHING** ME ISN'T THE ANSWER, FATHER. IF WE CAN JUST STOP AND TALK ABOUT--
TALK?! BOY, ONCE YOU'VE RAISED A SWORD AGAINST YOUR KING...
...THE TIME FOR TALK HAS ***PASSED!***

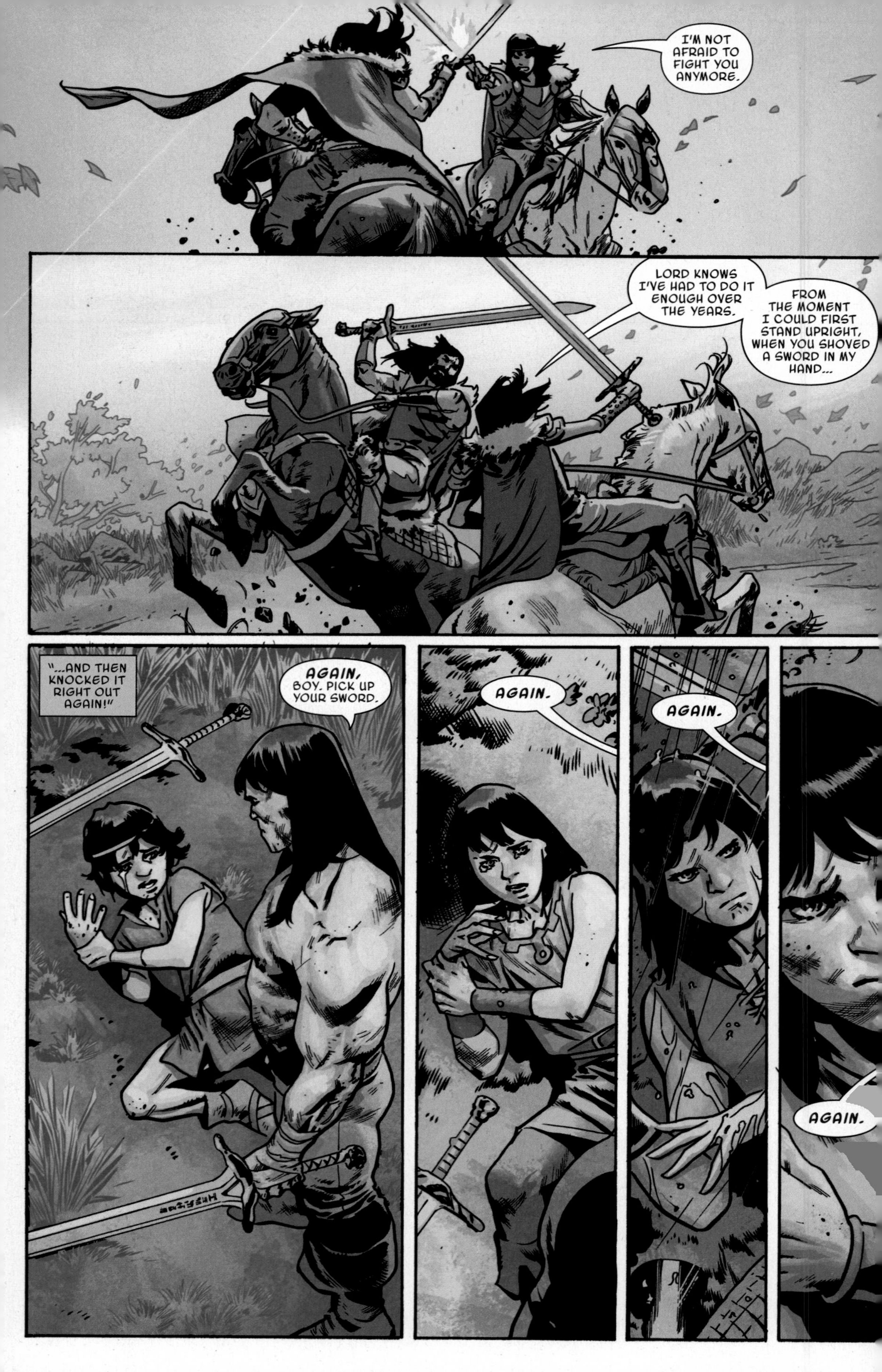
I'M NOT AFRAID TO FIGHT YOU ANYMORE.
LORD KNOWS I'VE HAD TO DO IT ENOUGH OVER THE YEARS.
FROM THE MOMENT I COULD FIRST STAND UPRIGHT, WHEN YOU SHOVED A SWORD IN MY HAND...
"...AND THEN KNOCKED IT RIGHT OUT AGAIN!"
AGAIN, BOY. PICK UP YOUR SWORD.
AGAIN.
AGAIN.
AGAIN.

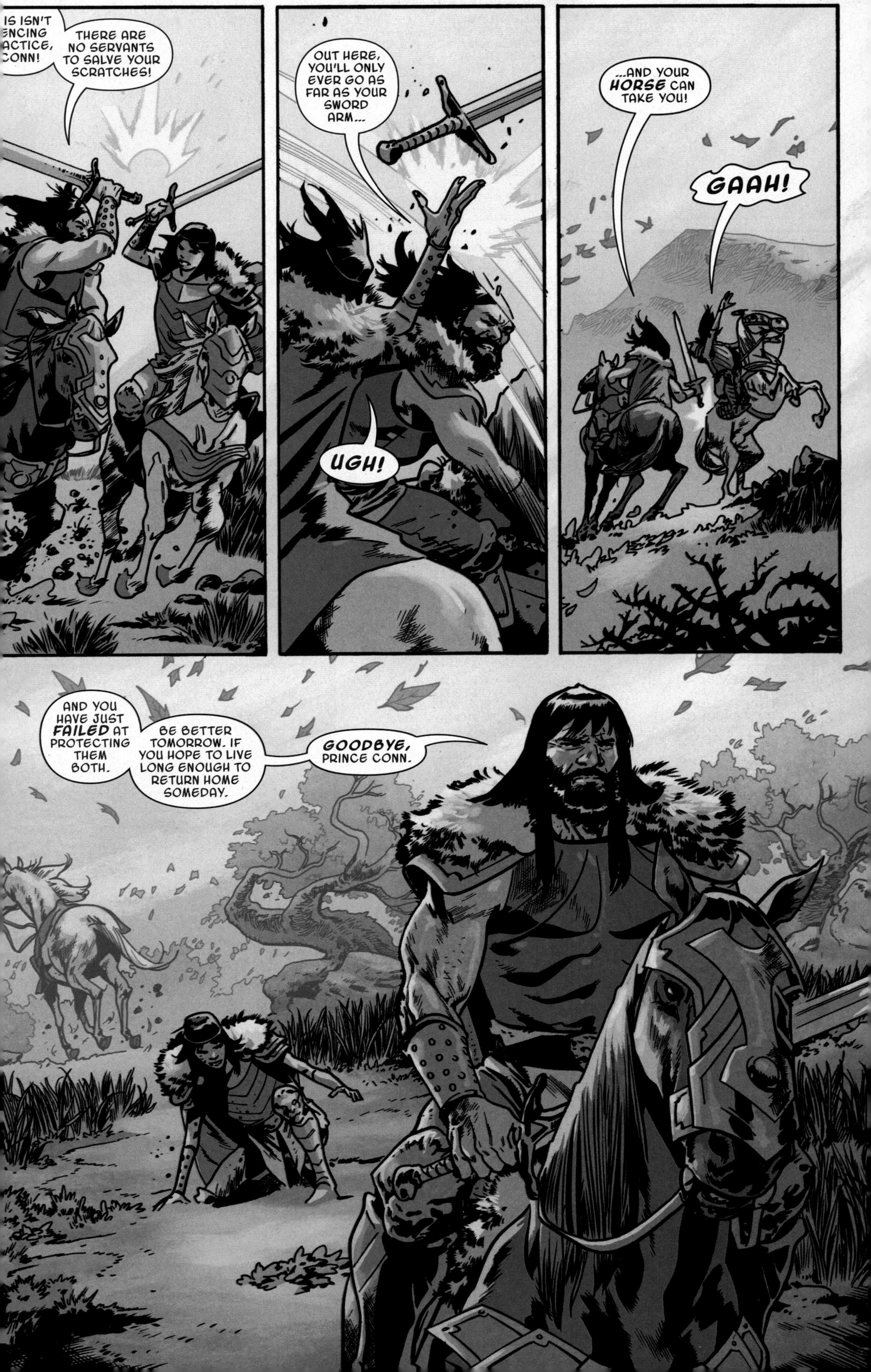
IS ISN'T
ENCING
ACTICE,
CONN!
THERE ARE NO SERVANTS TO SALVE YOUR SCRATCHES!
OUT HERE, YOU'LL ONLY EVER GO AS FAR AS YOUR SWORD ARM...
UGH!
...AND YOUR HORSE CAN TAKE YOU!
GAAH!
AND YOU HAVE JUST FAILED AT PROTECTING THEM BOTH.
BE BETTER TOMORROW. IF YOU HOPE TO LIVE LONG ENOUGH TO RETURN HOME SOMEDAY.
GOODBYE, PRINCE CONN.

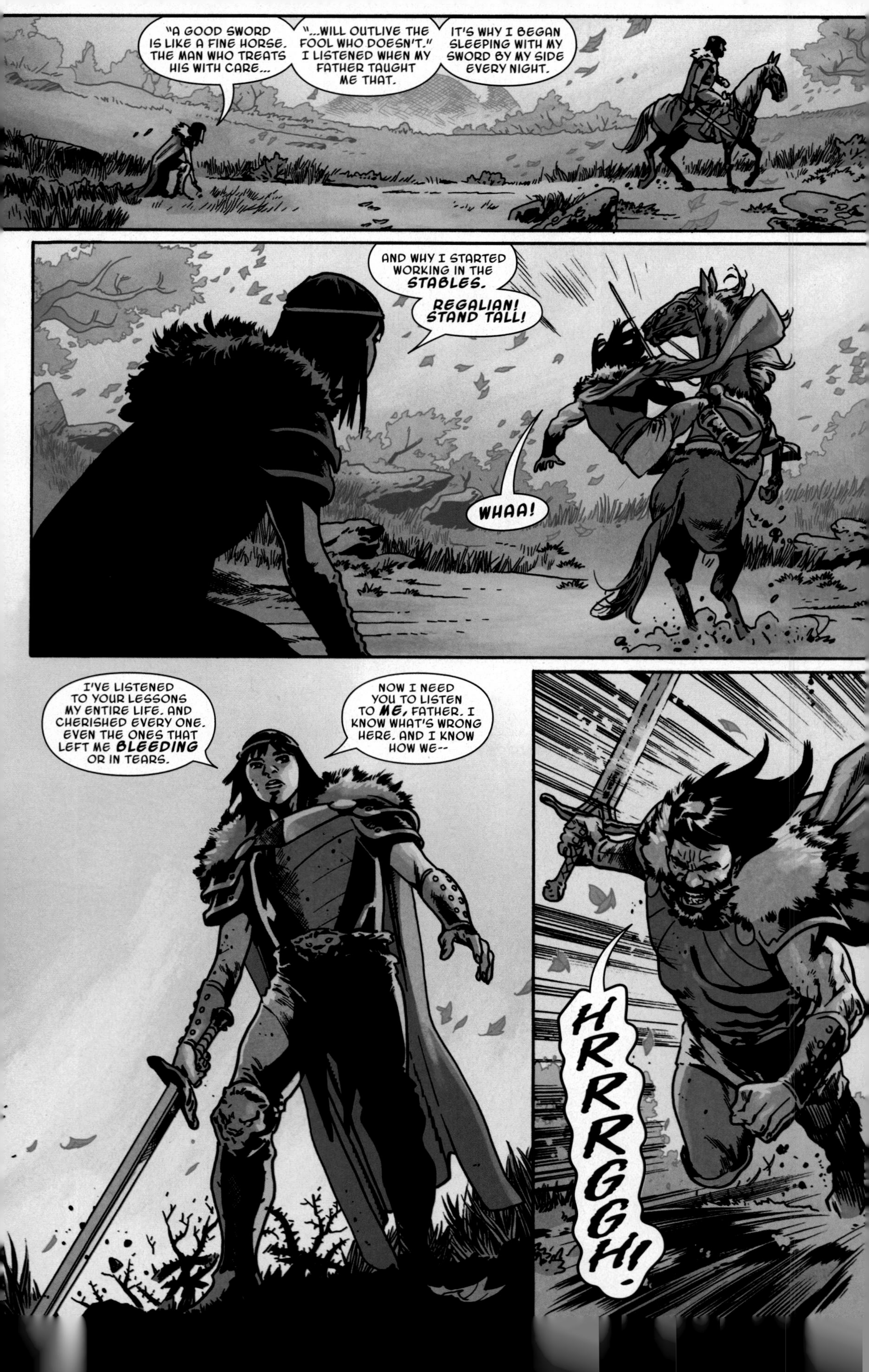
"A GOOD SWORD IS LIKE A FINE HORSE. THE MAN WHO TREATS HIS WITH CARE...
"...WILL OUTLIVE THE FOOL WHO DOESN'T." I LISTENED WHEN MY FATHER TAUGHT ME THAT.
IT'S WHY I BEGAN SLEEPING WITH MY SWORD BY MY SIDE EVERY NIGHT.
AND WHY I STARTED WORKING IN THE STABLES.
REGALIAN! STAND TALL!
WHAA!
I'VE LISTENED TO YOUR LESSONS MY ENTIRE LIFE. AND CHERISHED EVERY ONE. EVEN THE ONES THAT LEFT ME BLEEDING OR IN TEARS.
NOW I NEED YOU TO LISTEN TO ME, FATHER. I KNOW WHAT'S WRONG HERE. AND I KNOW HOW WE--
HRRRGGH!

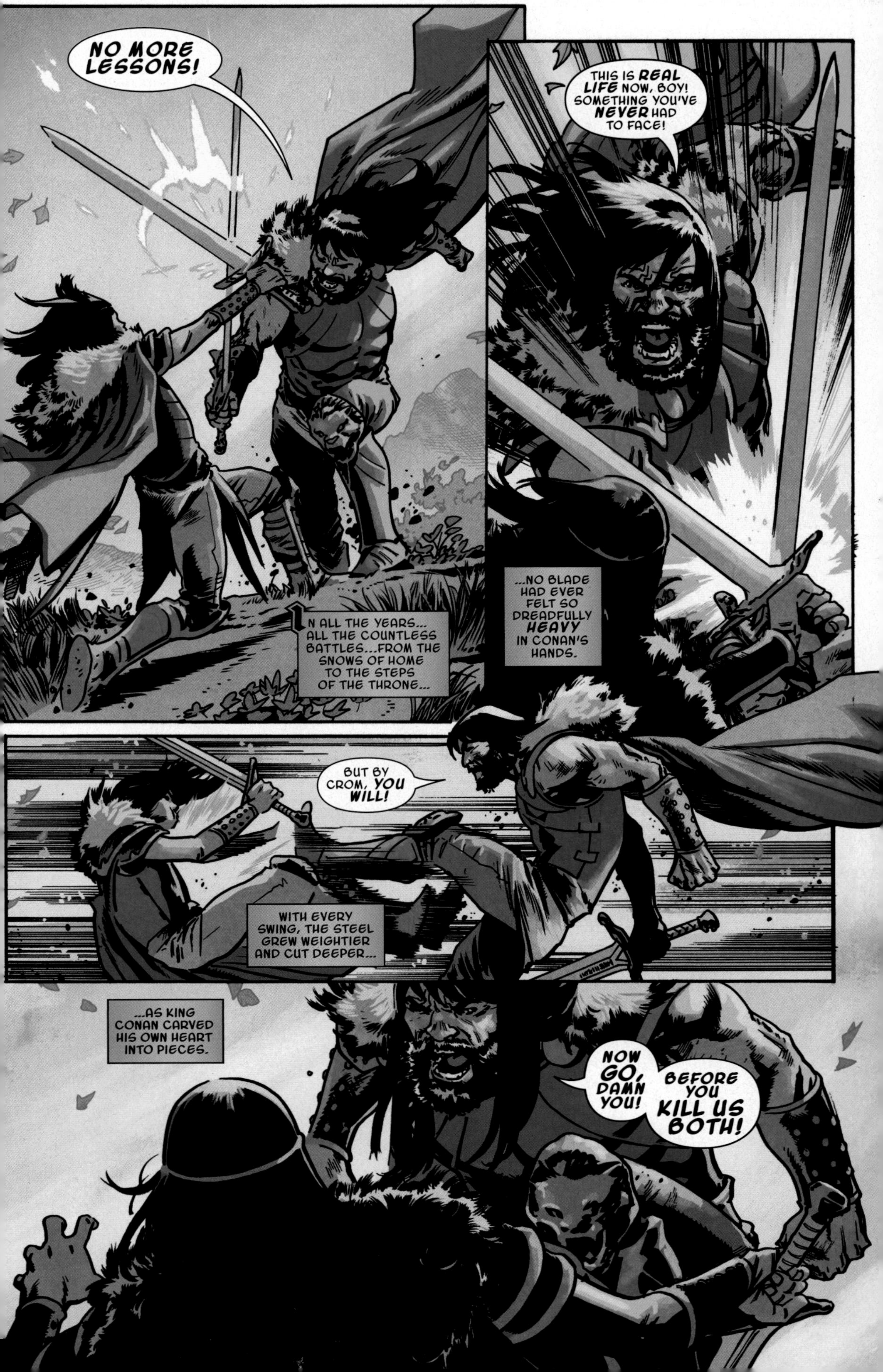
NO MORE LESSONS!
IN ALL THE YEARS... ALL THE COUNTLESS BATTLES...FROM THE SNOWS OF HOME TO THE STEPS OF THE THRONE...
THIS IS REAL LIFE NOW, BOY! SOMETHING YOU'VE NEVER HAD TO FACE!
...NO BLADE HAD EVER FELT SO DREADFULLY HEAVY IN CONAN'S HANDS.
BUT BY CROM, YOU WILL!
WITH EVERY SWING, THE STEEL GREW WEIGHTIER AND CUT DEEPER...
...AS KING CONAN CARVED HIS OWN HEART INTO PIECES.
NOW GO, DAMN YOU!
BEFORE YOU KILL US BOTH!

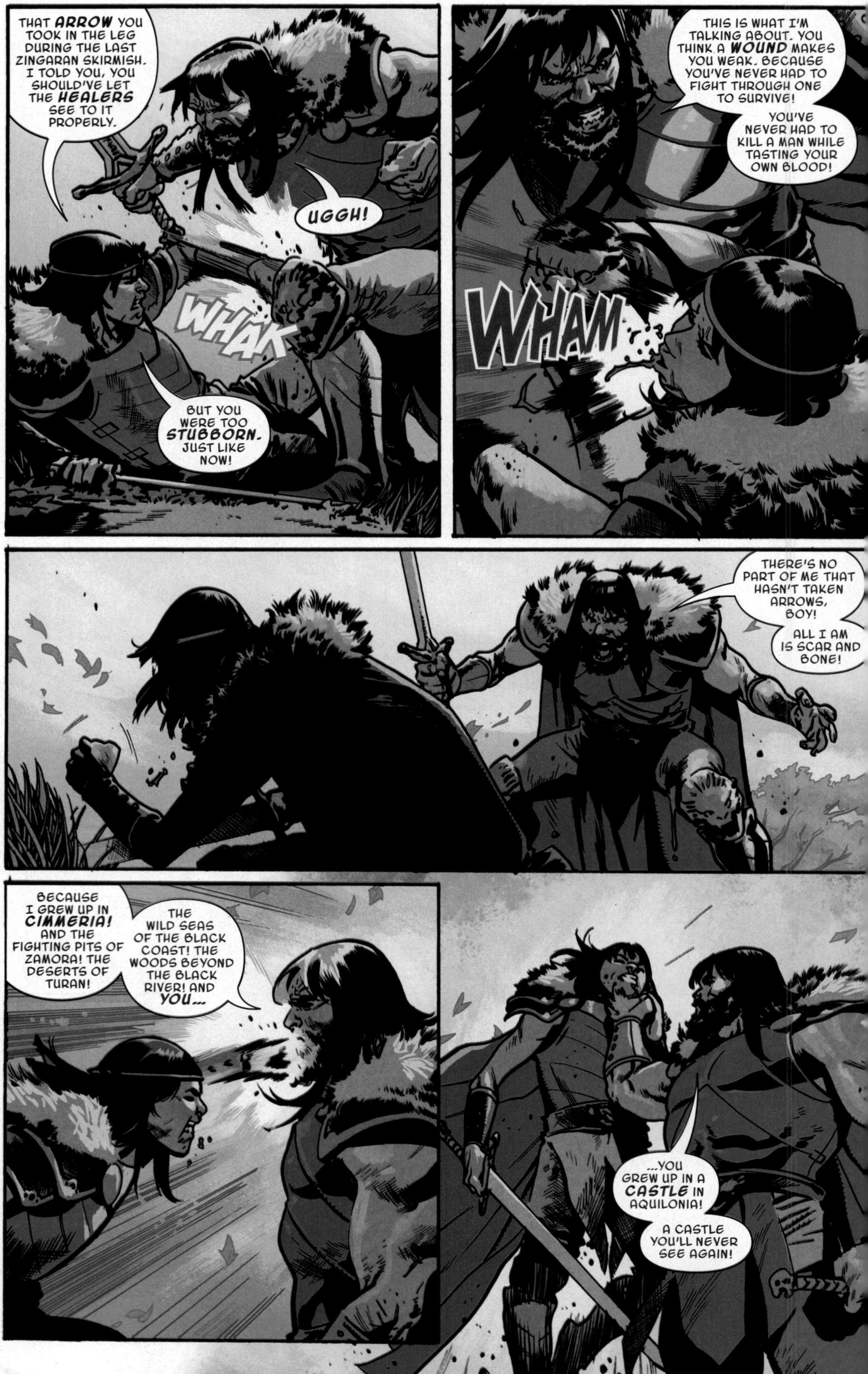

THAT ARROW YOU TOOK IN THE LEG DURING THE LAST ZINGARAN SKIRMISH. I TOLD YOU, YOU SHOULD'VE LET THE HEALERS SEE TO IT PROPERLY.
UGGH!
WHAK
BUT YOU WERE TOO STUBBORN. JUST LIKE NOW!
THIS IS WHAT I'M TALKING ABOUT. YOU THINK A WOUND MAKES YOU WEAK. BECAUSE YOU'VE NEVER HAD TO FIGHT THROUGH ONE TO SURVIVE!
YOU'VE NEVER HAD TO KILL A MAN WHILE TASTING YOUR OWN BLOOD!
WHAM
THERE'S NO PART OF ME THAT HASN'T TAKEN ARROWS, BOY!
ALL I AM IS SCAR AND BONE!
BECAUSE I GREW UP IN CIMMERIA! AND THE FIGHTING PITS OF ZAMORA! THE DESERTS OF TURAN!
THE WILD SEAS OF THE BLACK COAST! THE WOODS BEYOND THE BLACK RIVER! AND YOU...
...YOU GREW UP IN A CASTLE IN AQUILONIA!
A CASTLE YOU'LL NEVER SEE AGAIN!

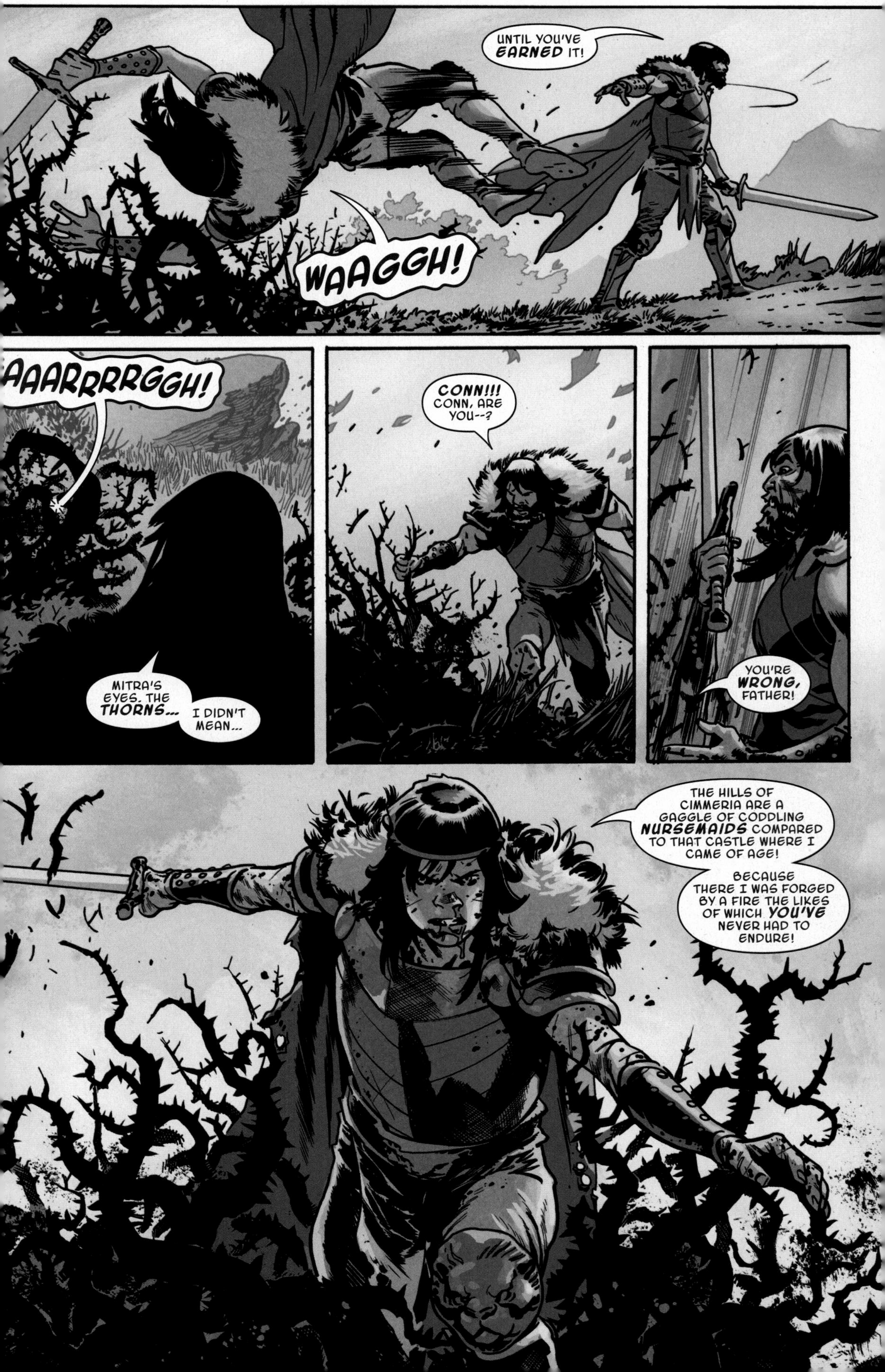
UNTIL YOU'VE EARNED IT!
WAAGGH!
AAARRRRRGGH!
CONN!!! CONN, ARE YOU--?
YOU'RE WRONG, FATHER!
MITRA'S EYES. THE THORNS...
I DIDN'T MEAN...
THE HILLS OF CIMMERIA ARE A GAGGLE OF CODDLING NURSEMAIDS COMPARED TO THAT CASTLE WHERE I CAME OF AGE!
BECAUSE THERE I WAS FORGED BY A FIRE THE LIKES OF WHICH YOU'VE NEVER HAD TO ENDURE!

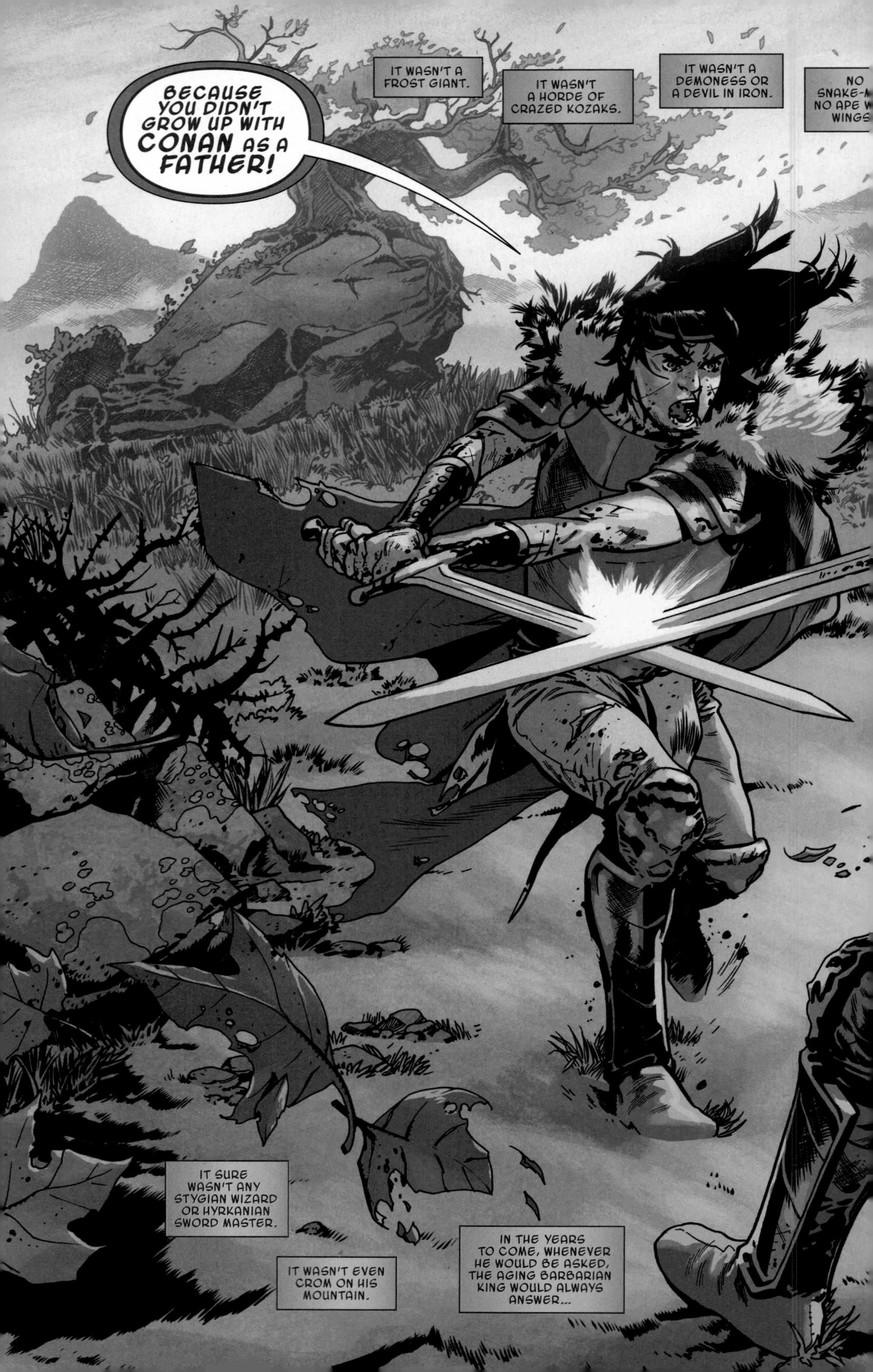

BECAUSE YOU DIDN'T GROW UP WITH CONAN AS A FATHER!
IT WASN'T A FROST GIANT.
IT WASN'T A HORDE OF CRAZED KOZAKS.
IT WASN'T A DEMONESS OR A DEVIL IN IRON.
IT SURE WASN'T ANY STYGIAN WIZARD OR HYRKANIAN SWORD MASTER.
IT WASN'T EVEN CROM ON HIS MOUNTAIN.
IN THE YEARS TO COME, WHENEVER HE WOULD BE ASKED, THE AGING BARBARIAN KING WOULD ALWAYS ANSWER...

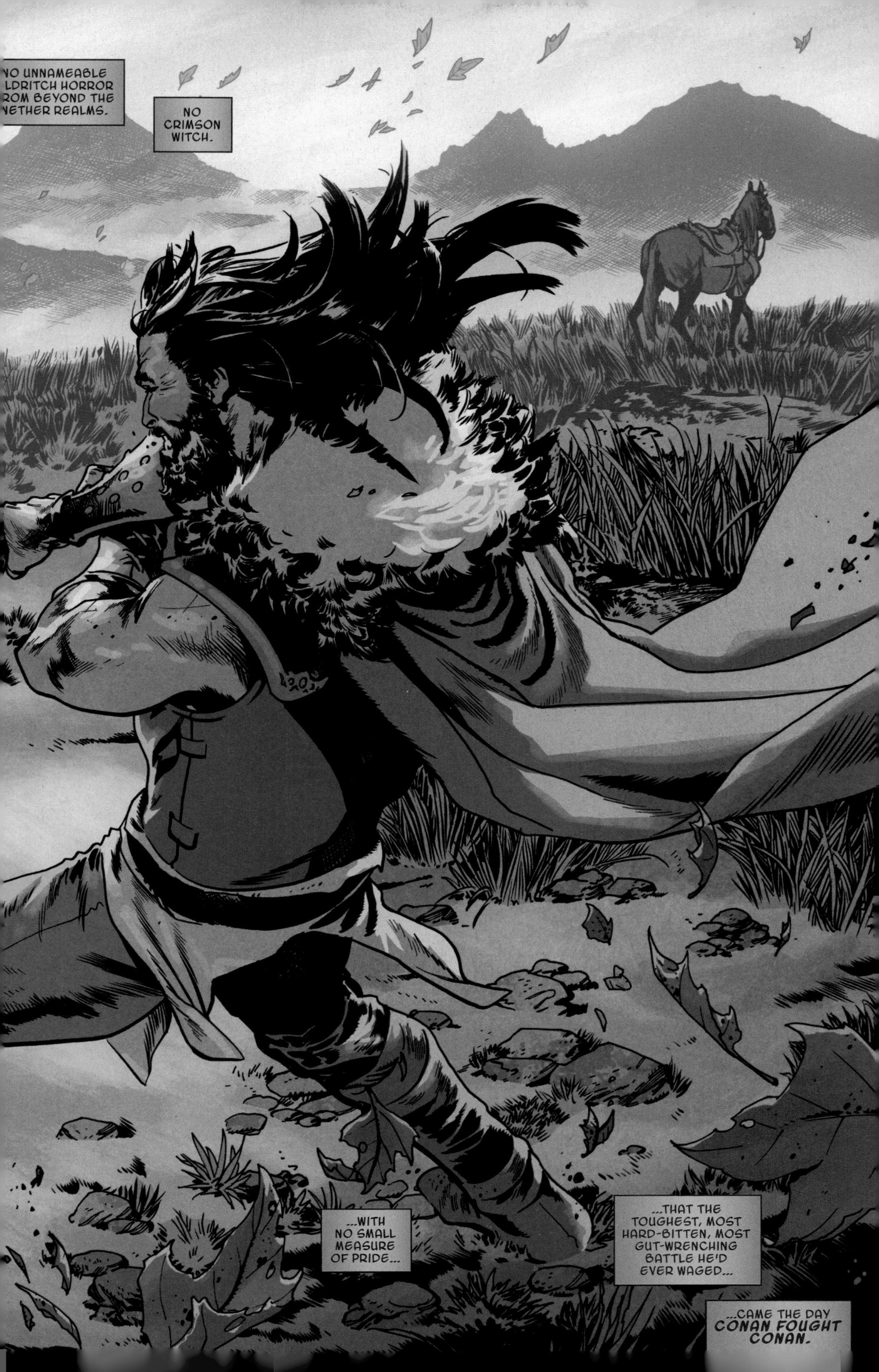
NO UNNAMEABLE LDRITCH HORROR ROM BEYOND THE NETHER REALMS.
NO CRIMSON WITCH.
...WITH NO SMALL MEASURE OF PRIDE...
...THAT THE TOUGHEST, MOST HARD-BITTEN, MOST GUT-WRENCHING BATTLE HE'D EVER WAGED...
...CAME THE DAY CONAN FOUGHT CONAN.

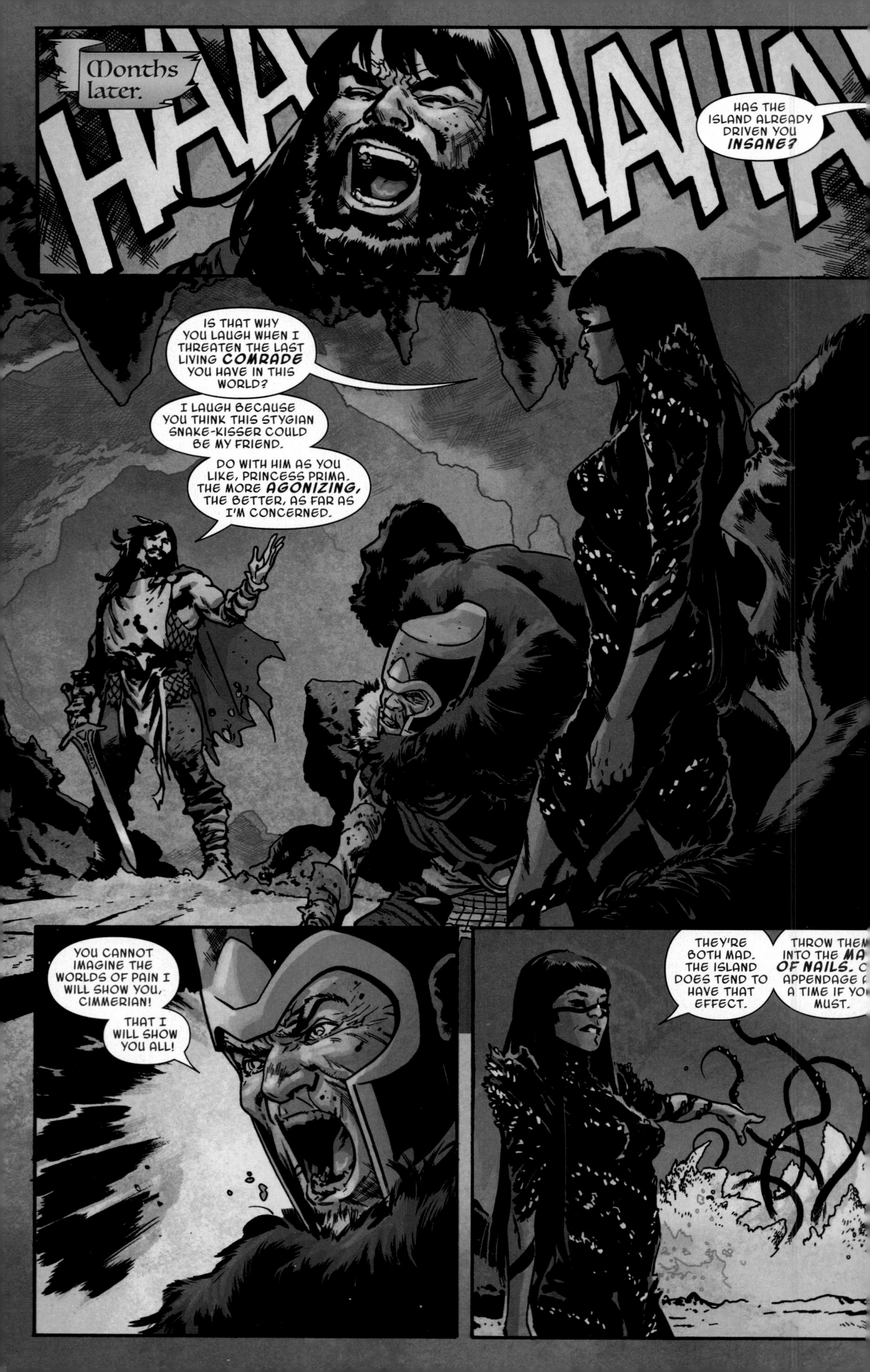
Months later.
HA HAHA
HAS THE ISLAND ALREADY DRIVEN YOU INSANE?
IS THAT WHY YOU LAUGH WHEN I THREATEN THE LAST LIVING COMRADE YOU HAVE IN THIS WORLD?
I LAUGH BECAUSE YOU THINK THIS STYGIAN SNAKE-KISSER COULD BE MY FRIEND.
DO WITH HIM AS YOU LIKE, PRINCESS PRIMA. THE MORE AGONIZING, THE BETTER, AS FAR AS I'M CONCERNED.
YOU CANNOT IMAGINE THE WORLDS OF PAIN I WILL SHOW YOU, CIMMERIAN!
THAT I WILL SHOW YOU ALL!
THEY'RE BOTH MAD. THE ISLAND DOES TEND TO HAVE THAT EFFECT.
THROW THEM INTO THE MA OF NAILS. APPENDAGE A TIME IF YO MUST.

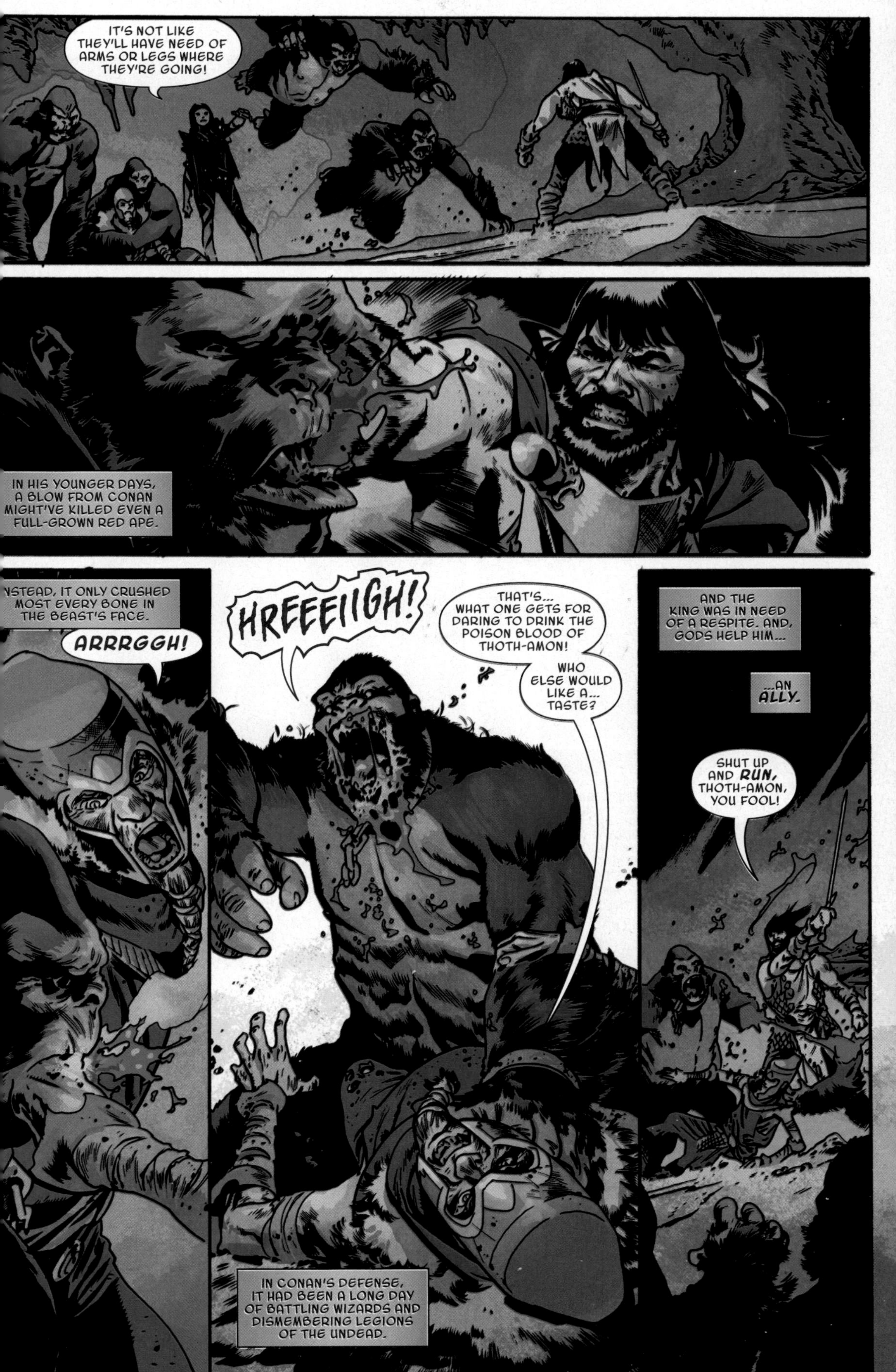
IT'S NOT LIKE THEY'LL HAVE NEED OF ARMS OR LEGS WHERE THEY'RE GOING!
IN HIS YOUNGER DAYS, A BLOW FROM CONAN MIGHT'VE KILLED EVEN A FULL-GROWN RED APE.
NSTEAD, IT ONLY CRUSHED MOST EVERY BONE IN THE BEAST'S FACE.
ARRRGGH!
HREEEIIGH!
THAT'S... WHAT ONE GETS FOR DARING TO DRINK THE POISON BLOOD OF THOTH-AMON!
WHO ELSE WOULD LIKE A... TASTE?
IN CONAN'S DEFENSE, IT HAD BEEN A LONG DAY OF BATTLING WIZARDS AND DISMEMBERING LEGIONS OF THE UNDEAD.
AND THE KING WAS IN NEED OF A RESPITE. AND, GODS HELP HIM...
...AN ALLY.
SHUT UP AND RUN, THOTH-AMON, YOU FOOL!

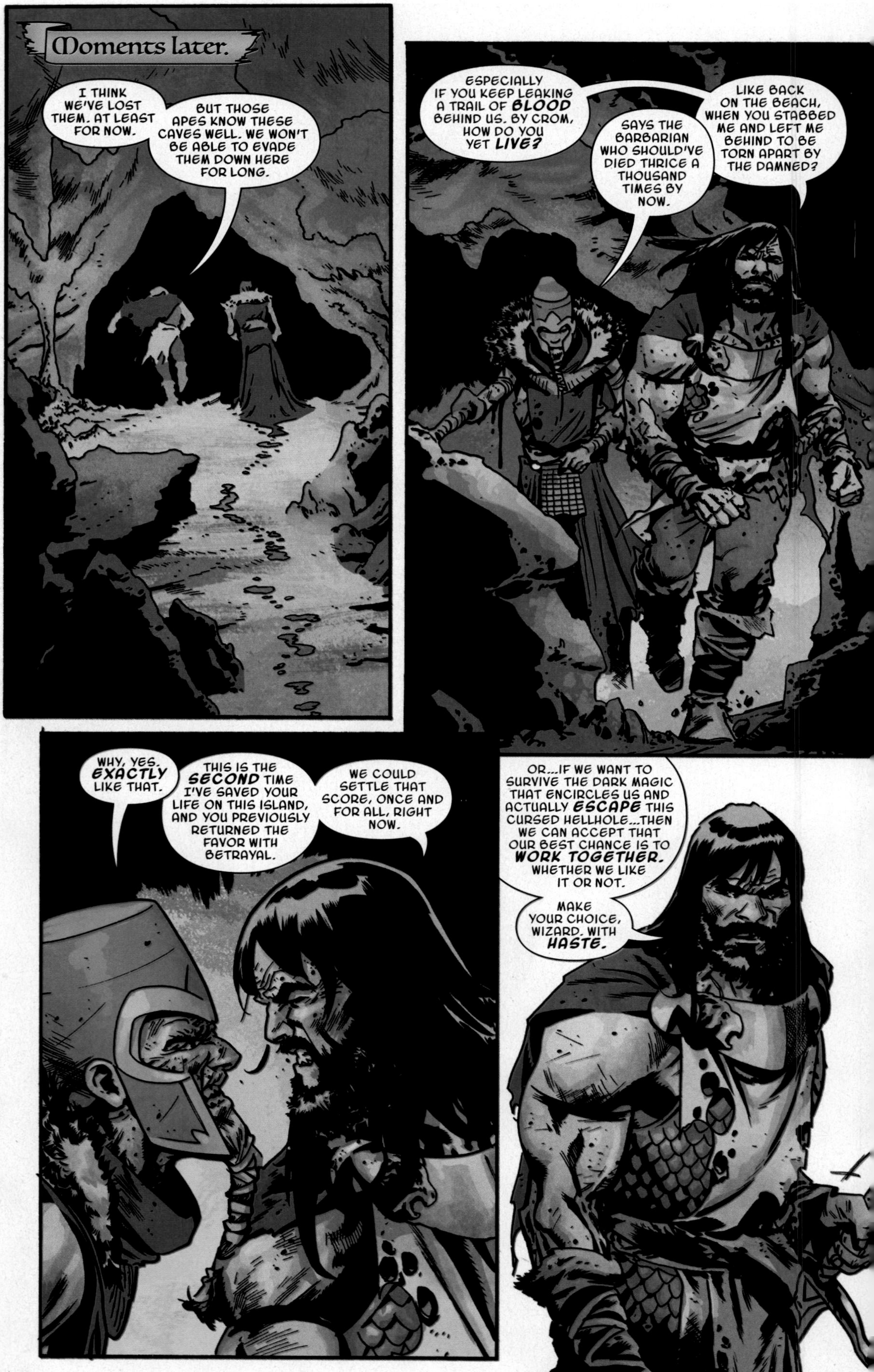
Moments later.
I THINK WE'VE LOST THEM. AT LEAST FOR NOW.
BUT THOSE APES KNOW THESE CAVES WELL. WE WON'T BE ABLE TO EVADE THEM DOWN HERE FOR LONG.
ESPECIALLY IF YOU KEEP LEAKING A TRAIL OF BLOOD BEHIND US. BY CROM, HOW DO YOU YET LIVE?
SAYS THE BARBARIAN WHO SHOULD'VE DIED THRICE A THOUSAND TIMES BY NOW.
LIKE BACK ON THE BEACH, WHEN YOU STABBED ME AND LEFT ME BEHIND TO BE TORN APART BY THE DAMNED?
WHY, YES. EXACTLY LIKE THAT.
THIS IS THE SECOND TIME I'VE SAVED YOUR LIFE ON THIS ISLAND, AND YOU PREVIOUSLY RETURNED THE FAVOR WITH BETRAYAL.
WE COULD SETTLE THAT SCORE, ONCE AND FOR ALL, RIGHT NOW.
OR...IF WE WANT TO SURVIVE THE DARK MAGIC THAT ENCIRCLES US AND ACTUALLY ESCAPE THIS CURSED HELLHOLE...THEN WE CAN ACCEPT THAT OUR BEST CHANCE IS TO WORK TOGETHER. WHETHER WE LIKE IT OR NOT.
MAKE YOUR CHOICE, WIZARD. WITH HASTE.

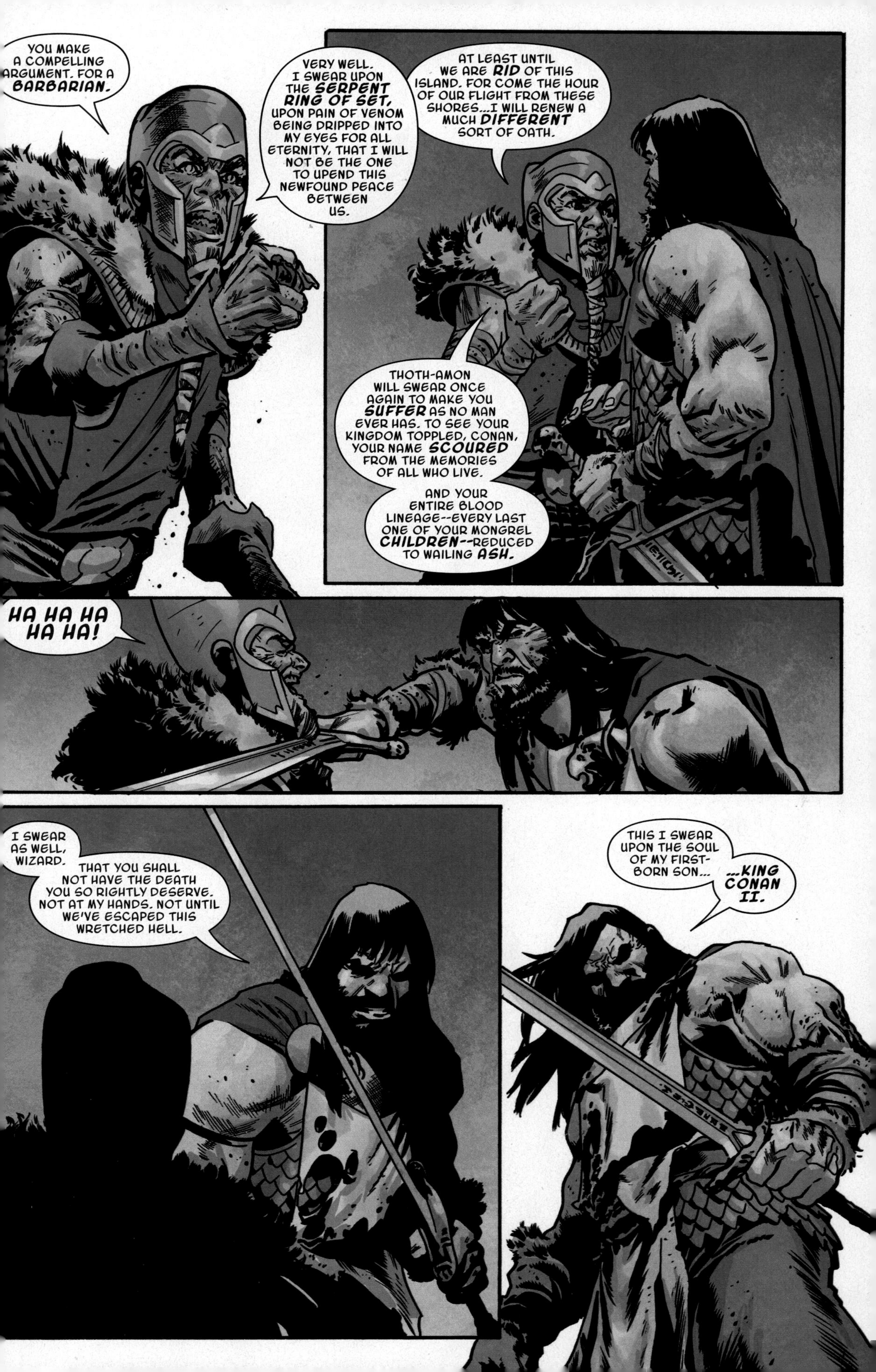
YOU MAKE A COMPELLING ARGUMENT. FOR A BARBARIAN.
VERY WELL. I SWEAR UPON THE SERPENT RING OF SET, UPON PAIN OF VENOM BEING DRIPPED INTO MY EYES FOR ALL ETERNITY, THAT I WILL NOT BE THE ONE TO UPEND THIS NEWFOUND PEACE BETWEEN US.
AT LEAST UNTIL WE ARE RID OF THIS ISLAND. FOR COME THE HOUR OF OUR FLIGHT FROM THESE SHORES...I WILL RENEW A MUCH DIFFERENT SORT OF OATH.
THOTH-AMON WILL SWEAR ONCE AGAIN TO MAKE YOU SUFFER AS NO MAN EVER HAS. TO SEE YOUR KINGDOM TOPPLED, CONAN, YOUR NAME SCOURED FROM THE MEMORIES OF ALL WHO LIVE.
AND YOUR ENTIRE BLOOD LINEAGE--EVERY LAST ONE OF YOUR MONGREL CHILDREN--REDUCED TO WAILING ASH.
HA HA HA HA HA!
I SWEAR AS WELL, WIZARD.
THAT YOU SHALL NOT HAVE THE DEATH YOU SO RIGHTLY DESERVE. NOT AT MY HANDS. NOT UNTIL WE'VE ESCAPED THIS WRETCHED HELL.
THIS I SWEAR UPON THE SOUL OF MY FIRST-BORN SON...
...KING CONAN II.

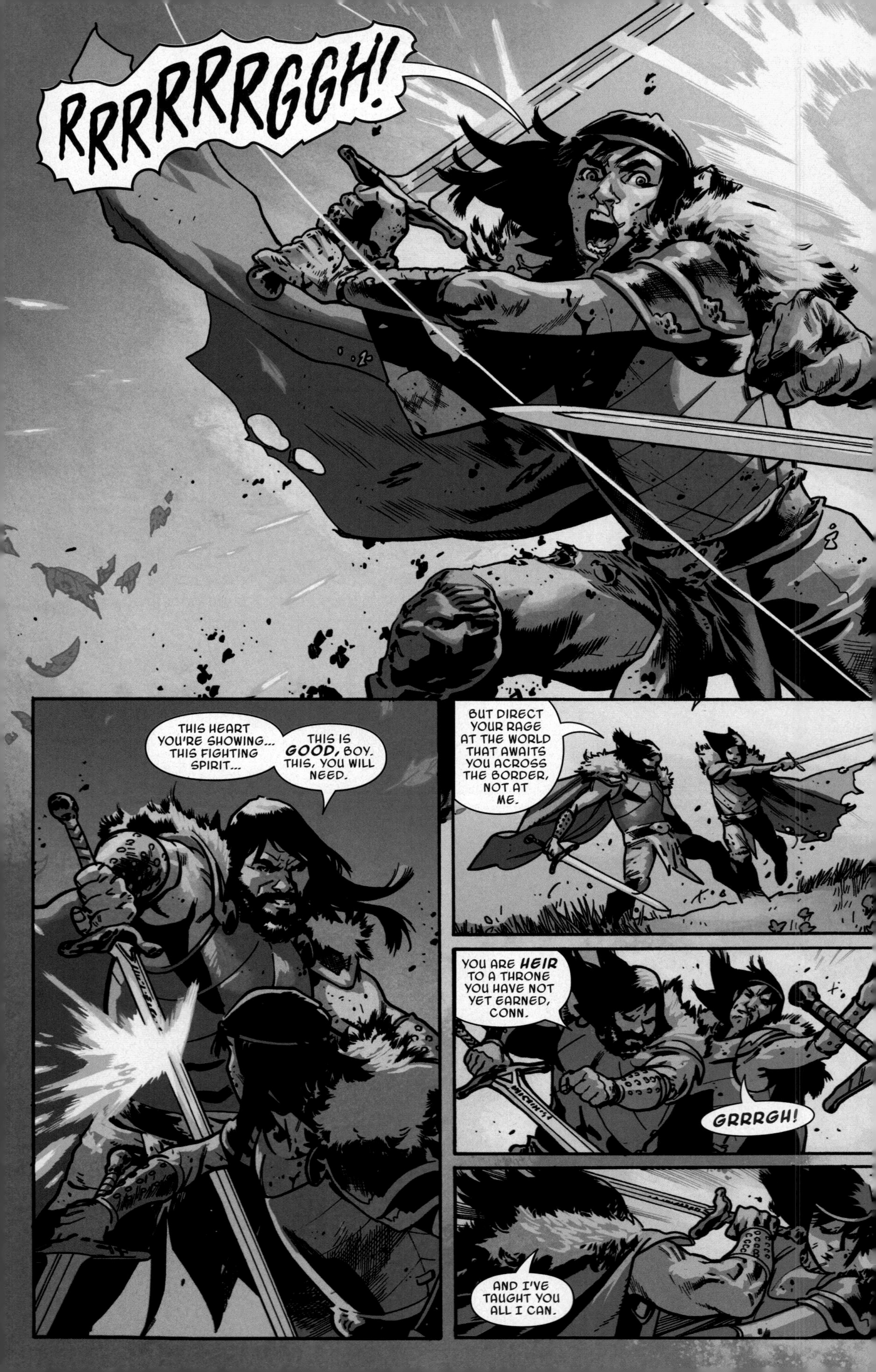
RRRRRRGGH!
THIS HEART YOU'RE SHOWING... THIS FIGHTING SPIRIT...
THIS IS GOOD, BOY. THIS, YOU WILL NEED.
BUT DIRECT YOUR RAGE AT THE WORLD THAT AWAITS YOU ACROSS THE BORDER, NOT AT ME.
YOU ARE HEIR TO A THRONE YOU HAVE NOT YET EARNED, CONN.
GRRRGH!
AND I'VE TAUGHT YOU ALL I CAN.

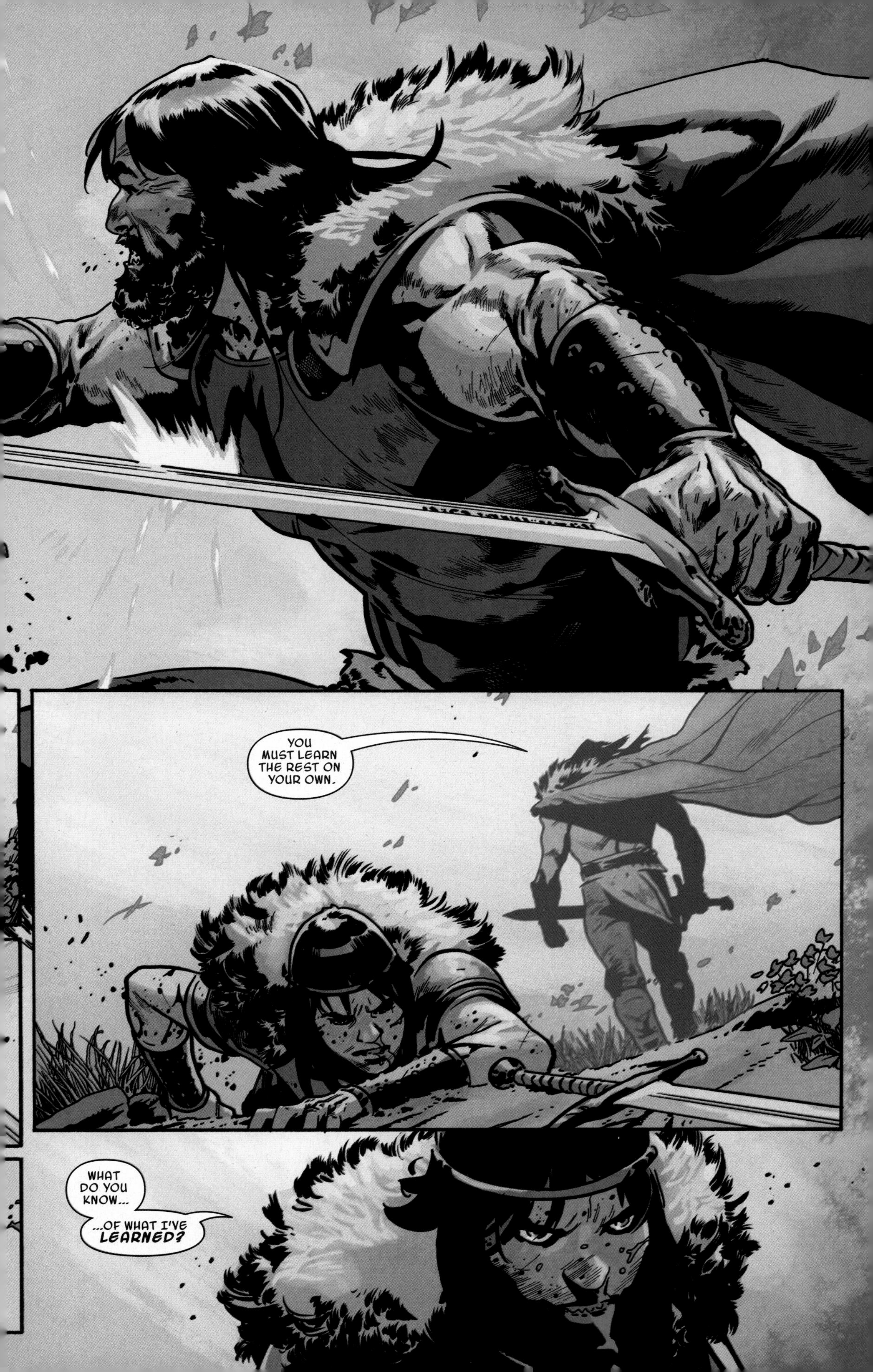
YOU MUST LEARN THE REST ON YOUR OWN.
WHAT DO YOU KNOW...
...OF WHAT I'VE LEARNED?

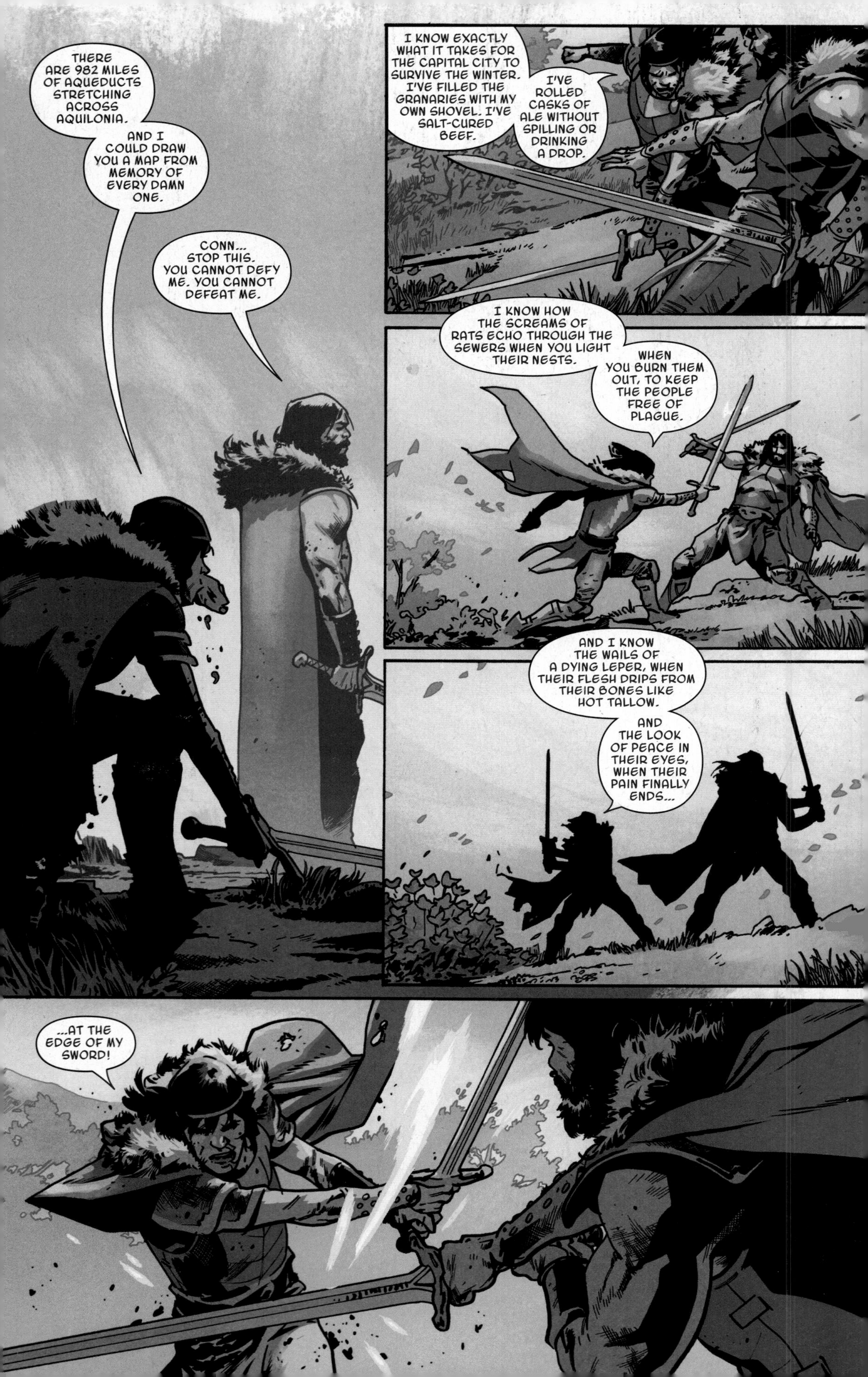
THERE ARE 982 MILES OF AQUEDUCTS STRETCHING ACROSS AQUILONIA.
AND I COULD DRAW YOU A MAP FROM MEMORY OF EVERY DAMN ONE.
CONN... STOP THIS. YOU CANNOT DEFY ME. YOU CANNOT DEFEAT ME.
I KNOW EXACTLY WHAT IT TAKES FOR THE CAPITAL CITY TO SURVIVE THE WINTER. I'VE FILLED THE GRANARIES WITH MY OWN SHOVEL. I'VE SALT-CURED BEEF.
I'VE ROLLED CASKS OF ALE WITHOUT SPILLING OR DRINKING A DROP.
I KNOW HOW THE SCREAMS OF RATS ECHO THROUGH THE SEWERS WHEN YOU LIGHT THEIR NESTS.
WHEN YOU BURN THEM OUT, TO KEEP THE PEOPLE FREE OF PLAGUE.
AND I KNOW THE WAILS OF A DYING LEPER, WHEN THEIR FLESH DRIPS FROM THEIR BONES LIKE HOT TALLOW.
AND THE LOOK OF PEACE IN THEIR EYES, WHEN THEIR PAIN FINALLY ENDS...
...AT THE EDGE OF MY SWORD!

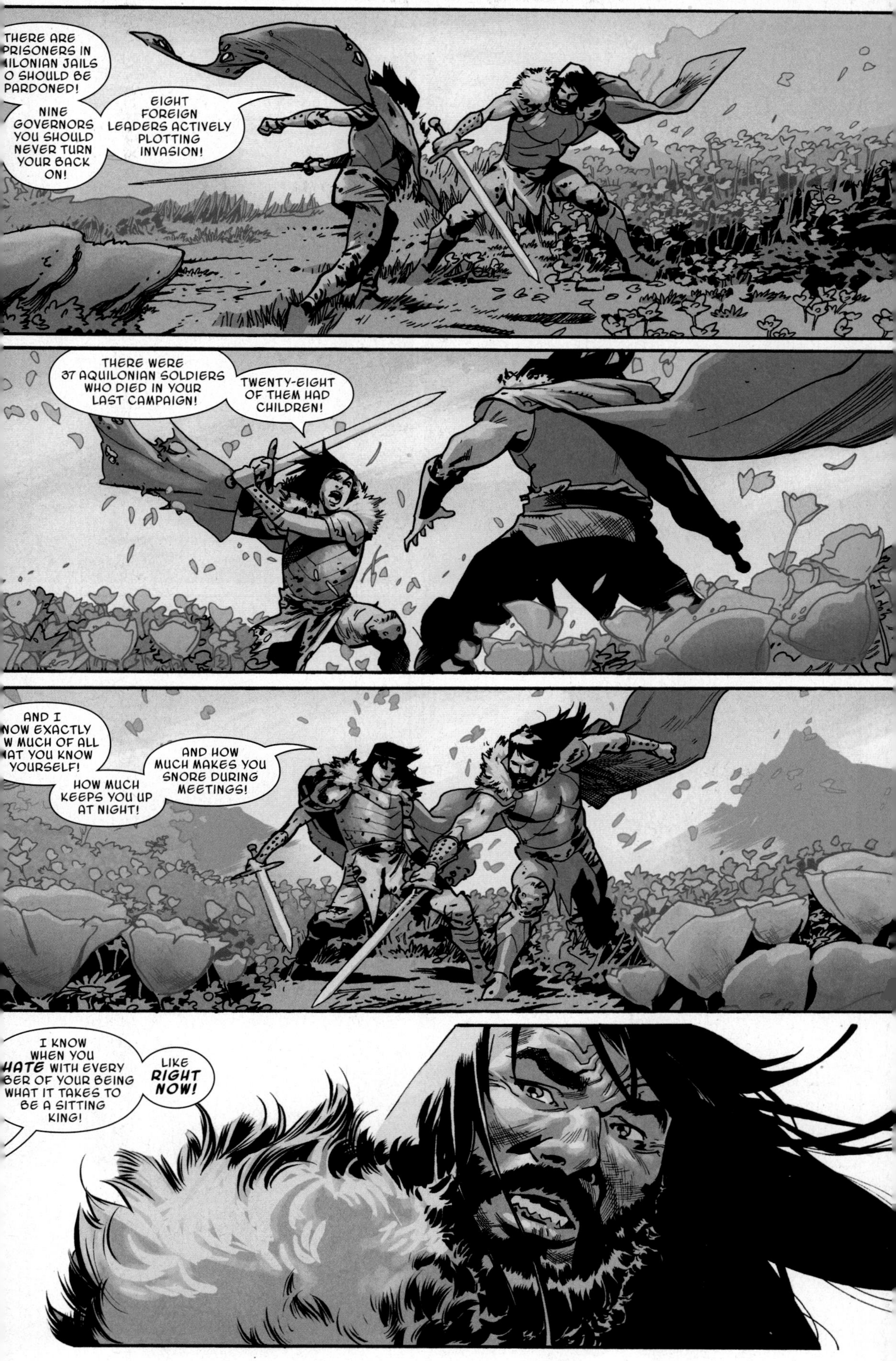
THERE ARE PRISONERS IN ILONIAN JAILS O SHOULD BE PARDONED!
NINE GOVERNORS YOU SHOULD NEVER TURN YOUR BACK ON!
EIGHT FOREIGN LEADERS ACTIVELY PLOTTING INVASION!
THERE WERE 37 AQUILONIAN SOLDIERS WHO DIED IN YOUR LAST CAMPAIGN!
TWENTY-EIGHT OF THEM HAD CHILDREN!
AND I NOW EXACTLY W MUCH OF ALL IAT YOU KNOW YOURSELF!
HOW MUCH KEEPS YOU UP AT NIGHT!
AND HOW MUCH MAKES YOU SNORE DURING MEETINGS!
I KNOW WHEN YOU ***HATE*** WITH EVERY BER OF YOUR BEING WHAT IT TAKES TO BE A SITTING KING!
LIKE ***RIGHT NOW!***

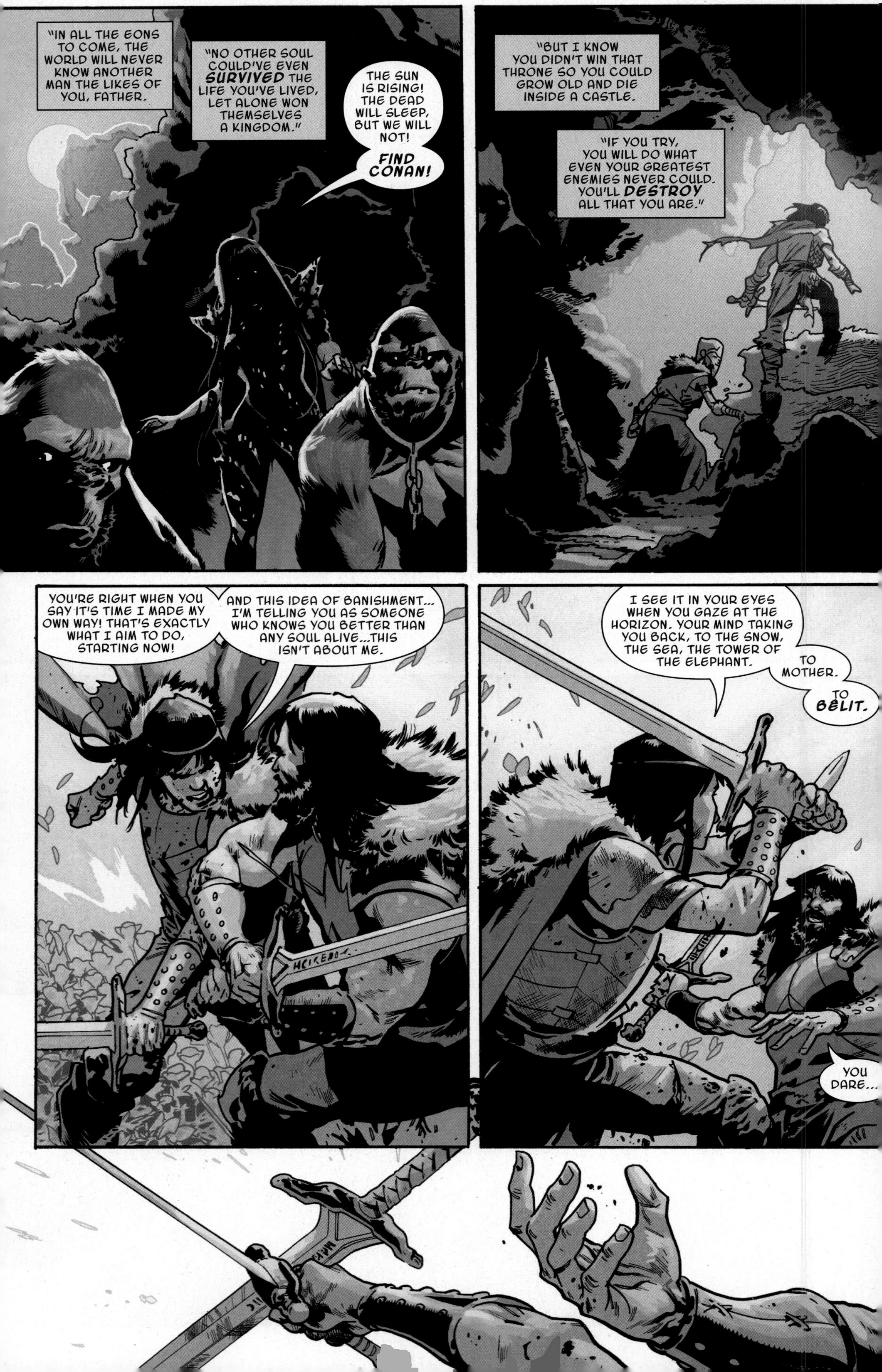
"IN ALL THE EONS TO COME, THE WORLD WILL NEVER KNOW ANOTHER MAN THE LIKES OF YOU, FATHER.
"NO OTHER SOUL COULD'VE EVEN SURVIVED THE LIFE YOU'VE LIVED, LET ALONE WON THEMSELVES A KINGDOM."
THE SUN IS RISING! THE DEAD WILL SLEEP, BUT WE WILL NOT!
FIND CONAN!
"BUT I KNOW YOU DIDN'T WIN THAT THRONE SO YOU COULD GROW OLD AND DIE INSIDE A CASTLE.
"IF YOU TRY, YOU WILL DO WHAT EVEN YOUR GREATEST ENEMIES NEVER COULD. YOU'LL DESTROY ALL THAT YOU ARE."
YOU'RE RIGHT WHEN YOU SAY IT'S TIME I MADE MY OWN WAY! THAT'S EXACTLY WHAT I AIM TO DO, STARTING NOW!
AND THIS IDEA OF BANISHMENT... I'M TELLING YOU AS SOMEONE WHO KNOWS YOU BETTER THAN ANY SOUL ALIVE...THIS ISN'T ABOUT ME.
I SEE IT IN YOUR EYES WHEN YOU GAZE AT THE HORIZON. YOUR MIND TAKING YOU BACK, TO THE SNOW, THE SEA, THE TOWER OF THE ELEPHANT.
TO MOTHER.
TO BÊLIT.
YOU DARE...

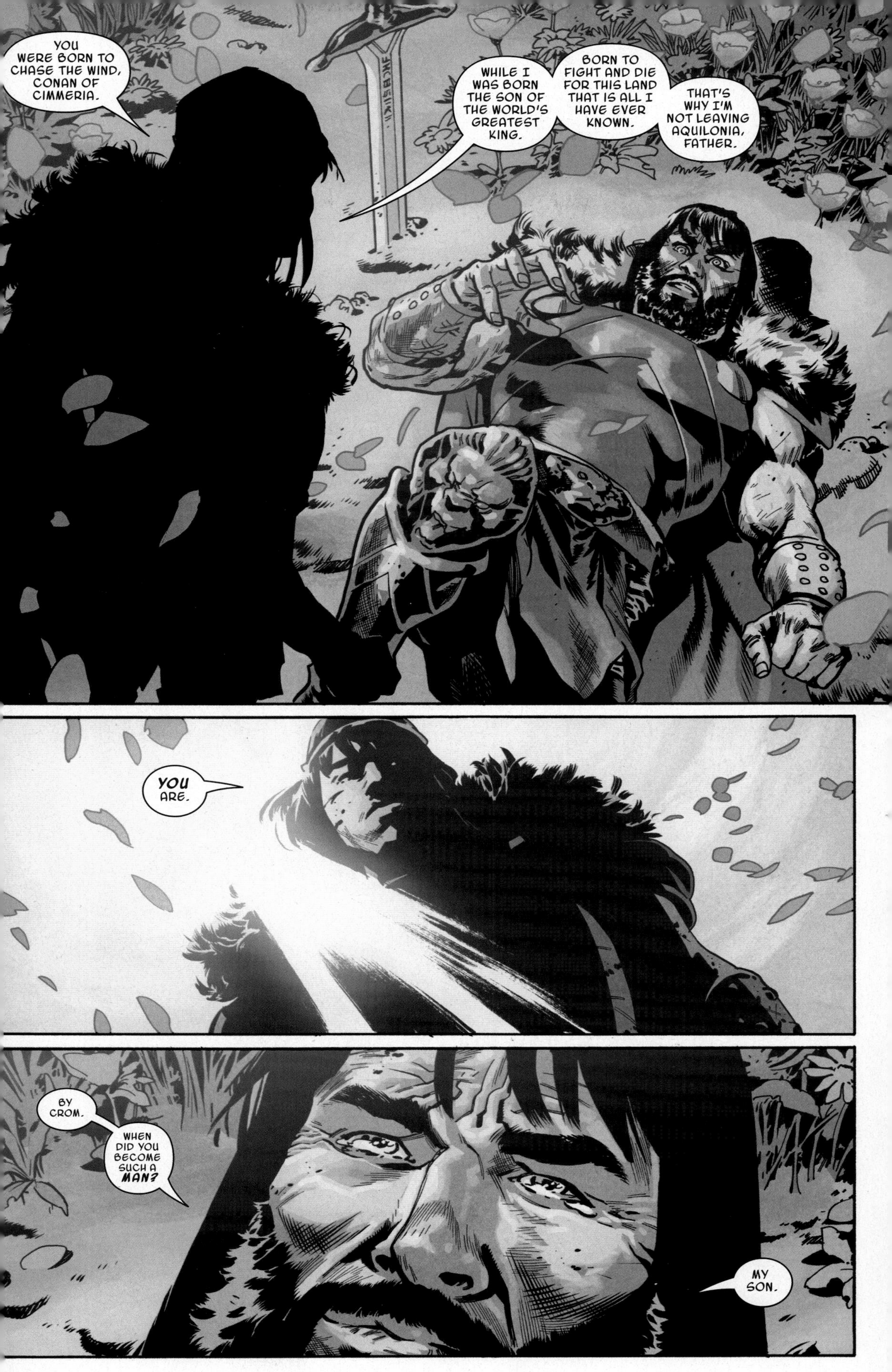
YOU WERE BORN TO CHASE THE WIND, CONAN OF CIMMERIA.
WHILE I WAS BORN THE SON OF THE WORLD'S GREATEST KING.
BORN TO FIGHT AND DIE FOR THIS LAND THAT IS ALL I HAVE EVER KNOWN.
THAT'S WHY I'M NOT LEAVING AQUILONIA, FATHER.
YOU ARE.
BY CROM.
WHEN DID YOU BECOME SUCH A MAN?
MY SON.

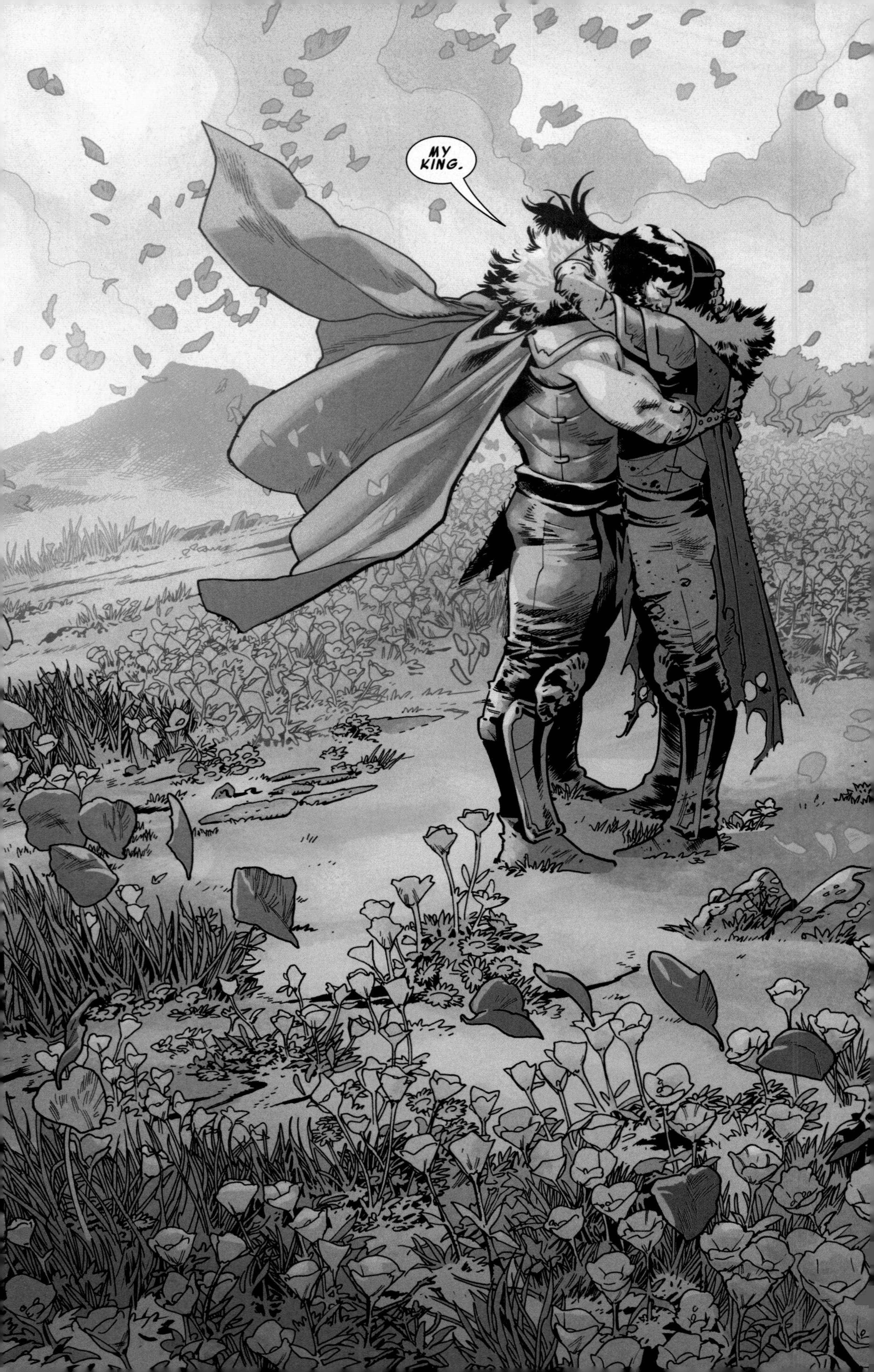
MY KING.

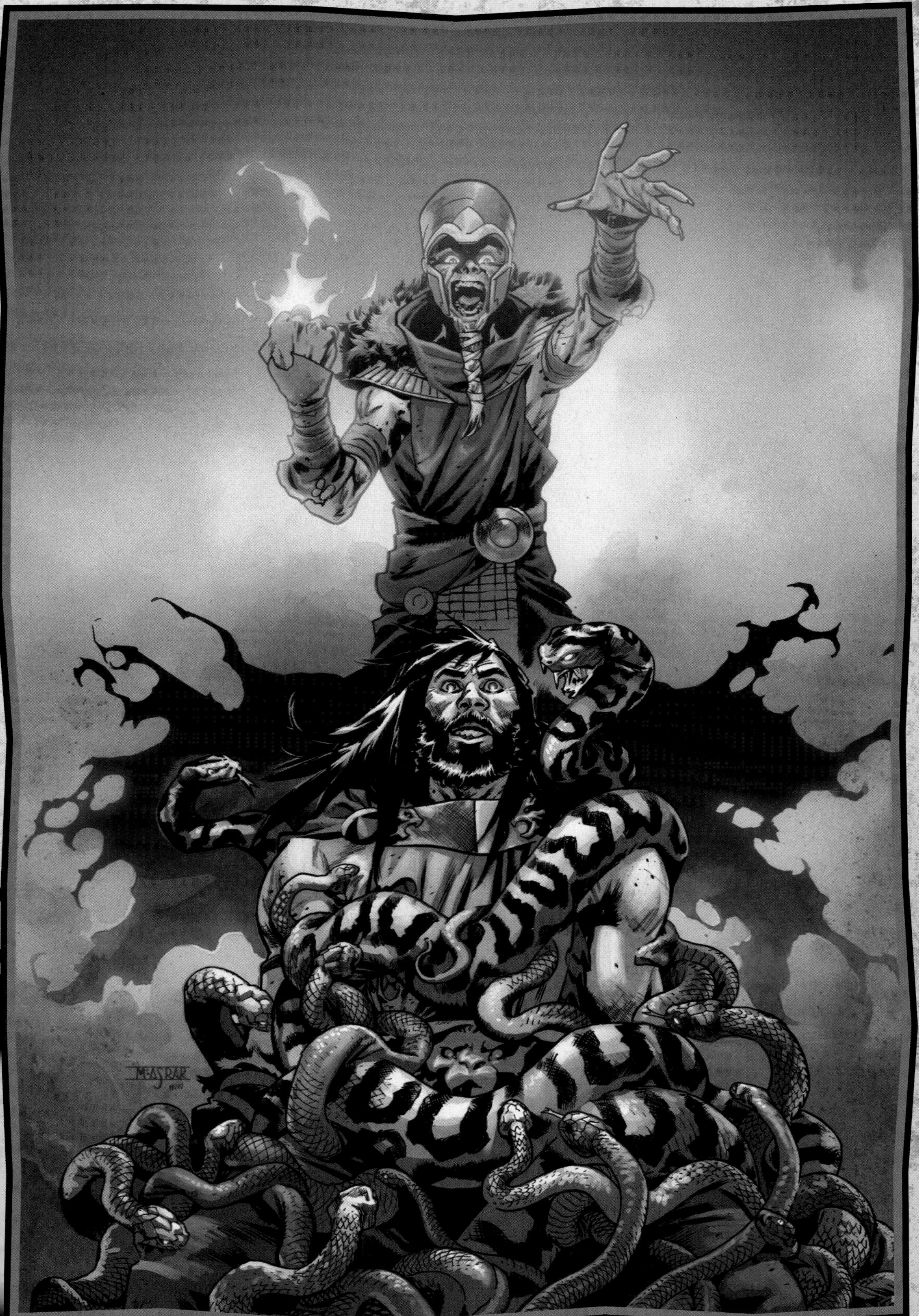

5

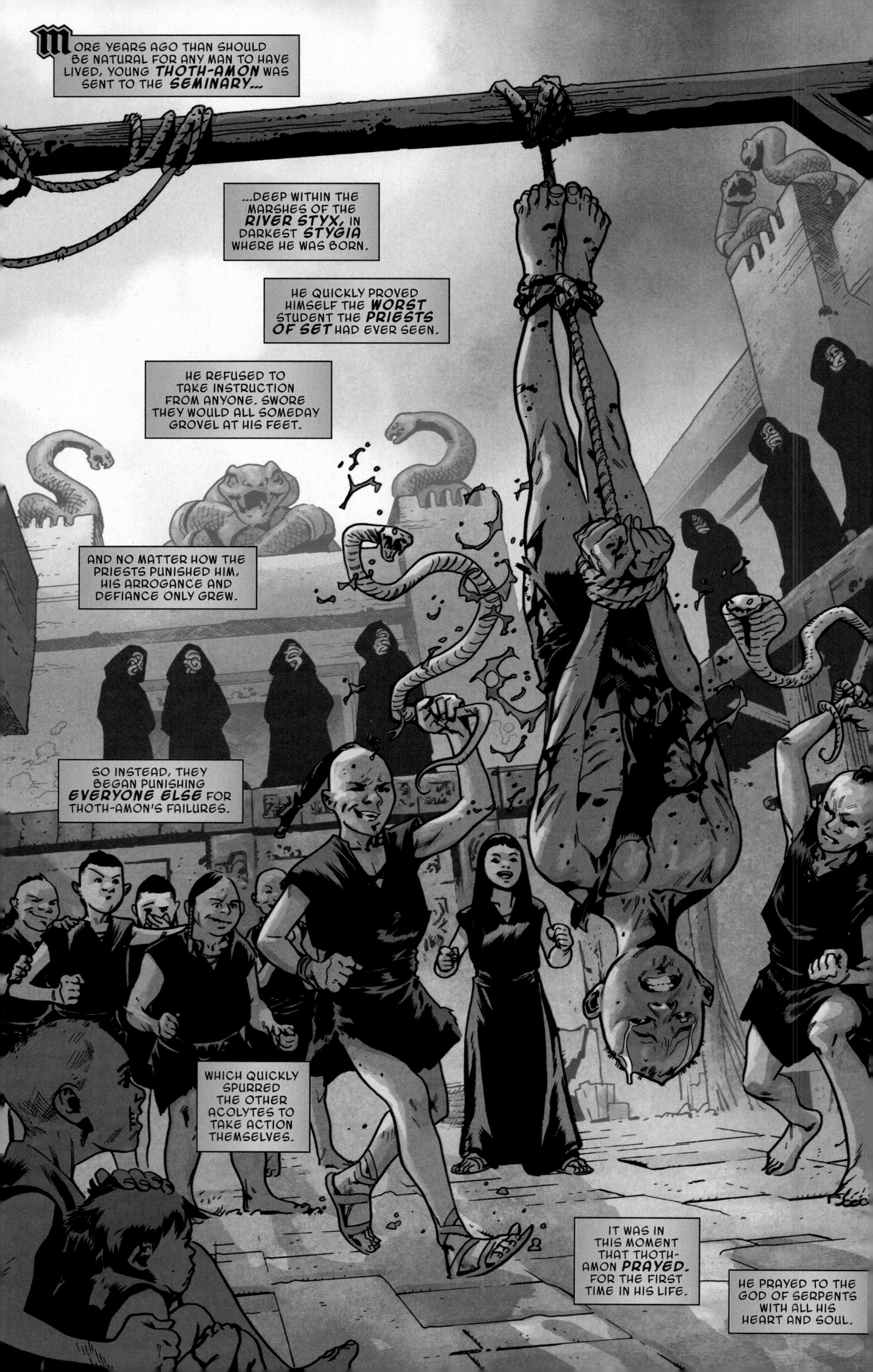
MORE YEARS AGO THAN SHOULD BE NATURAL FOR ANY MAN TO HAVE LIVED, YOUNG THOTH-AMON WAS SENT TO THE SEMINARY...
...DEEP WITHIN THE MARSHES OF THE RIVER STYX, IN DARKEST STYGIA WHERE HE WAS BORN.
HE QUICKLY PROVED HIMSELF THE WORST STUDENT THE PRIESTS OF SET HAD EVER SEEN.
HE REFUSED TO TAKE INSTRUCTION FROM ANYONE. SWORE THEY WOULD ALL SOMEDAY GROVEL AT HIS FEET.
AND NO MATTER HOW THE PRIESTS PUNISHED HIM, HIS ARROGANCE AND DEFIANCE ONLY GREW.
SO INSTEAD, THEY BEGAN PUNISHING EVERYONE ELSE FOR THOTH-AMON'S FAILURES.
WHICH QUICKLY SPURRED THE OTHER ACOLYTES TO TAKE ACTION THEMSELVES.
IT WAS IN THIS MOMENT THAT THOTH-AMON PRAYED. FOR THE FIRST TIME IN HIS LIFE.
HE PRAYED TO THE GOD OF SERPENTS WITH ALL HIS HEART AND SOUL.

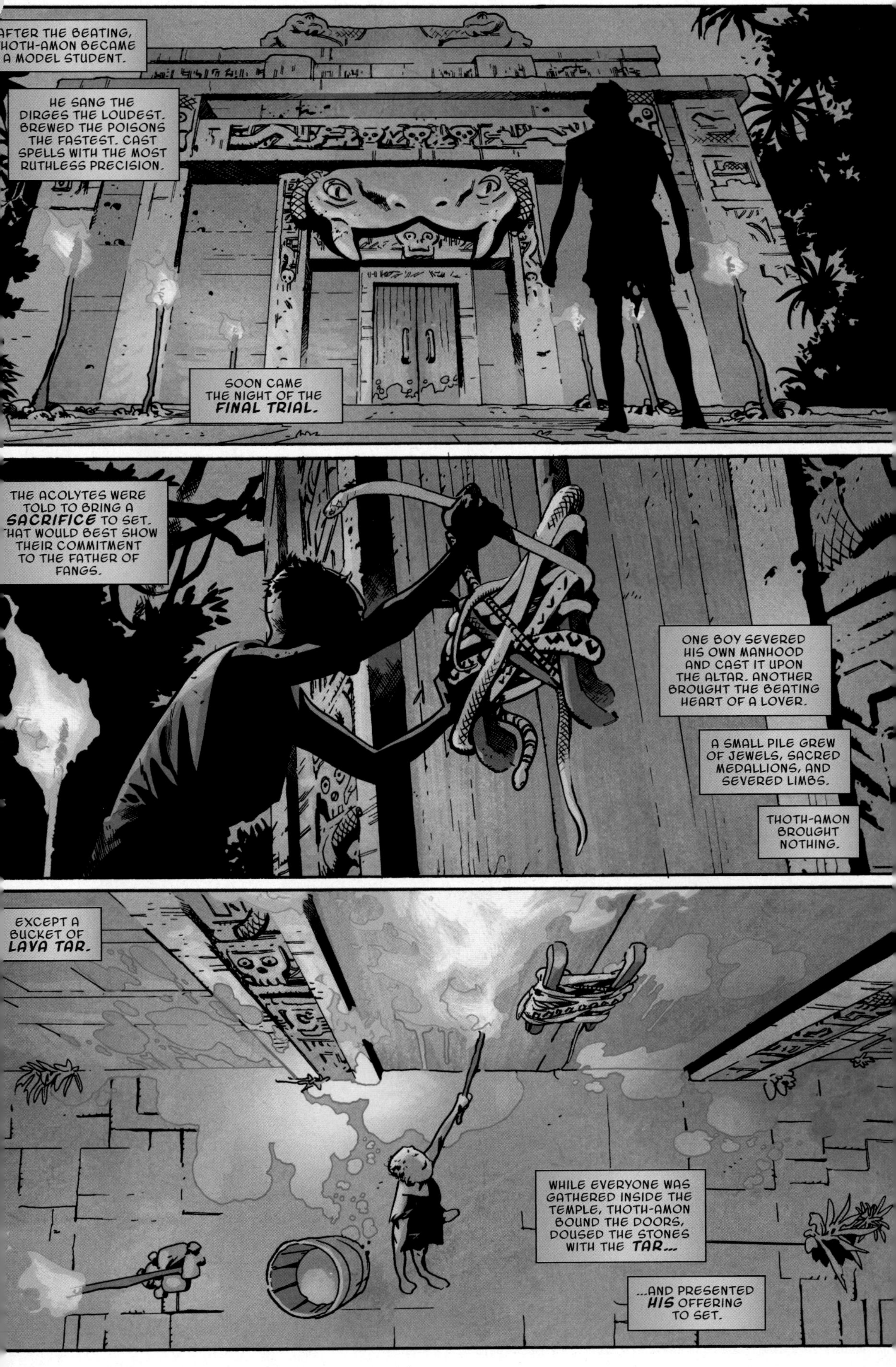
AFTER THE BEATING, THOTH-AMON BECAME A MODEL STUDENT.
HE SANG THE DIRGES THE LOUDEST. BREWED THE POISONS THE FASTEST. CAST SPELLS WITH THE MOST RUTHLESS PRECISION.
SOON CAME THE NIGHT OF THE FINAL TRIAL.
THE ACOLYTES WERE TOLD TO BRING A SACRIFICE TO SET THAT WOULD BEST SHOW THEIR COMMITMENT TO THE FATHER OF FANGS.
ONE BOY SEVERED HIS OWN MANHOOD AND CAST IT UPON THE ALTAR. ANOTHER BROUGHT THE BEATING HEART OF A LOVER.
A SMALL PILE GREW OF JEWELS, SACRED MEDALLIONS, AND SEVERED LIMBS.
THOTH-AMON BROUGHT NOTHING.
EXCEPT A BUCKET OF LAVA TAR.
WHILE EVERYONE WAS GATHERED INSIDE THE TEMPLE, THOTH-AMON BOUND THE DOORS, DOUSED THE STONES WITH THE TAR...
...AND PRESENTED HIS OFFERING TO SET.

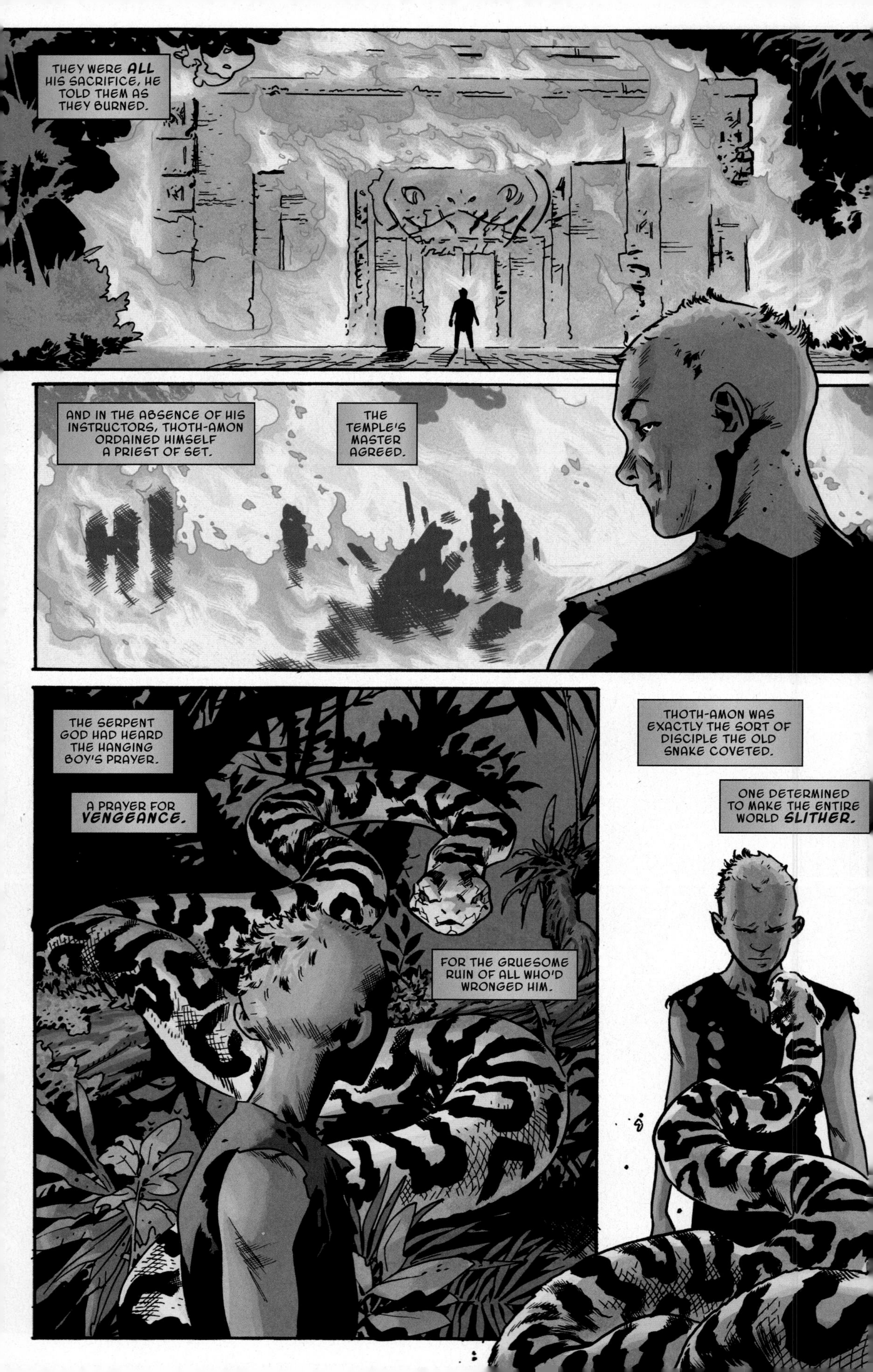
THEY WERE ALL HIS SACRIFICE, HE TOLD THEM AS THEY BURNED.
AND IN THE ABSENCE OF HIS INSTRUCTORS, THOTH-AMON ORDAINED HIMSELF A PRIEST OF SET.
THE TEMPLE'S MASTER AGREED.
THE SERPENT GOD HAD HEARD THE HANGING BOY'S PRAYER.
A PRAYER FOR VENGEANCE.
FOR THE GRUESOME RUIN OF ALL WHO'D WRONGED HIM.
THOTH-AMON WAS EXACTLY THE SORT OF DISCIPLE THE OLD SNAKE COVETED.
ONE DETERMINED TO MAKE THE ENTIRE WORLD SLITHER.

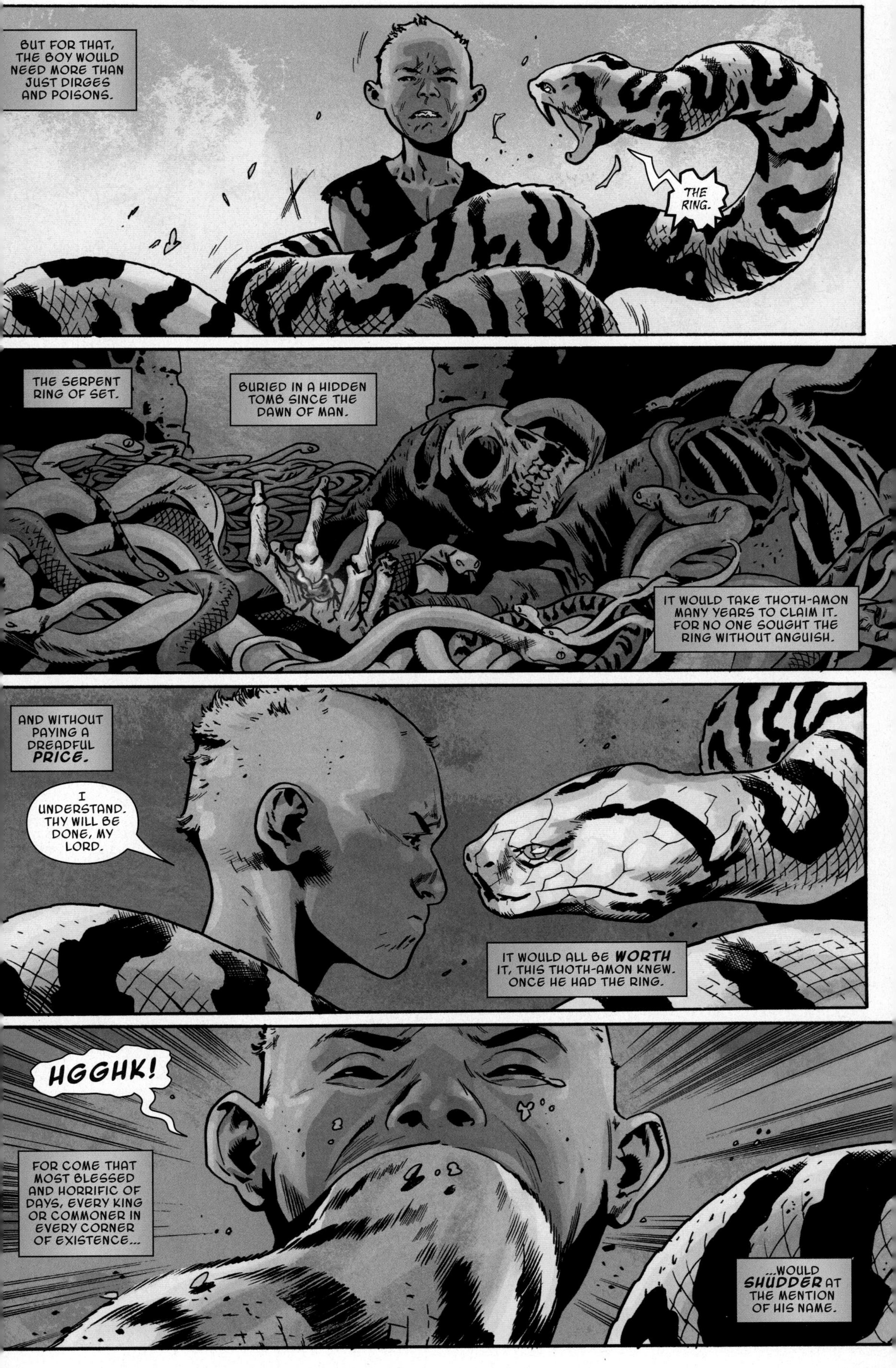
BUT FOR THAT, THE BOY WOULD NEED MORE THAN JUST DIRGES AND POISONS.
THE RING.
THE SERPENT RING OF SET.
BURIED IN A HIDDEN TOMB SINCE THE DAWN OF MAN.
IT WOULD TAKE THOTH-AMON MANY YEARS TO CLAIM IT. FOR NO ONE SOUGHT THE RING WITHOUT ANGUISH.
AND WITHOUT PAYING A DREADFUL PRICE.
I UNDERSTAND. THY WILL BE DONE, MY LORD.
IT WOULD ALL BE WORTH IT, THIS THOTH-AMON KNEW. ONCE HE HAD THE RING.
HGGHK!
FOR COME THAT MOST BLESSED AND HORRIFIC OF DAYS, EVERY KING OR COMMONER IN EVERY CORNER OF EXISTENCE...
...WOULD SHUDDER AT THE MENTION OF HIS NAME.

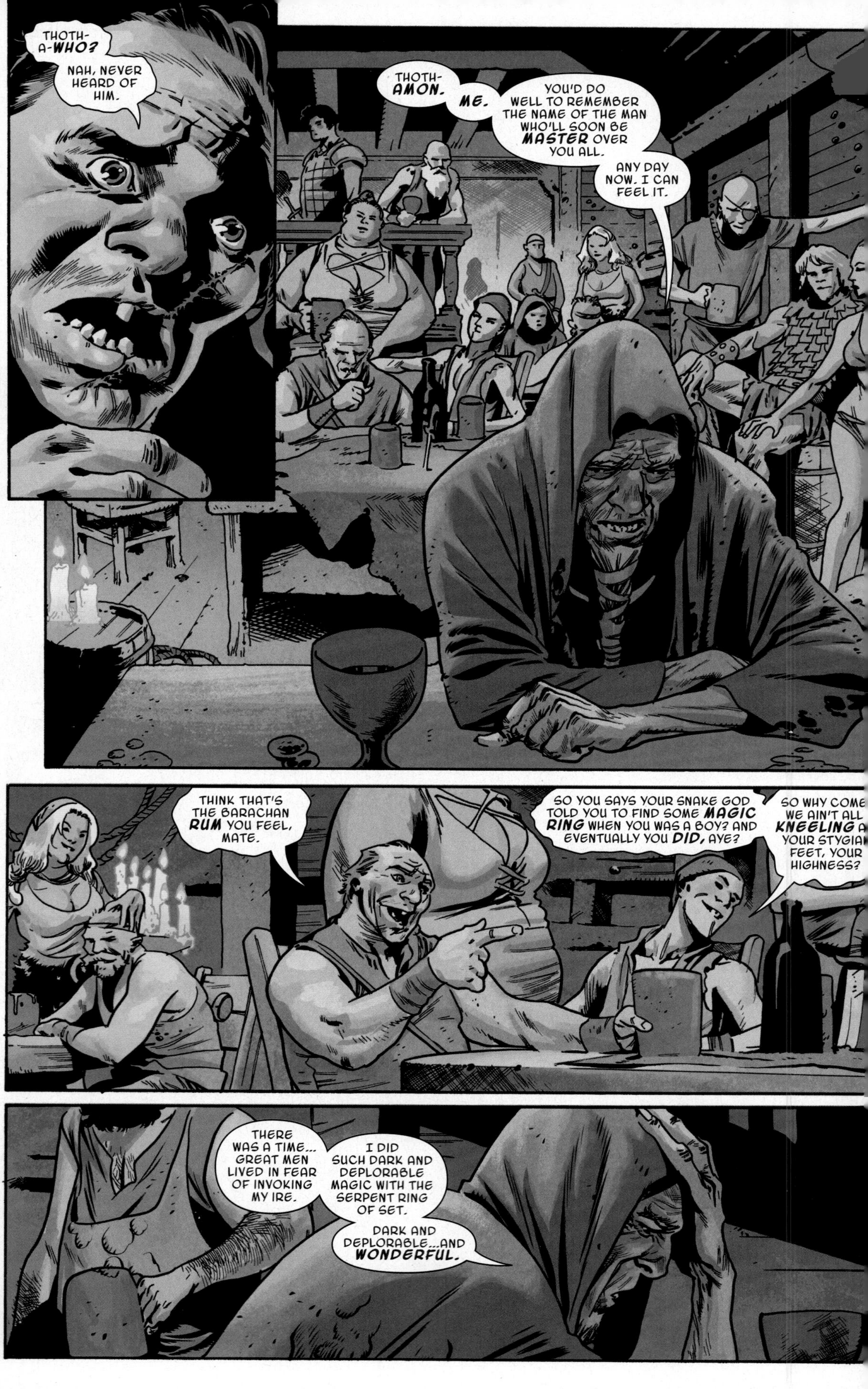
THOTH-A-WHO?
NAH, NEVER HEARD OF HIM.
THOTH-AMON.
ME.
YOU'D DO WELL TO REMEMBER THE NAME OF THE MAN WHO'LL SOON BE MASTER OVER YOU ALL.
ANY DAY NOW. I CAN FEEL IT.
THINK THAT'S THE BARACHAN RUM YOU FEEL, MATE.
SO YOU SAYS YOUR SNAKE GOD TOLD YOU TO FIND SOME MAGIC RING WHEN YOU WAS A BOY? AND EVENTUALLY YOU DID, AYE?
SO WHY COME WE AIN'T ALL KNEELING A YOUR STYGIA FEET, YOUR HIGHNESS?
THERE WAS A TIME... GREAT MEN LIVED IN FEAR OF INVOKING MY IRE.
I DID SUCH DARK AND DEPLORABLE MAGIC WITH THE SERPENT RING OF SET.
DARK AND DEPLORABLE...AND WONDERFUL.

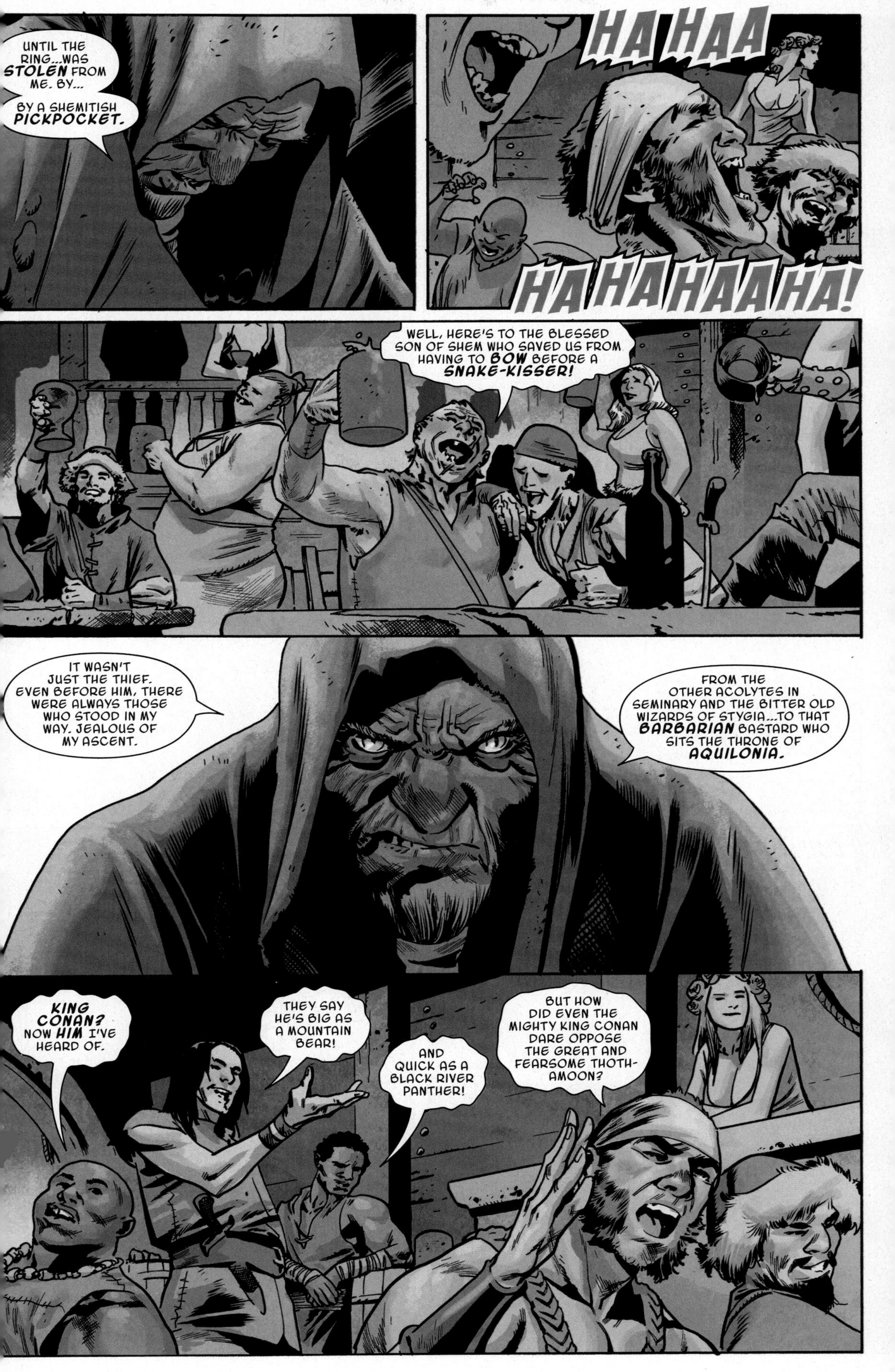

UNTIL THE RING...WAS STOLEN FROM ME. BY...
BY A SHEMITISH PICKPOCKET.
HA HAA
HA HA HA HAA HA!
WELL, HERE'S TO THE BLESSED SON OF SHEM WHO SAVED US FROM HAVING TO BOW BEFORE A SNAKE-KISSER!
IT WASN'T JUST THE THIEF. EVEN BEFORE HIM, THERE WERE ALWAYS THOSE WHO STOOD IN MY WAY. JEALOUS OF MY ASCENT.
FROM THE OTHER ACOLYTES IN SEMINARY AND THE BITTER OLD WIZARDS OF STYGIA...TO THAT BARBARIAN BASTARD WHO SITS THE THRONE OF AQUILONIA.
KING CONAN? NOW HIM I'VE HEARD OF.
THEY SAY HE'S BIG AS A MOUNTAIN BEAR!
AND QUICK AS A BLACK RIVER PANTHER!
BUT HOW DID EVEN THE MIGHTY KING CONAN DARE OPPOSE THE GREAT AND FEARSOME THOTH-AMOON?

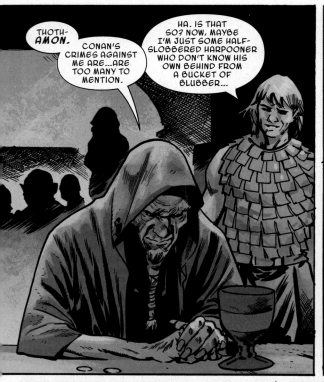

THOTH-**AMON.**

CONAN'S CRIMES AGAINST ME ARE...ARE TOO MANY TO MENTION.

HA. IS THAT SO? NOW, MAYBE I'M JUST SOME HALF-SLOBBERED HARPOONER WHO DON'T KNOW HIS OWN BEHIND FROM A BUCKET OF BLUBBER...

...BUT I'D WAGER MY SORRY SKIN THAT OL' CONAN'S NEVER EVEN **HEARD** OF THOTH-AMOK.

AND THAT YOU ONLY HATE THE KING SO MUCH 'CAUSE HE WENT AND DID WHAT YOU NEVER COULD.

CONAN WENT FROM NOTHING TO **GREATNESS.** WITH NO GOD TO THANK FOR IT.

WHILE YOU--WELL, YOU LOST YOUR FANCY RING, AND BY THE LOOKS OF YOU, MANAGED TO GO FROM NOTHING... TO A BIT MORE NOTHING.

AM I RIGHT?

BHLRRUUUUGHH!!!

HA! I'D SAY MY HARPOON FOUND THE MARK.

YOU FOOLS MISUNDERSTAND. THE RING MAY HAVE ONCE BEEN LOST. BUT, SET BE PRAISED...

...IT HAS BEEN **FOUND.**

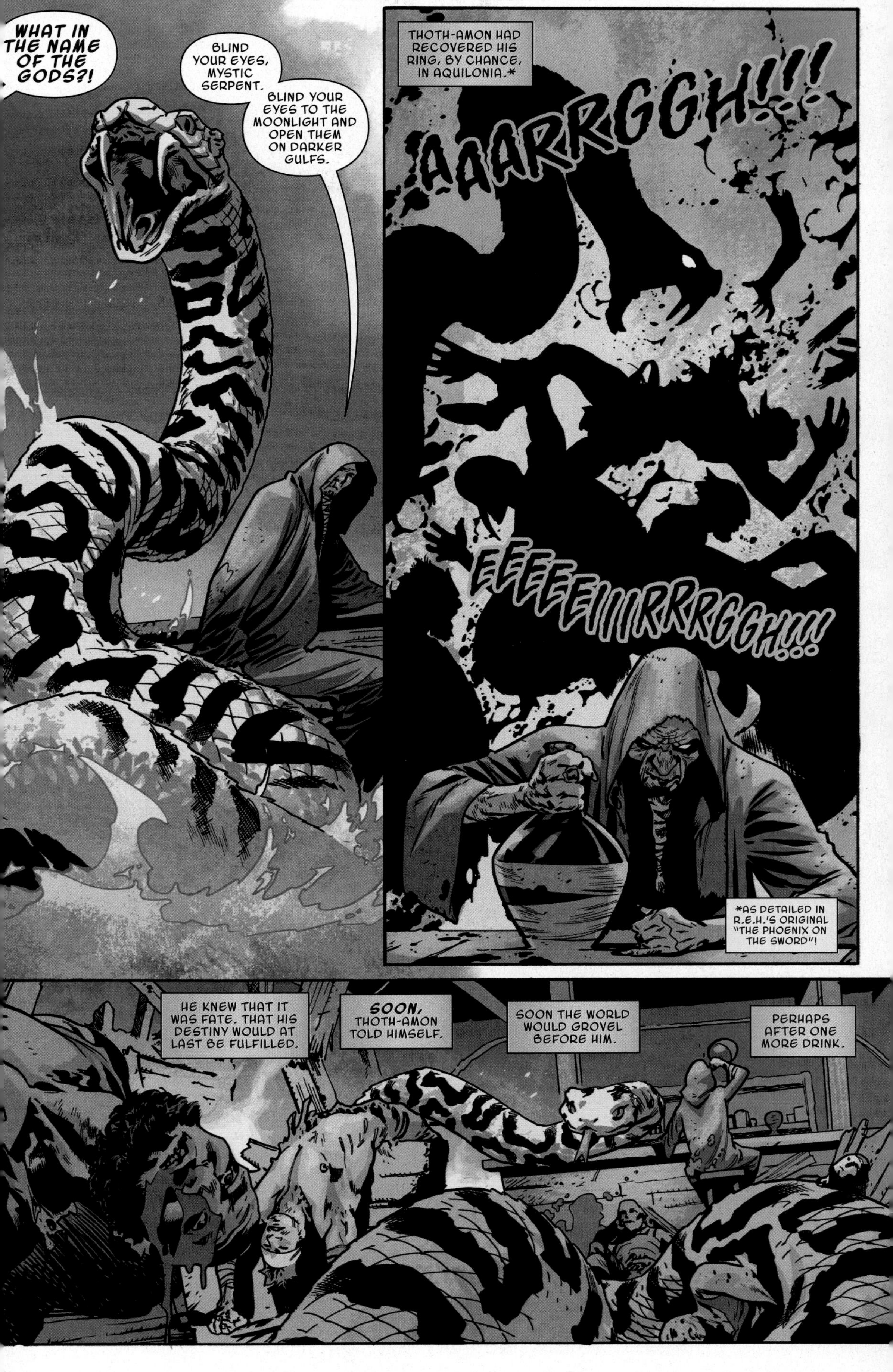
WHAT IN THE NAME OF THE GODS?!
BLIND YOUR EYES, MYSTIC SERPENT.
BLIND YOUR EYES TO THE MOONLIGHT AND OPEN THEM ON DARKER GULFS.
THOTH-AMON HAD RECOVERED HIS RING, BY CHANCE, IN AQUILONIA.*
AAARRGGH!!!
EEEEEIIIRRRGGH!!!
*AS DETAILED IN R.E.H.'S ORIGINAL "THE PHOENIX ON THE SWORD"!
HE KNEW THAT IT WAS FATE. THAT HIS DESTINY WOULD AT LAST BE FULFILLED.
SOON, THOTH-AMON TOLD HIMSELF.
SOON THE WORLD WOULD GROVEL BEFORE HIM.
PERHAPS AFTER ONE MORE DRINK.

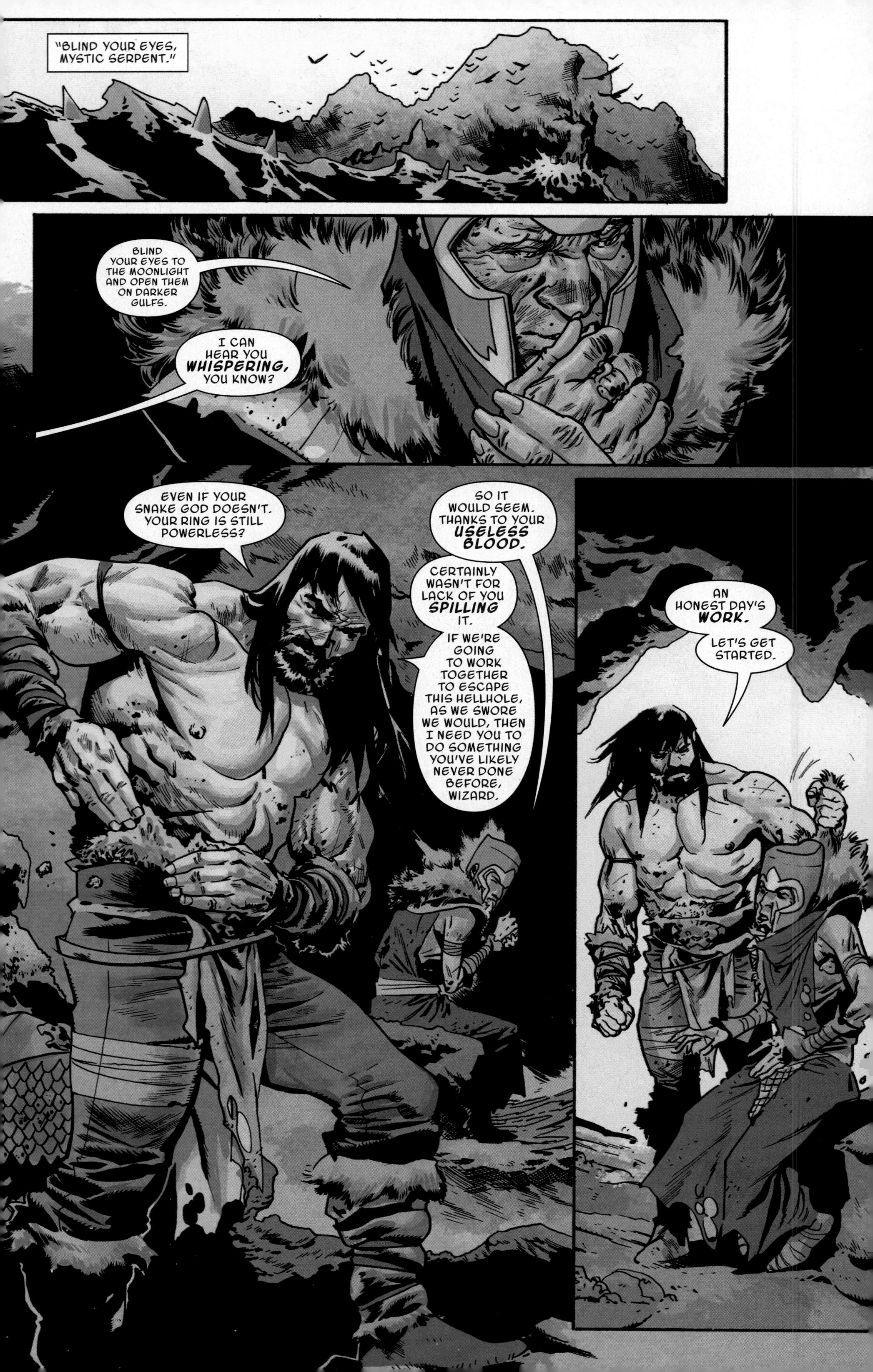
"BLIND YOUR EYES, MYSTIC SERPENT."
BLIND YOUR EYES TO THE MOONLIGHT AND OPEN THEM ON DARKER GULFS.
I CAN HEAR YOU WHISPERING, YOU KNOW?
EVEN IF YOUR SNAKE GOD DOESN'T. YOUR RING IS STILL POWERLESS?
SO IT WOULD SEEM. THANKS TO YOUR USELESS BLOOD.
CERTAINLY WASN'T FOR LACK OF YOU SPILLING IT.
IF WE'RE GOING TO WORK TOGETHER TO ESCAPE THIS HELLHOLE, AS WE SWORE WE WOULD, THEN I NEED YOU TO DO SOMETHING YOU'VE LIKELY NEVER DONE BEFORE, WIZARD.
AN HONEST DAY'S WORK.
LET'S GET STARTED.

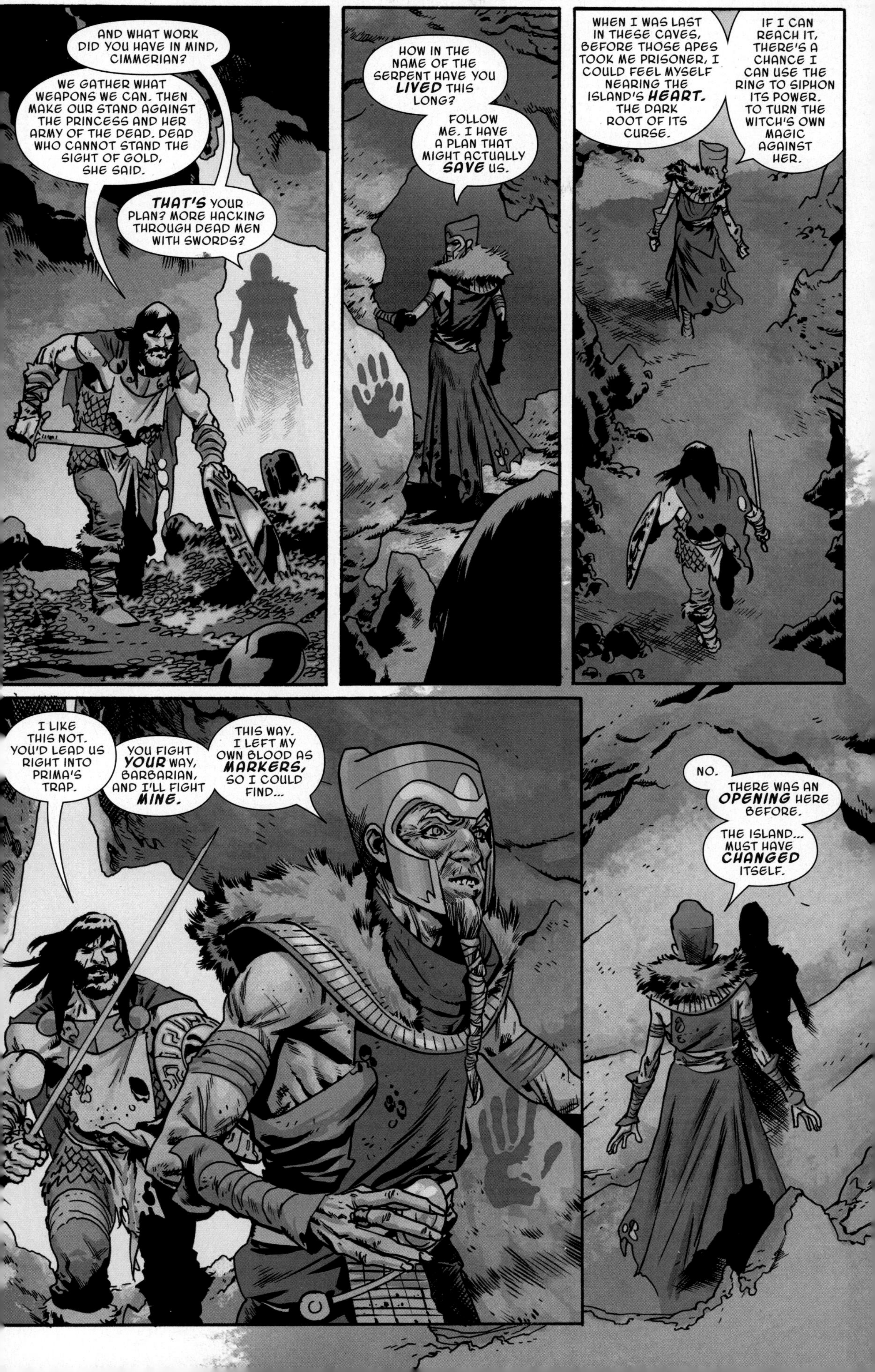

AND WHAT WORK DID YOU HAVE IN MIND, CIMMERIAN?
WE GATHER WHAT WEAPONS WE CAN. THEN MAKE OUR STAND AGAINST THE PRINCESS AND HER ARMY OF THE DEAD. DEAD WHO CANNOT STAND THE SIGHT OF GOLD, SHE SAID.
THAT'S YOUR PLAN? MORE HACKING THROUGH DEAD MEN WITH SWORDS?
HOW IN THE NAME OF THE SERPENT HAVE YOU LIVED THIS LONG?
FOLLOW ME. I HAVE A PLAN THAT MIGHT ACTUALLY SAVE US.
WHEN I WAS LAST IN THESE CAVES, BEFORE THOSE APES TOOK ME PRISONER, I COULD FEEL MYSELF NEARING THE ISLAND'S HEART. THE DARK ROOT OF ITS CURSE.
IF I CAN REACH IT, THERE'S A CHANCE I CAN USE THE RING TO SIPHON ITS POWER. TO TURN THE WITCH'S OWN MAGIC AGAINST HER.
I LIKE THIS NOT. YOU'D LEAD US RIGHT INTO PRIMA'S TRAP.
YOU FIGHT YOUR WAY, BARBARIAN, AND I'LL FIGHT MINE.
THIS WAY. I LEFT MY OWN BLOOD AS MARKERS, SO I COULD FIND...
NO.
THERE WAS AN OPENING HERE BEFORE.
THE ISLAND... MUST HAVE CHANGED ITSELF.

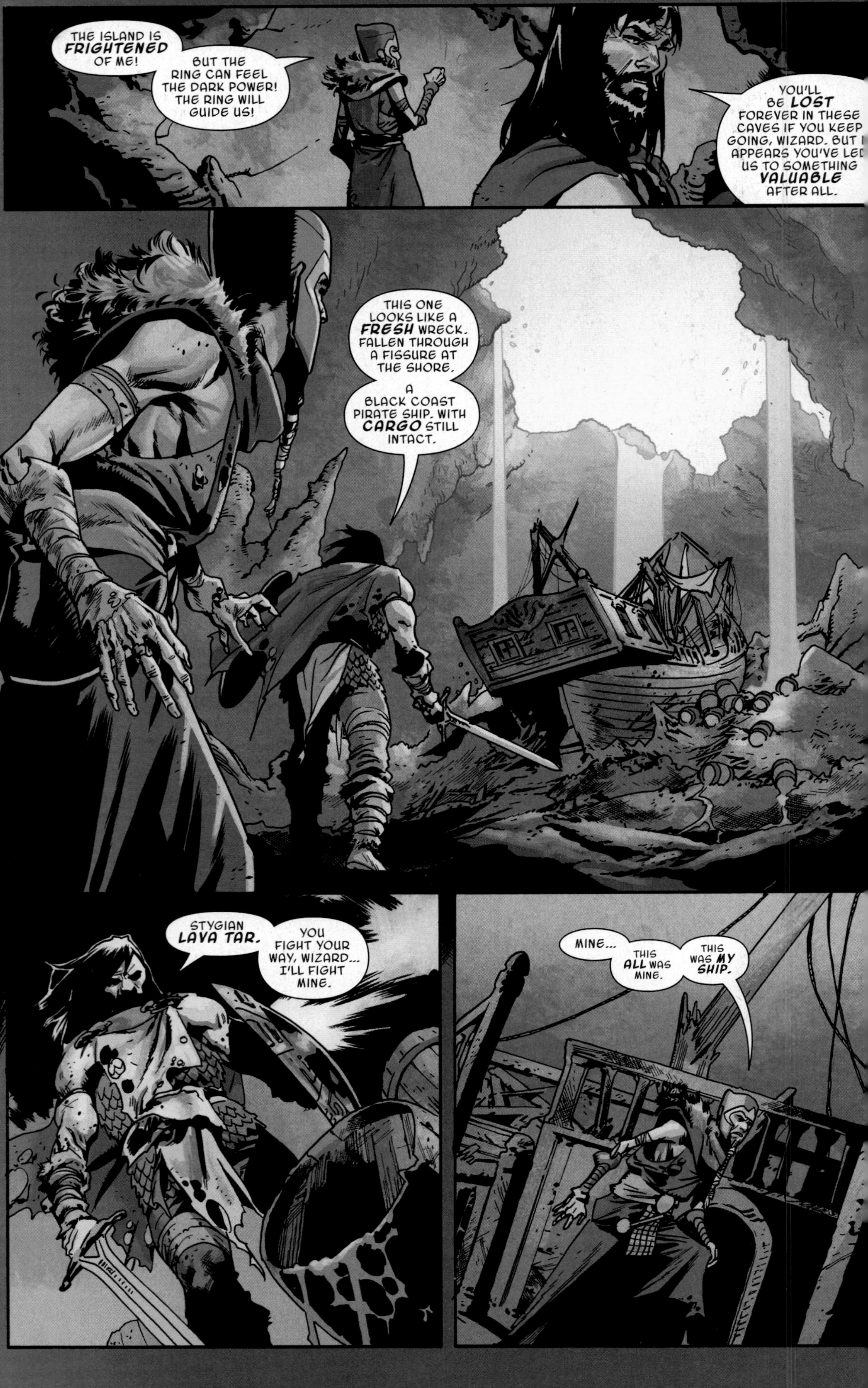
THE ISLAND IS FRIGHTENED OF ME!
BUT THE RING CAN FEEL THE DARK POWER! THE RING WILL GUIDE US!
YOU'LL BE LOST FOREVER IN THESE CAVES IF YOU KEEP GOING, WIZARD. BUT I APPEARS YOU'VE LED US TO SOMETHING VALUABLE AFTER ALL.
THIS ONE LOOKS LIKE A FRESH WRECK. FALLEN THROUGH A FISSURE AT THE SHORE.
A BLACK COAST PIRATE SHIP. WITH CARGO STILL INTACT.
STYGIAN LAVA TAR.
YOU FIGHT YOUR WAY, WIZARD... I'LL FIGHT MINE.
MINE...
THIS ALL WAS MINE.
THIS WAS MY SHIP.

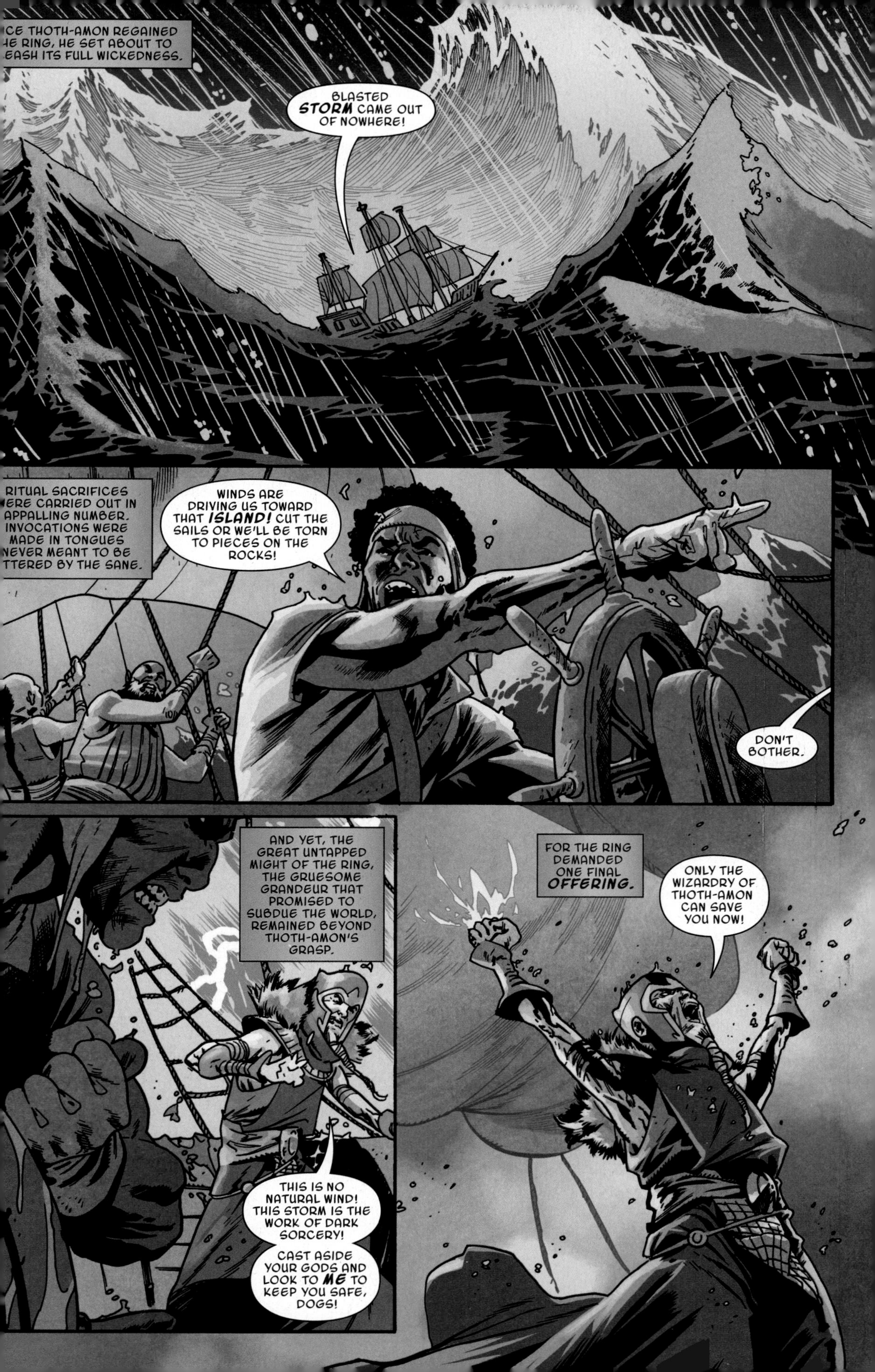

...CE THOTH-AMON REGAINED ...HE RING, HE SET ABOUT TO ...EASH ITS FULL WICKEDNESS.
BLASTED STORM CAME OUT OF NOWHERE!
RITUAL SACRIFICES ...ERE CARRIED OUT IN APPALLING NUMBER. INVOCATIONS WERE MADE IN TONGUES NEVER MEANT TO BE ...TTERED BY THE SANE.
WINDS ARE DRIVING US TOWARD THAT ISLAND! CUT THE SAILS OR WE'LL BE TORN TO PIECES ON THE ROCKS!
DON'T BOTHER.
AND YET, THE GREAT UNTAPPED MIGHT OF THE RING, THE GRUESOME GRANDEUR THAT PROMISED TO SUBDUE THE WORLD, REMAINED BEYOND THOTH-AMON'S GRASP.
THIS IS NO NATURAL WIND! THIS STORM IS THE WORK OF DARK SORCERY!
CAST ASIDE YOUR GODS AND LOOK TO ME TO KEEP YOU SAFE, DOGS!
FOR THE RING DEMANDED ONE FINAL OFFERING.
ONLY THE WIZARDRY OF THOTH-AMON CAN SAVE YOU NOW!

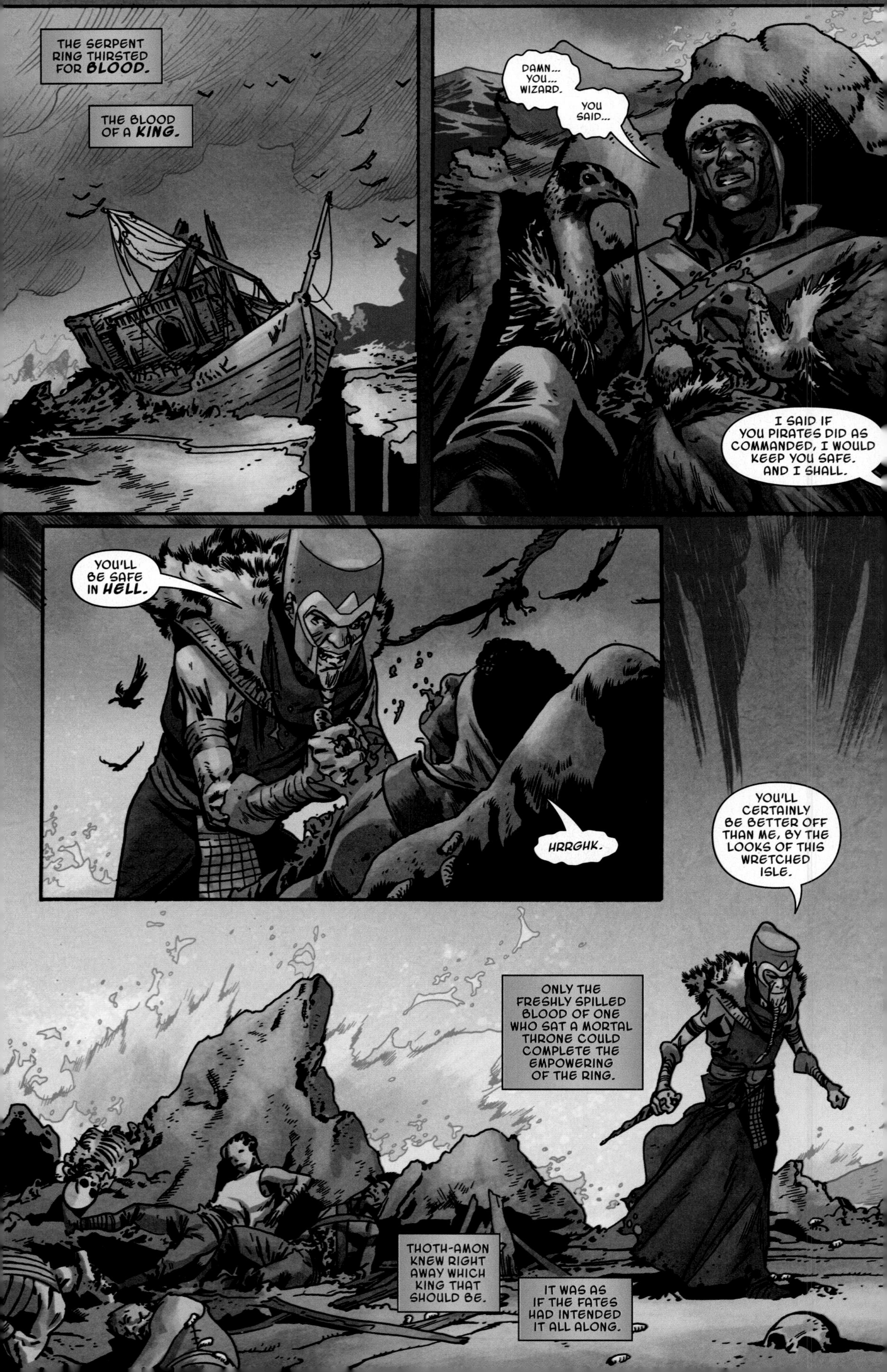
THE SERPENT RING THIRSTED FOR BLOOD.
THE BLOOD OF A KING.
DAMN... YOU... WIZARD.
YOU SAID...
I SAID IF YOU PIRATES DID AS COMMANDED, I WOULD KEEP YOU SAFE. AND I SHALL.
YOU'LL BE SAFE IN HELL.
HRRGHK.
YOU'LL CERTAINLY BE BETTER OFF THAN ME, BY THE LOOKS OF THIS WRETCHED ISLE.
ONLY THE FRESHLY SPILLED BLOOD OF ONE WHO SAT A MORTAL THRONE COULD COMPLETE THE EMPOWERING OF THE RING.
THOTH-AMON KNEW RIGHT AWAY WHICH KING THAT SHOULD BE.
IT WAS AS IF THE FATES HAD INTENDED IT ALL ALONG.

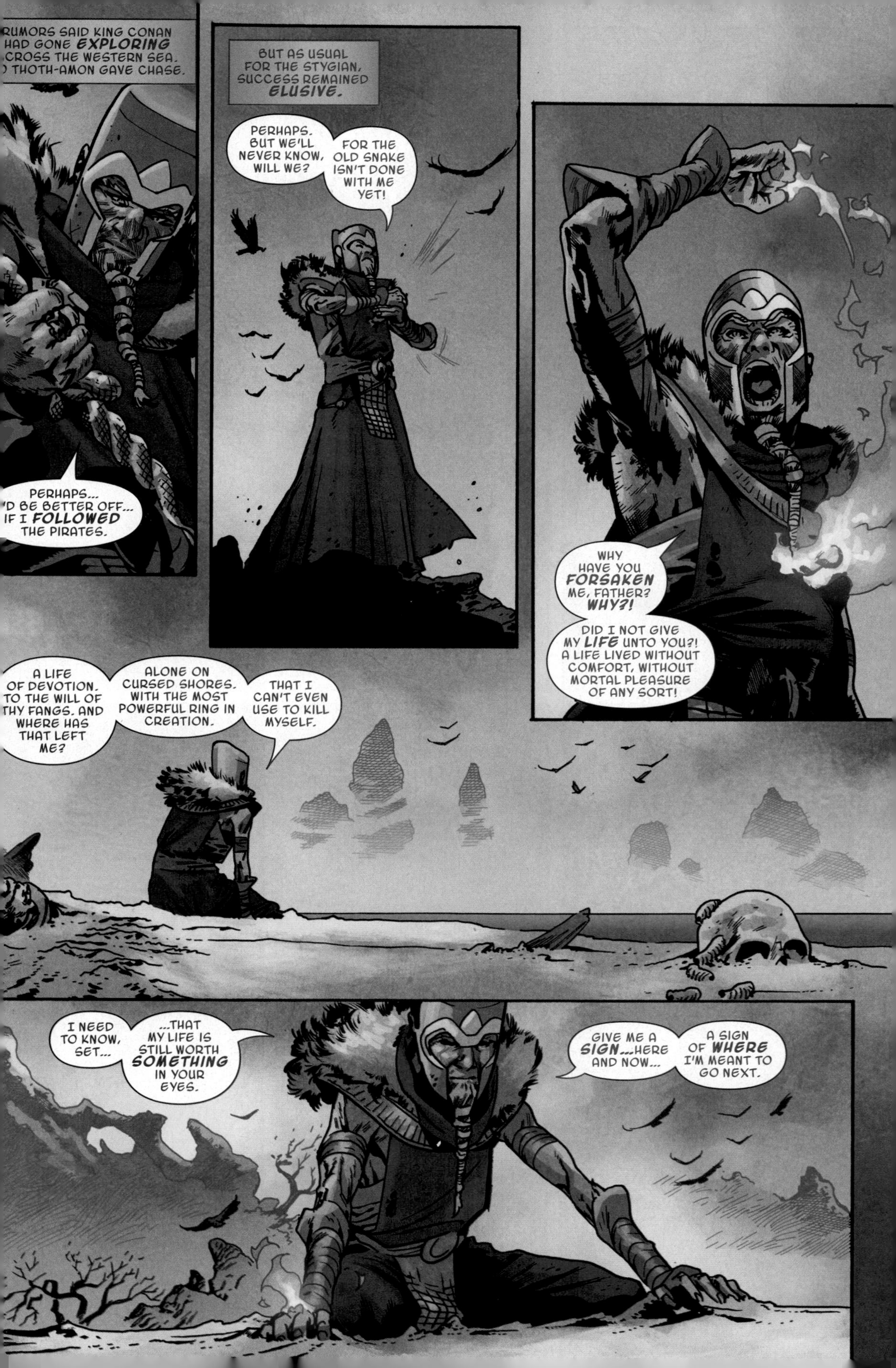
RUMORS SAID KING CONAN HAD GONE EXPLORING CROSS THE WESTERN SEA. O THOTH-AMON GAVE CHASE.
PERHAPS... 'D BE BETTER OFF... IF I FOLLOWED THE PIRATES.
BUT AS USUAL FOR THE STYGIAN, SUCCESS REMAINED ELUSIVE.
PERHAPS. BUT WE'LL NEVER KNOW, WILL WE?
FOR THE OLD SNAKE ISN'T DONE WITH ME YET!
WHY HAVE YOU FORSAKEN ME, FATHER? WHY?!
DID I NOT GIVE MY LIFE UNTO YOU?! A LIFE LIVED WITHOUT COMFORT, WITHOUT MORTAL PLEASURE OF ANY SORT!
A LIFE OF DEVOTION. TO THE WILL OF THY FANGS. AND WHERE HAS THAT LEFT ME?
ALONE ON CURSED SHORES. WITH THE MOST POWERFUL RING IN CREATION.
THAT I CAN'T EVEN USE TO KILL MYSELF.
I NEED TO KNOW, SET...
...THAT MY LIFE IS STILL WORTH SOMETHING IN YOUR EYES.
GIVE ME A SIGN...HERE AND NOW...
A SIGN OF WHERE I'M MEANT TO GO NEXT.

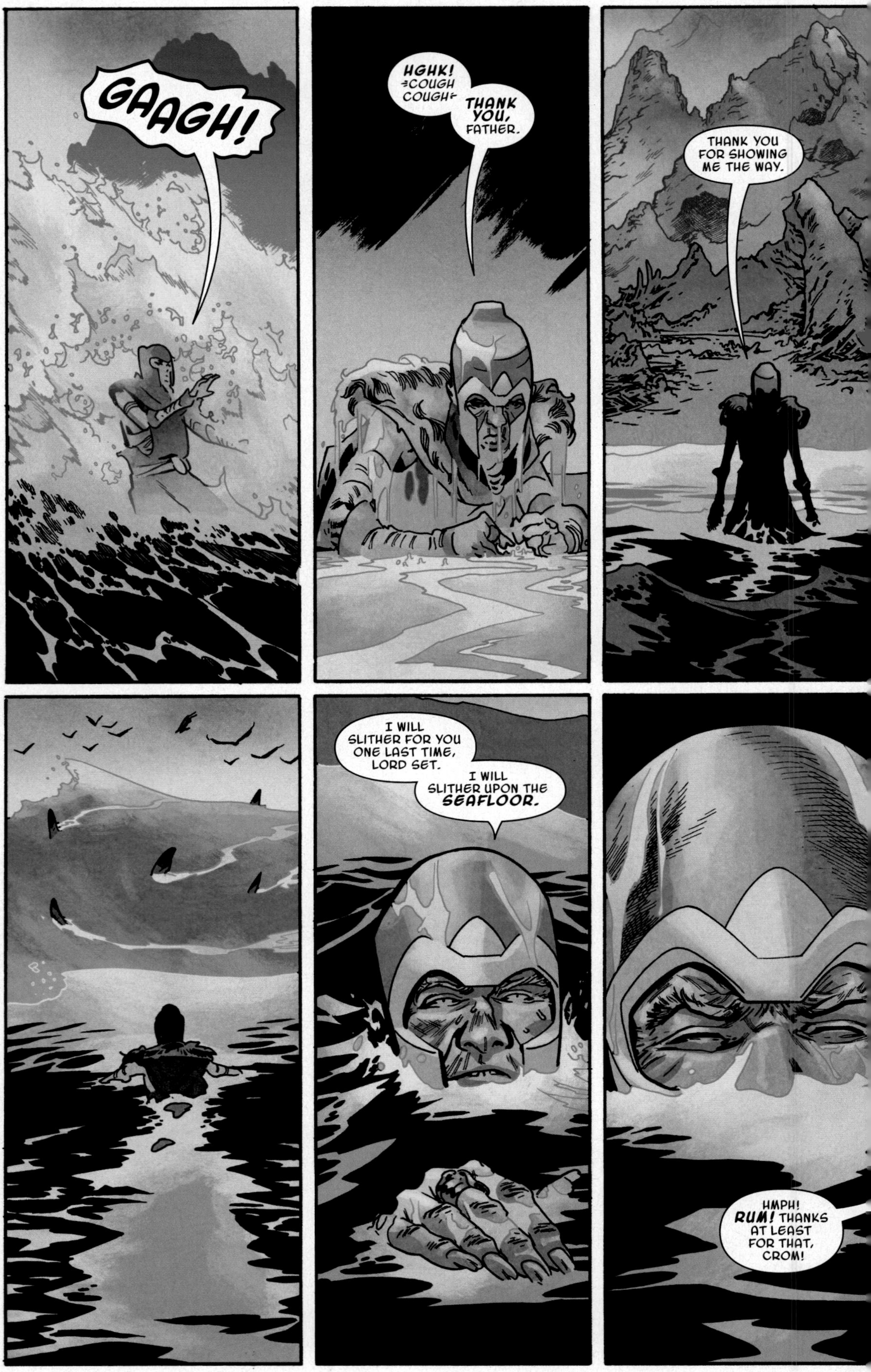
GAAGH!
HGHK! COUGH COUGH
THANK YOU, FATHER.
THANK YOU FOR SHOWING ME THE WAY.
I WILL SLITHER FOR YOU ONE LAST TIME, LORD SET.
I WILL SLITHER UPON THE SEAFLOOR.
HMPH! RUM! THANKS AT LEAST FOR THAT, CROM!

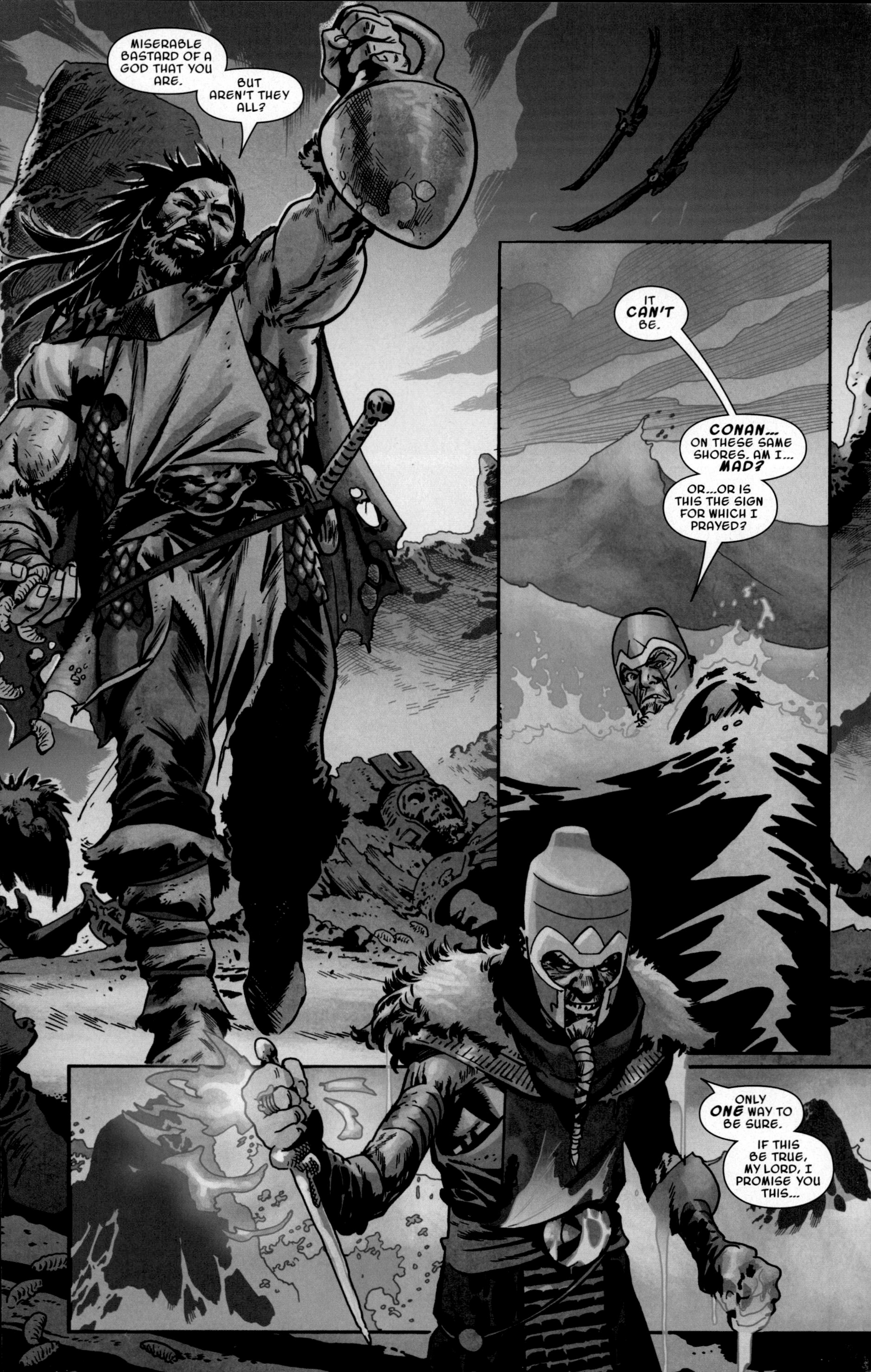
MISERABLE BASTARD OF A GOD THAT YOU ARE.
BUT AREN'T THEY ALL?
IT CAN'T BE.
CONAN... ON THESE SAME SHORES. AM I... MAD?
OR...OR IS THIS THE SIGN FOR WHICH I PRAYED?
ONLY ONE WAY TO BE SURE.
IF THIS BE TRUE, MY LORD, I PROMISE YOU THIS...

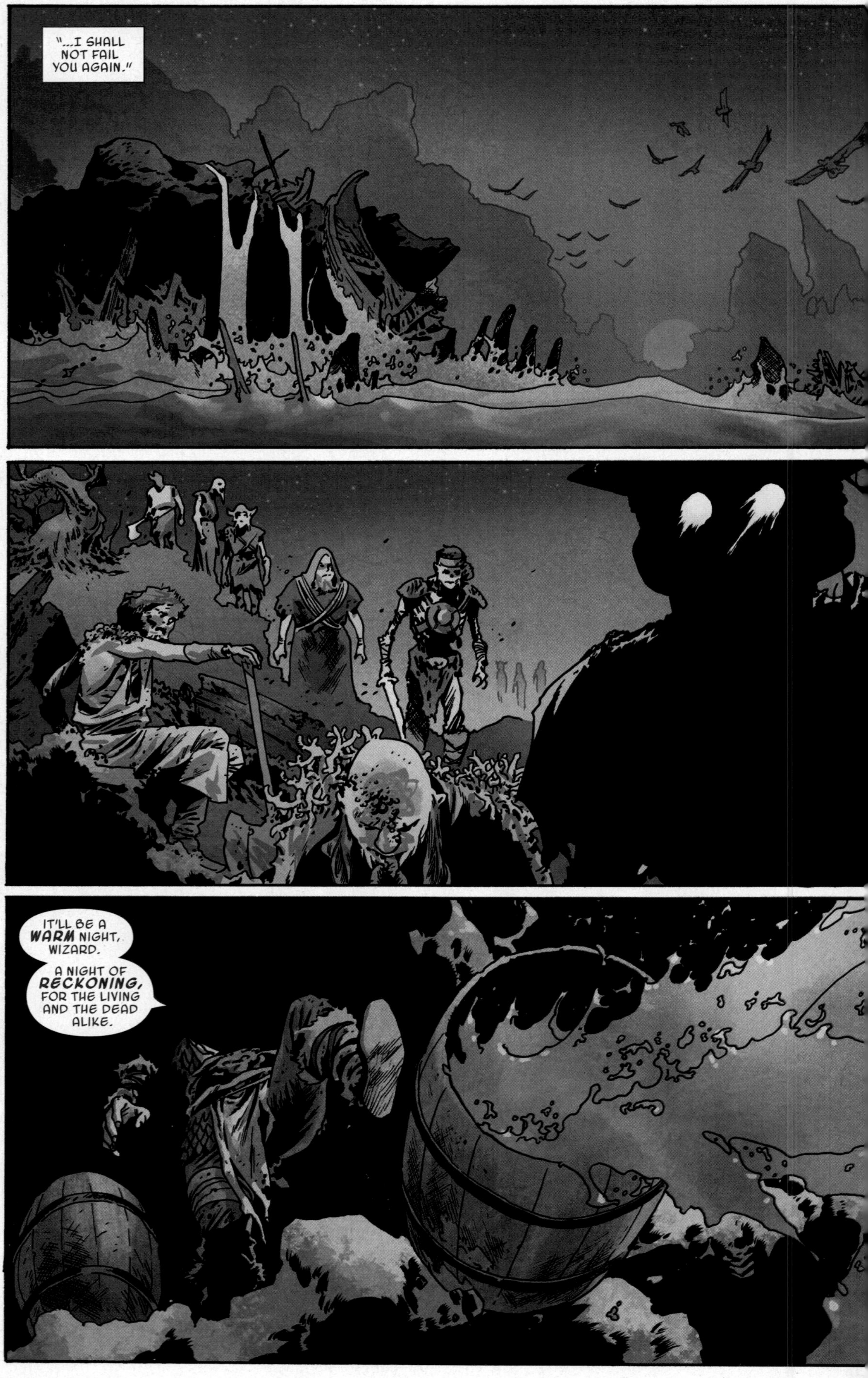
"...I SHALL NOT FAIL YOU AGAIN."
IT'LL BE A WARM NIGHT, WIZARD.
A NIGHT OF RECKONING, FOR THE LIVING AND THE DEAD ALIKE.

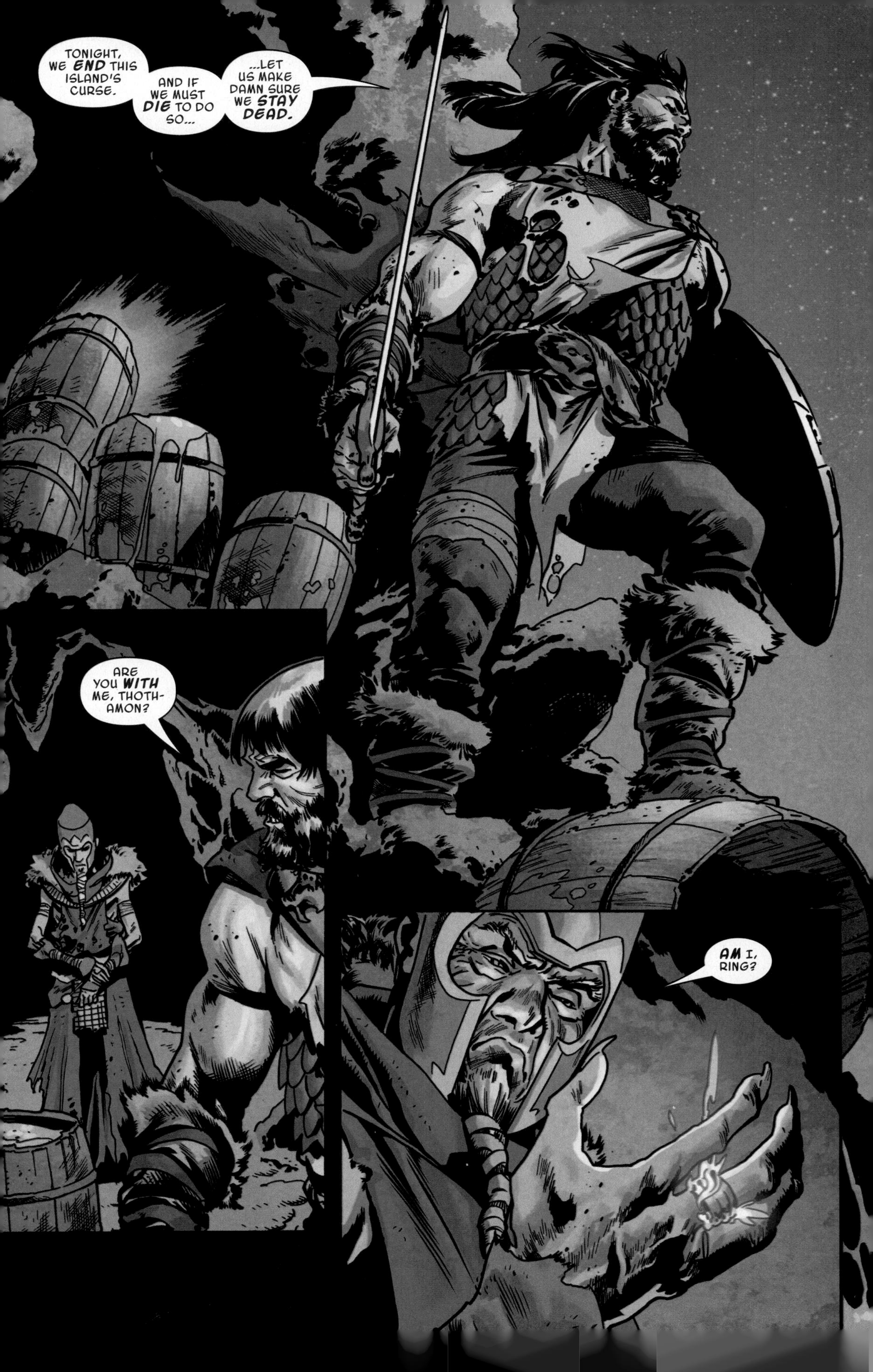
TONIGHT, WE END THIS ISLAND'S CURSE.
AND IF WE MUST DIE TO DO SO...
...LET US MAKE DAMN SURE WE STAY DEAD.
ARE YOU WITH ME, THOTH-AMON?
AM I, RING?

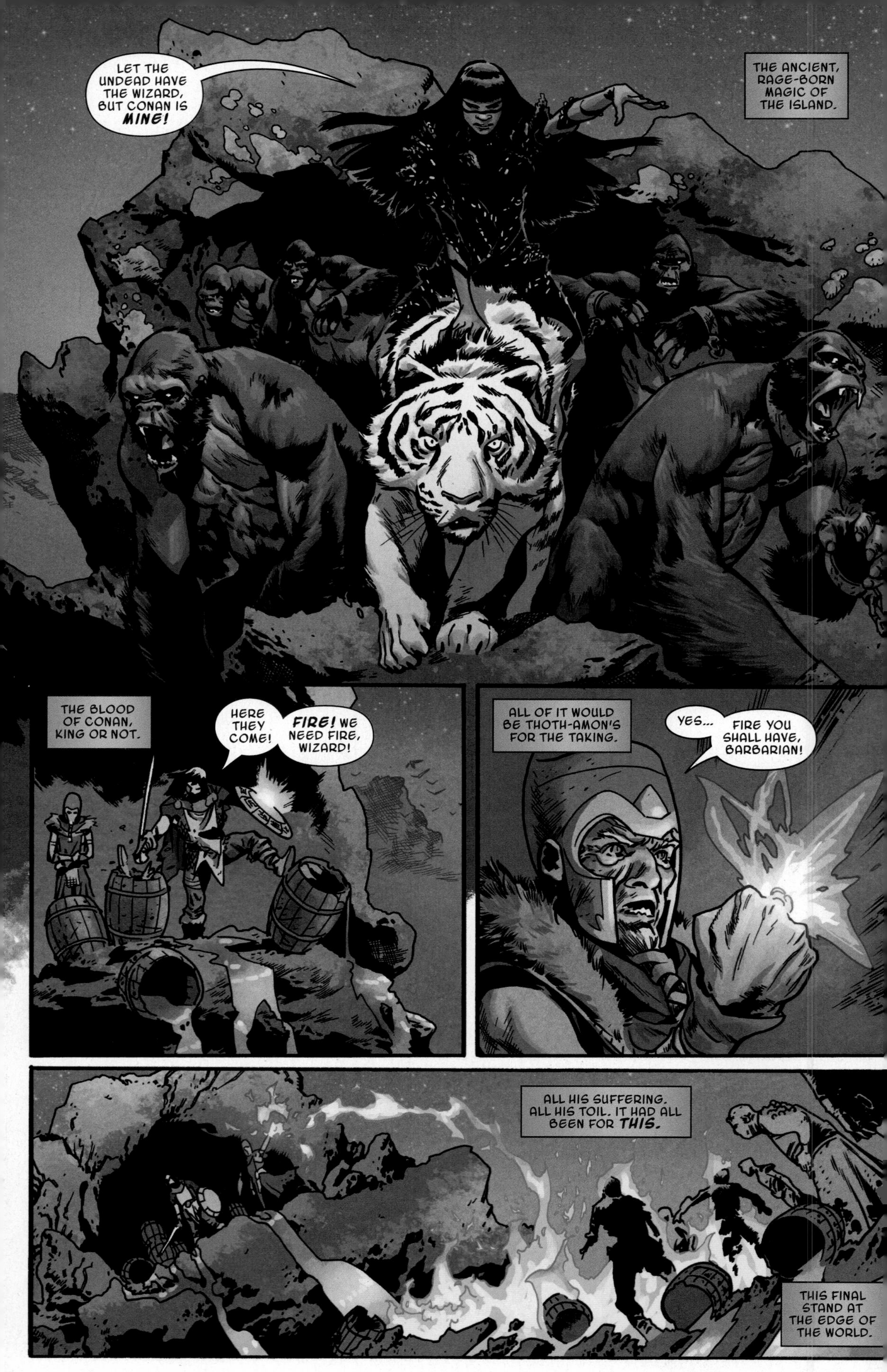
LET THE UNDEAD HAVE THE WIZARD, BUT CONAN IS MINE!
THE ANCIENT, RAGE-BORN MAGIC OF THE ISLAND.
THE BLOOD OF CONAN, KING OR NOT.
HERE THEY COME!
FIRE! WE NEED FIRE, WIZARD!
ALL OF IT WOULD BE THOTH-AMON'S FOR THE TAKING.
YES...
FIRE YOU SHALL HAVE, BARBARIAN!
ALL HIS SUFFERING. ALL HIS TOIL. IT HAD ALL BEEN FOR THIS.
THIS FINAL STAND AT THE EDGE OF THE WORLD.

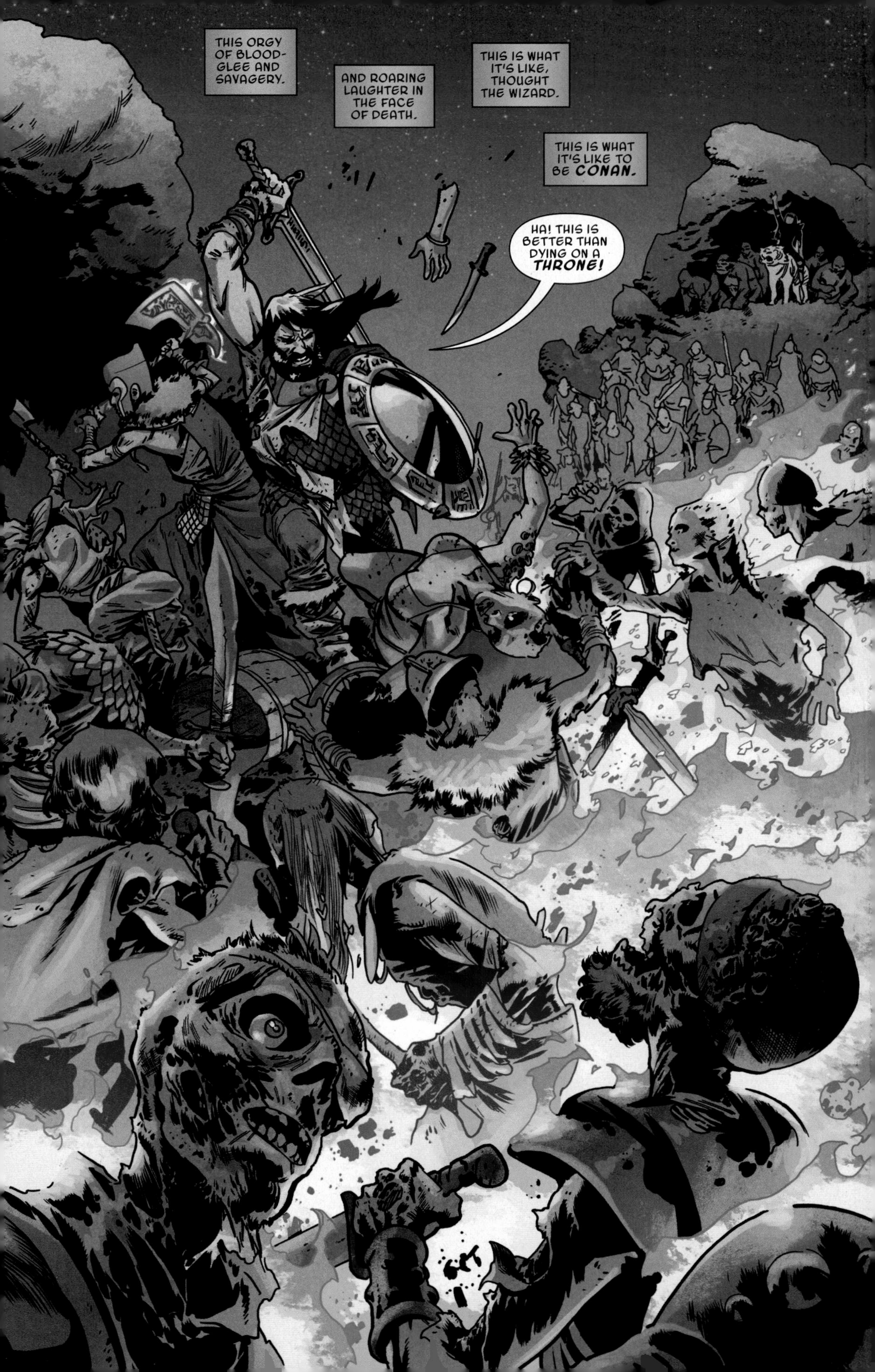

THIS ORGY OF BLOOD-GLEE AND SAVAGERY.
AND ROARING LAUGHTER IN THE FACE OF DEATH.
THIS IS WHAT IT'S LIKE, THOUGHT THE WIZARD.
THIS IS WHAT IT'S LIKE TO BE CONAN.
HA! THIS IS BETTER THAN DYING ON A THRONE!

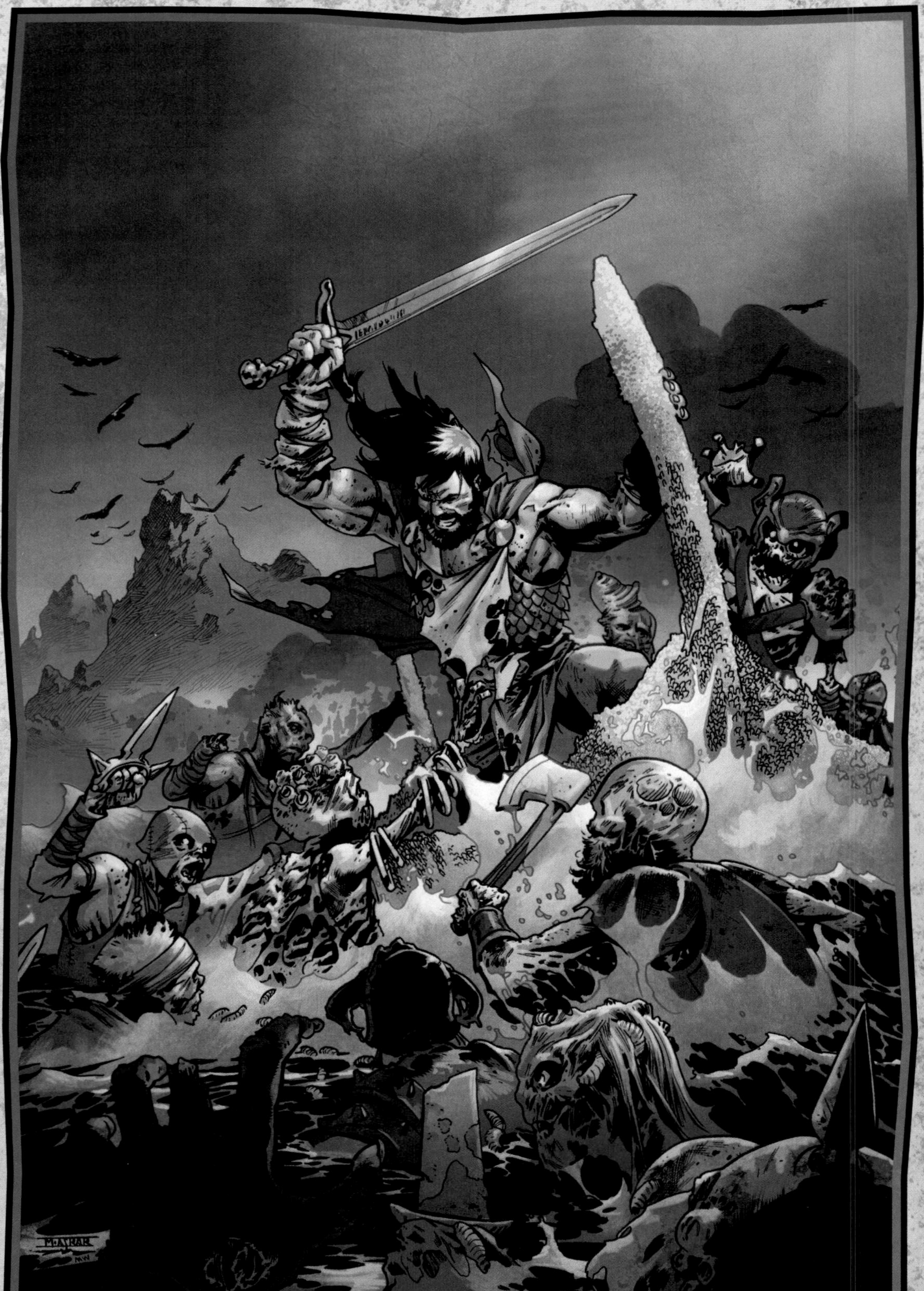

6

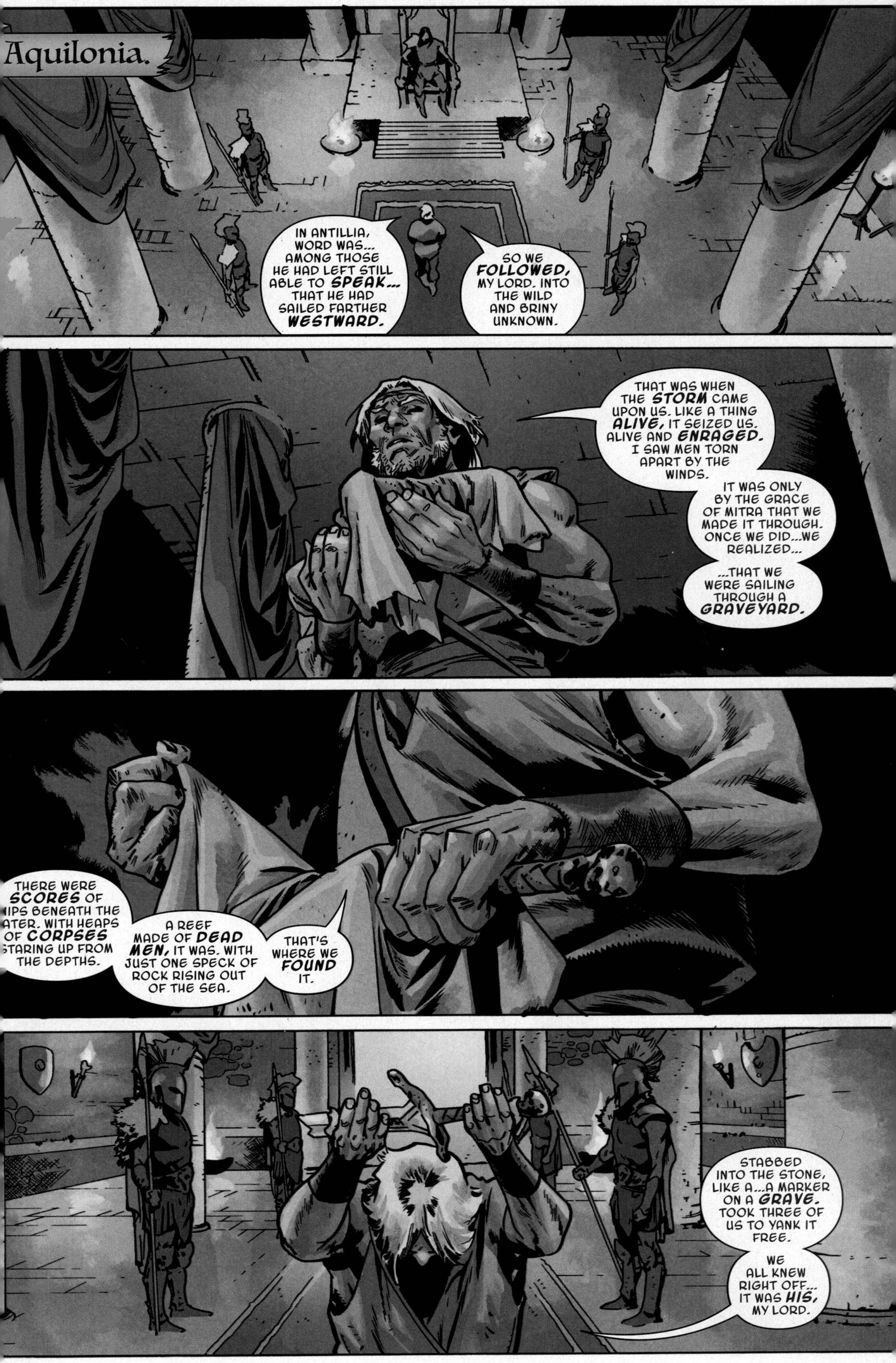
Aquilonia.
IN ANTILLIA, WORD WAS... AMONG THOSE HE HAD LEFT STILL ABLE TO SPEAK... THAT HE HAD SAILED FARTHER WESTWARD.
SO WE FOLLOWED, MY LORD. INTO THE WILD AND BRINY UNKNOWN.
THAT WAS WHEN THE STORM CAME UPON US. LIKE A THING ALIVE, IT SEIZED US. ALIVE AND ENRAGED. I SAW MEN TORN APART BY THE WINDS.
IT WAS ONLY BY THE GRACE OF MITRA THAT WE MADE IT THROUGH. ONCE WE DID...WE REALIZED...
...THAT WE WERE SAILING THROUGH A GRAVEYARD.
THERE WERE SCORES OF IPS BENEATH THE ATER. WITH HEAPS OF CORPSES STARING UP FROM THE DEPTHS.
A REEF MADE OF DEAD MEN, IT WAS. WITH JUST ONE SPECK OF ROCK RISING OUT OF THE SEA.
THAT'S WHERE WE FOUND IT.
STABBED INTO THE STONE, LIKE A...A MARKER ON A GRAVE. TOOK THREE OF US TO YANK IT FREE.
WE ALL KNEW RIGHT OFF... IT WAS HIS, MY LORD.

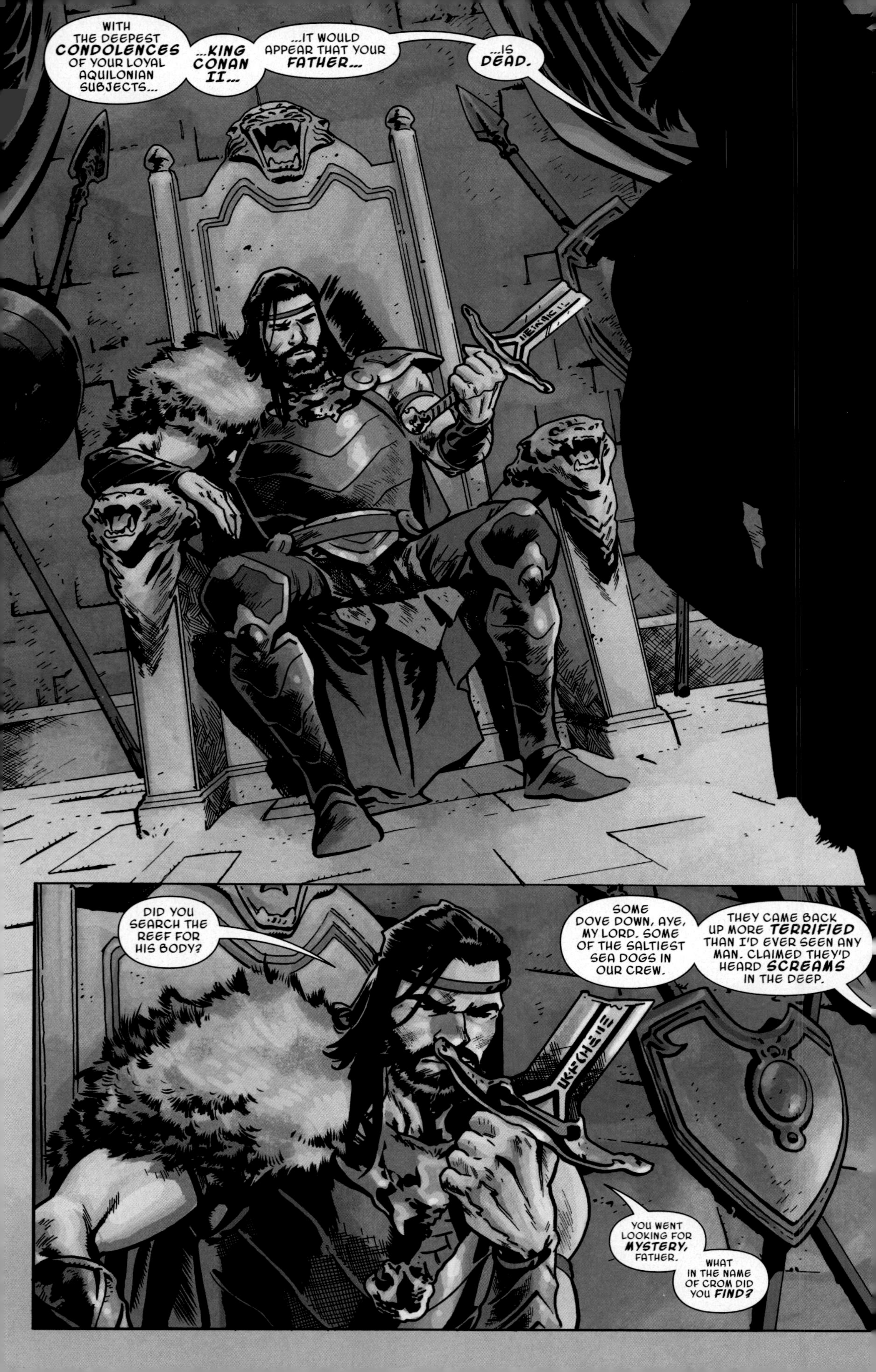
WITH THE DEEPEST CONDOLENCES OF YOUR LOYAL AQUILONIAN SUBJECTS...
...KING CONAN II...
...IT WOULD APPEAR THAT YOUR FATHER...
...IS DEAD.
DID YOU SEARCH THE REEF FOR HIS BODY?
SOME DOVE DOWN, AYE, MY LORD. SOME OF THE SALTIEST SEA DOGS IN OUR CREW.
THEY CAME BACK UP MORE TERRIFIED THAN I'D EVER SEEN ANY MAN. CLAIMED THEY'D HEARD SCREAMS IN THE DEEP.
YOU WENT LOOKING FOR MYSTERY, FATHER.
WHAT IN THE NAME OF CROM DID YOU FIND?

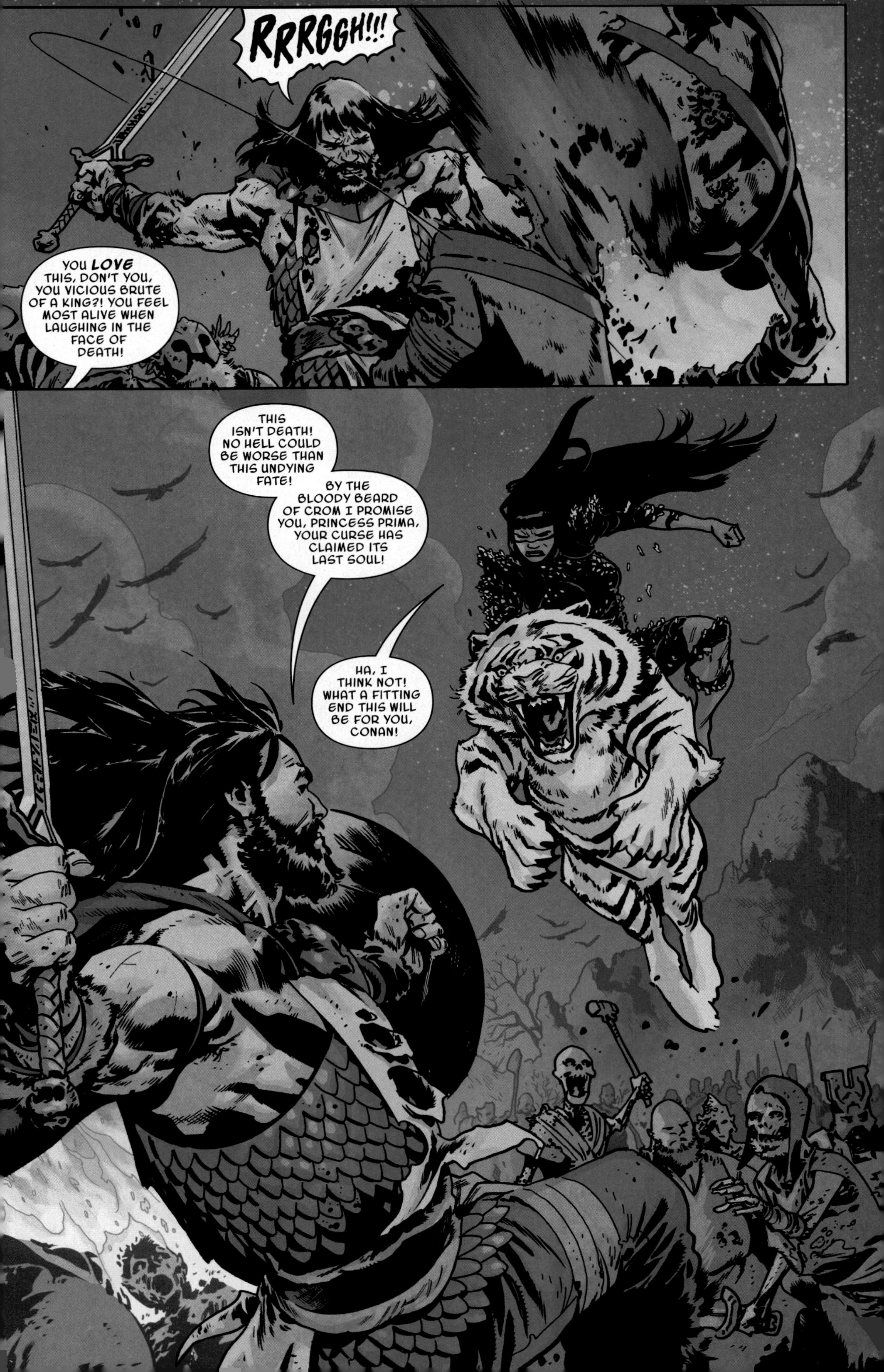
RRRGGH!!!
YOU LOVE THIS, DON'T YOU, YOU VICIOUS BRUTE OF A KING?! YOU FEEL MOST ALIVE WHEN LAUGHING IN THE FACE OF DEATH!
THIS ISN'T DEATH! NO HELL COULD BE WORSE THAN THIS UNDYING FATE!
BY THE BLOODY BEARD OF CROM I PROMISE YOU, PRINCESS PRIMA, YOUR CURSE HAS CLAIMED ITS LAST SOUL!
HA, I THINK NOT! WHAT A FITTING END THIS WILL BE FOR YOU, CONAN!

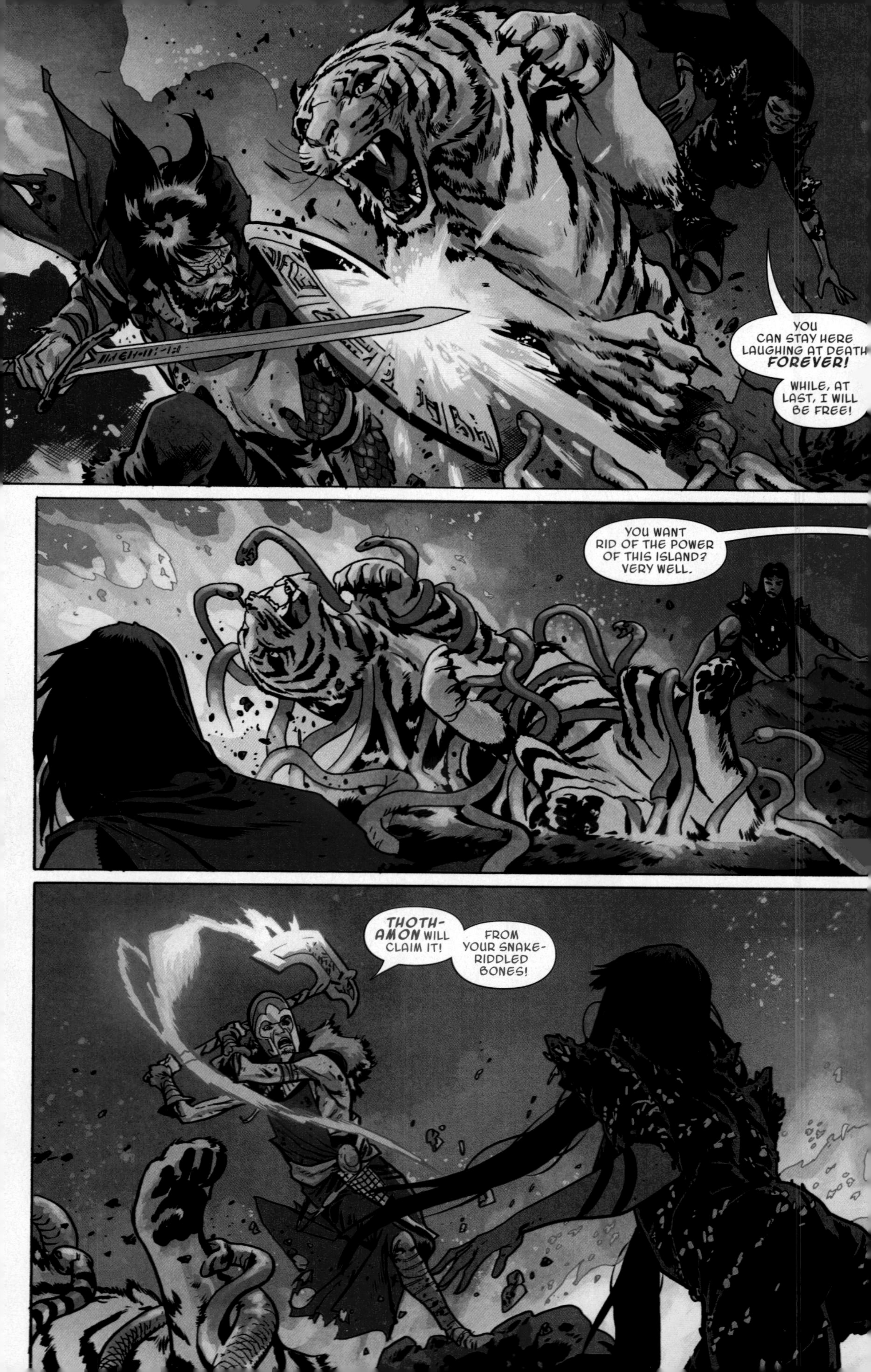
YOU CAN STAY HERE LAUGHING AT DEATH FOREVER!
WHILE, AT LAST, I WILL BE FREE!
YOU WANT RID OF THE POWER OF THIS ISLAND? VERY WELL.
THOTH-AMON WILL CLAIM IT!
FROM YOUR SNAKE-RIDDLED BONES!

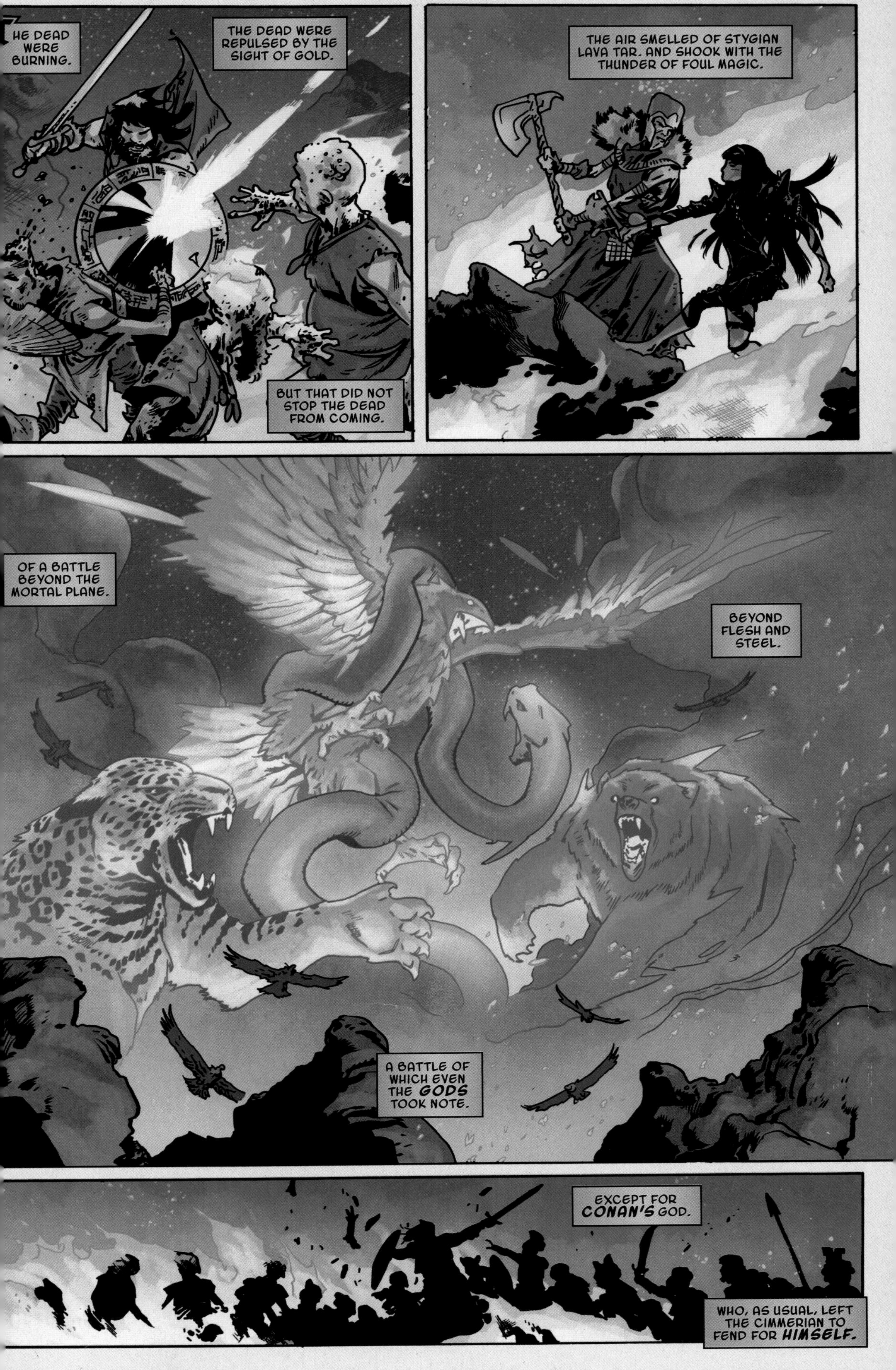
HE DEAD WERE BURNING.
THE DEAD WERE REPULSED BY THE SIGHT OF GOLD.
BUT THAT DID NOT STOP THE DEAD FROM COMING.
THE AIR SMELLED OF STYGIAN LAVA TAR. AND SHOOK WITH THE THUNDER OF FOUL MAGIC.
OF A BATTLE BEYOND THE MORTAL PLANE.
BEYOND FLESH AND STEEL.
A BATTLE OF WHICH EVEN THE GODS TOOK NOTE.
EXCEPT FOR CONAN'S GOD.
WHO, AS USUAL, LEFT THE CIMMERIAN TO FEND FOR HIMSELF.

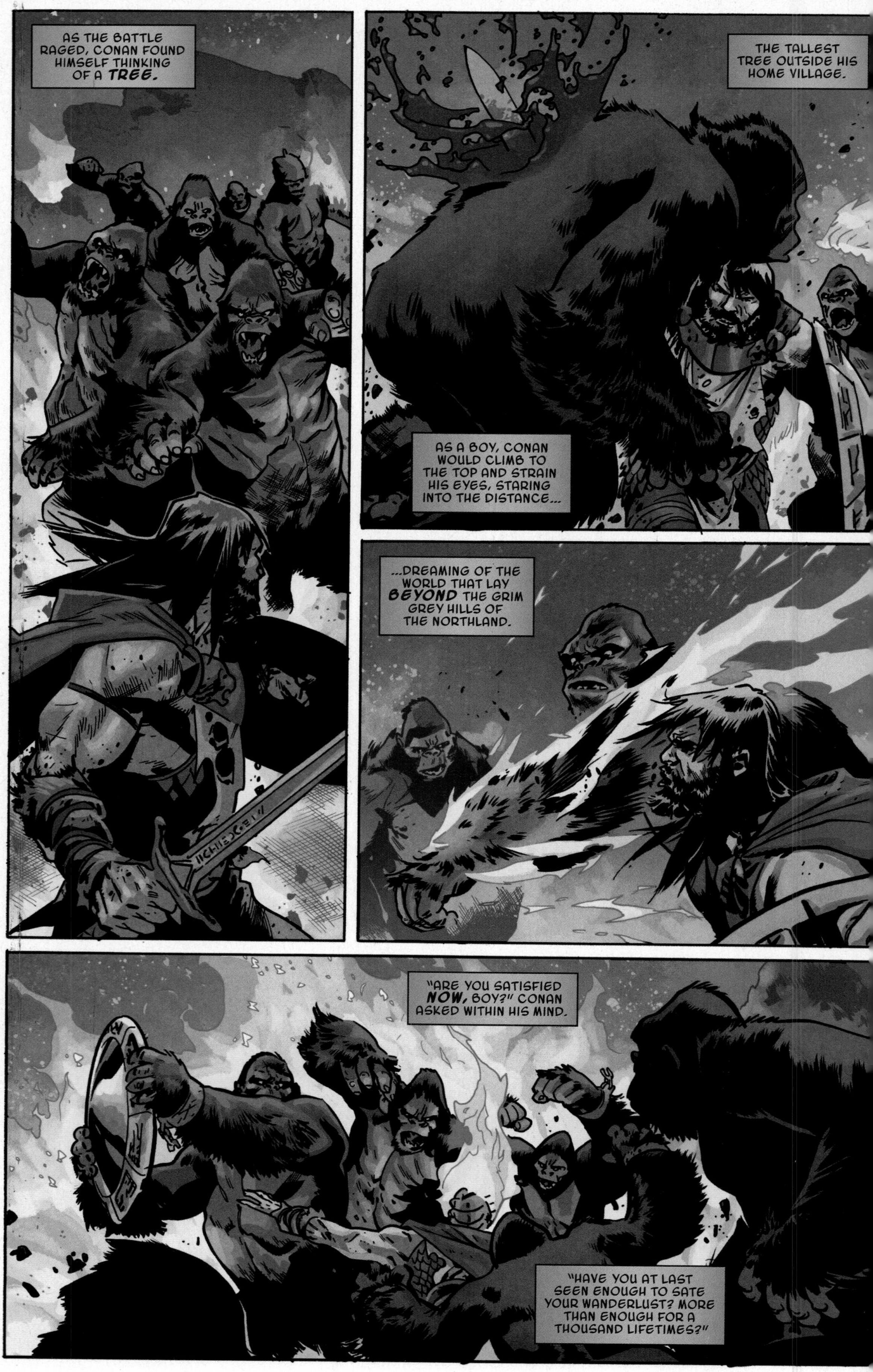
AS THE BATTLE RAGED, CONAN FOUND HIMSELF THINKING OF A TREE.
THE TALLEST TREE OUTSIDE HIS HOME VILLAGE.
AS A BOY, CONAN WOULD CLIMB TO THE TOP AND STRAIN HIS EYES, STARING INTO THE DISTANCE...
...DREAMING OF THE WORLD THAT LAY BEYOND THE GRIM GREY HILLS OF THE NORTHLAND.
"ARE YOU SATISFIED NOW, BOY?" CONAN ASKED WITHIN HIS MIND.
"HAVE YOU AT LAST SEEN ENOUGH TO SATE YOUR WANDERLUST? MORE THAN ENOUGH FOR A THOUSAND LIFETIMES?"

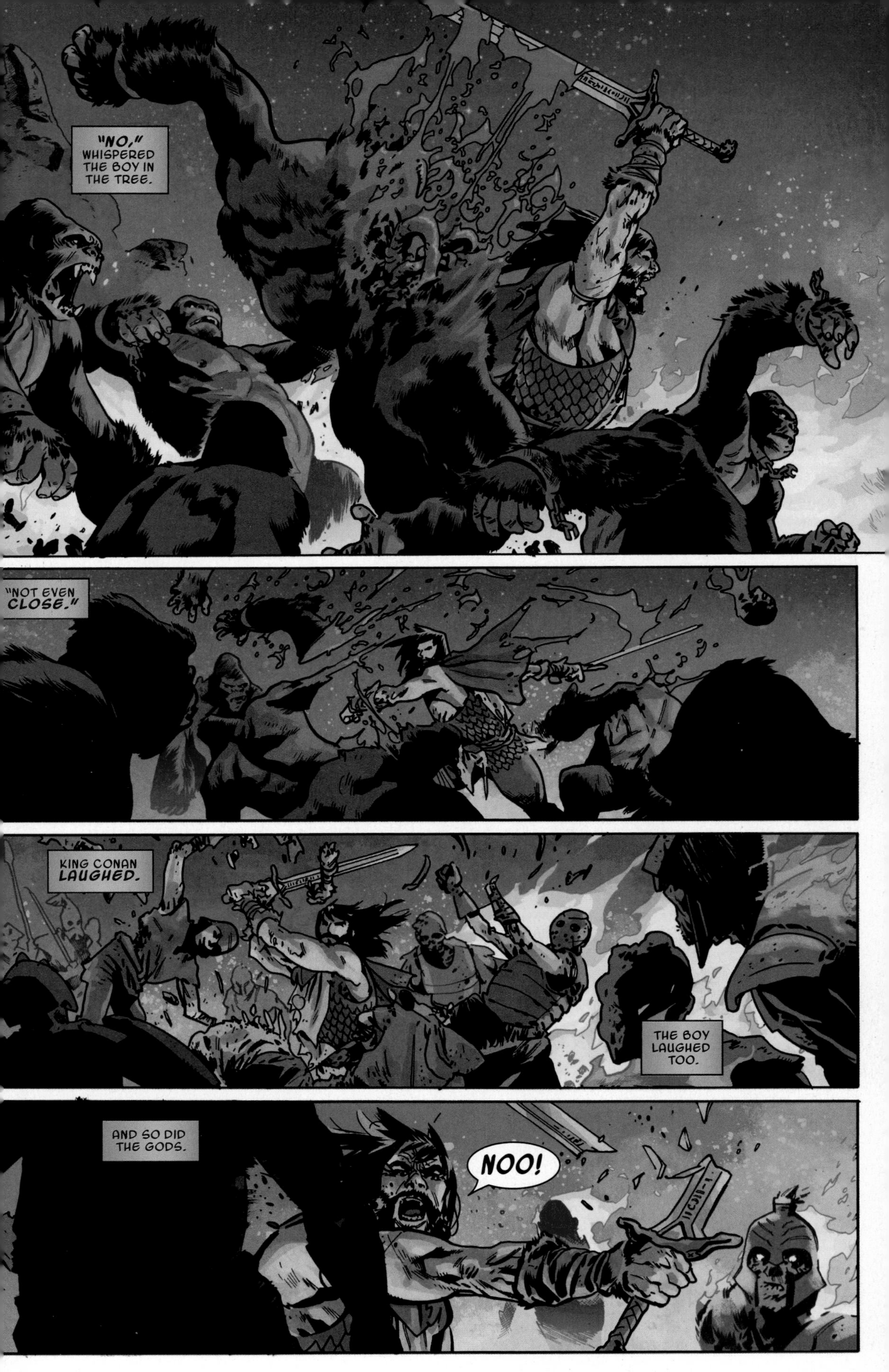
"NO," WHISPERED THE BOY IN THE TREE.
"NOT EVEN CLOSE."
KING CONAN LAUGHED.
THE BOY LAUGHED TOO.
AND SO DID THE GODS.
NOO!

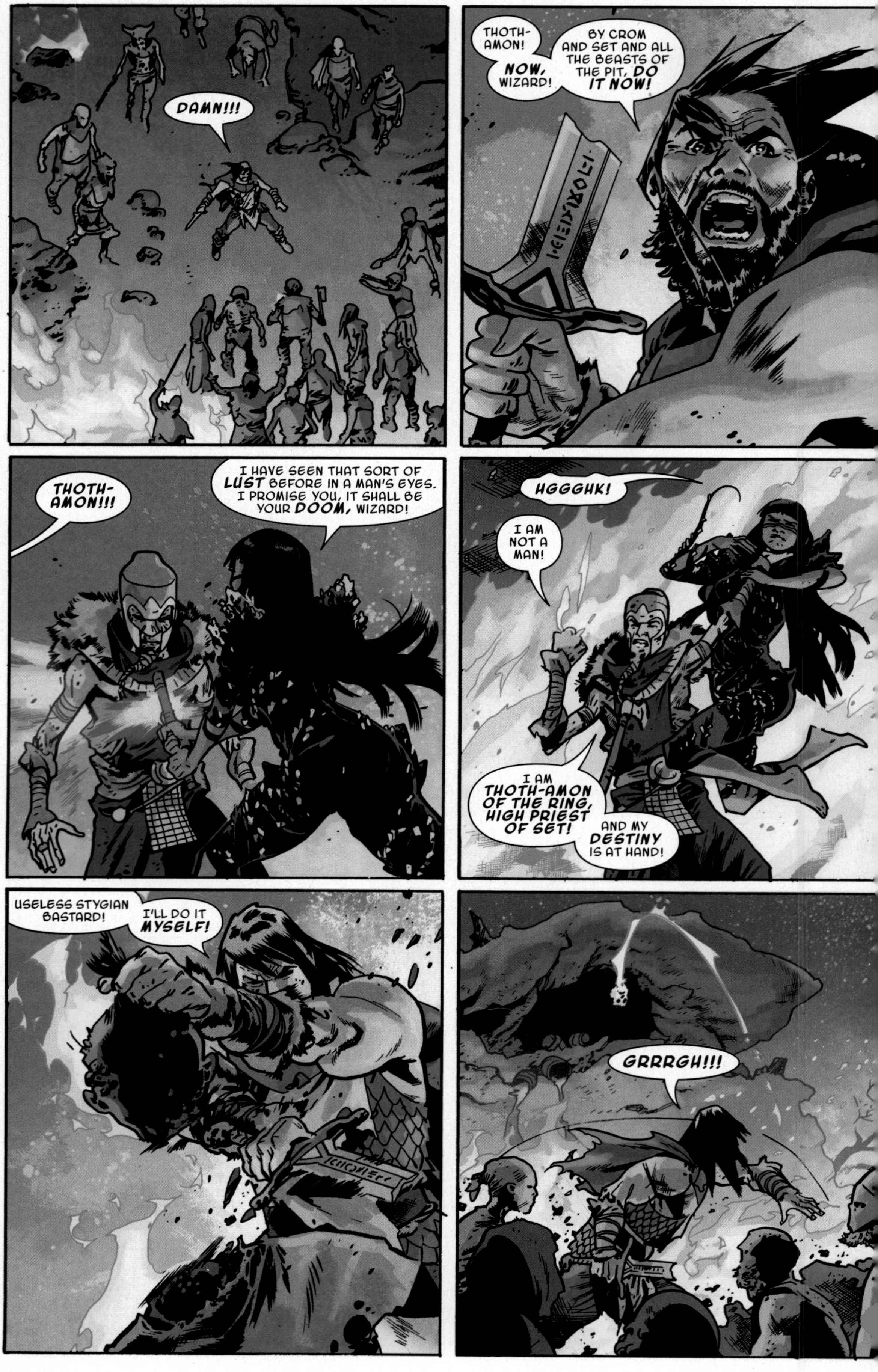

DAMN!!!
THOTH-AMON!
NOW, WIZARD!
BY CROM AND SET AND ALL THE BEASTS OF THE PIT, DO IT NOW!
THOTH-AMON!!!
I HAVE SEEN THAT SORT OF LUST BEFORE IN A MAN'S EYES. I PROMISE YOU, IT SHALL BE YOUR DOOM, WIZARD!
HGGGHK!
I AM NOT A MAN!
I AM THOTH-AMON OF THE RING, HIGH PRIEST OF SET!
AND MY DESTINY IS AT HAND!
USELESS STYGIAN BASTARD!
I'LL DO IT MYSELF!
GRRRGH!!!

IN THIS MOMENT... WHICH CONAN FULLY EXPECTED TO BE HIS *LAST*...

...IT WAS NOT A CURSE THAT CAME TO HIS LIPS, NOR A PRAYER, NOT EVEN AS HE PREPARED TO FACE HIS GOD.

ALL CONAN COULD UTTER WITH HIS LAST BREATH... WAS A *NAME*.

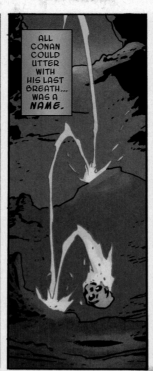

A CALL SENT ACROSS THE WAVES.

HEAVY WITH *REGRET*.

AND SOMETHING THAT WAS AS CLOSE AS A CIMMERIAN FATHER HAD EVER POSSIBLY COME...

...TO WHAT THE CIVILIZED MAN CALLED *"LOVE."*

CONN....

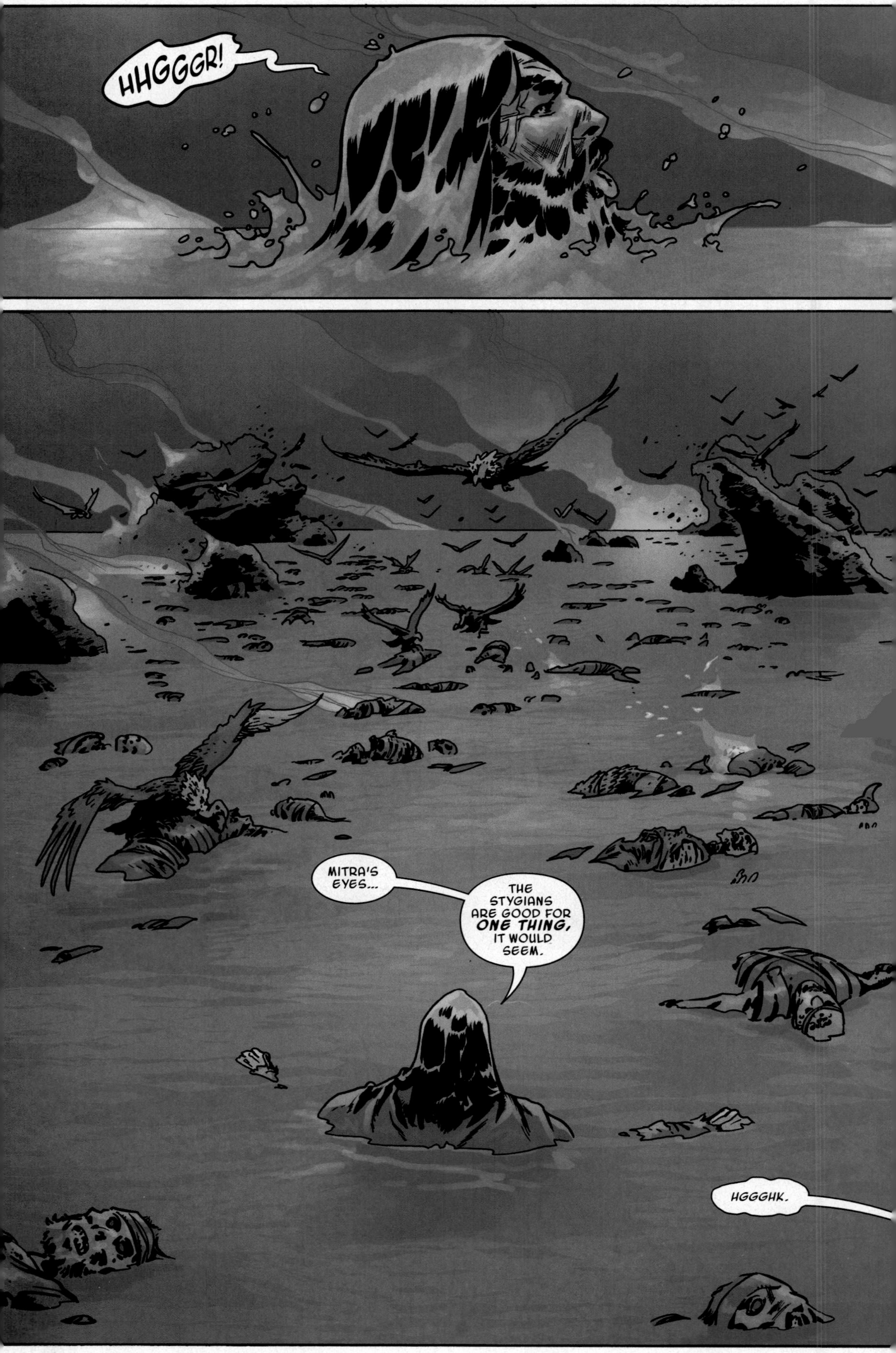
HHGGGR!
MITRA'S EYES...
THE STYGIANS ARE GOOD FOR ONE THING, IT WOULD SEEM.
HGGGHK.

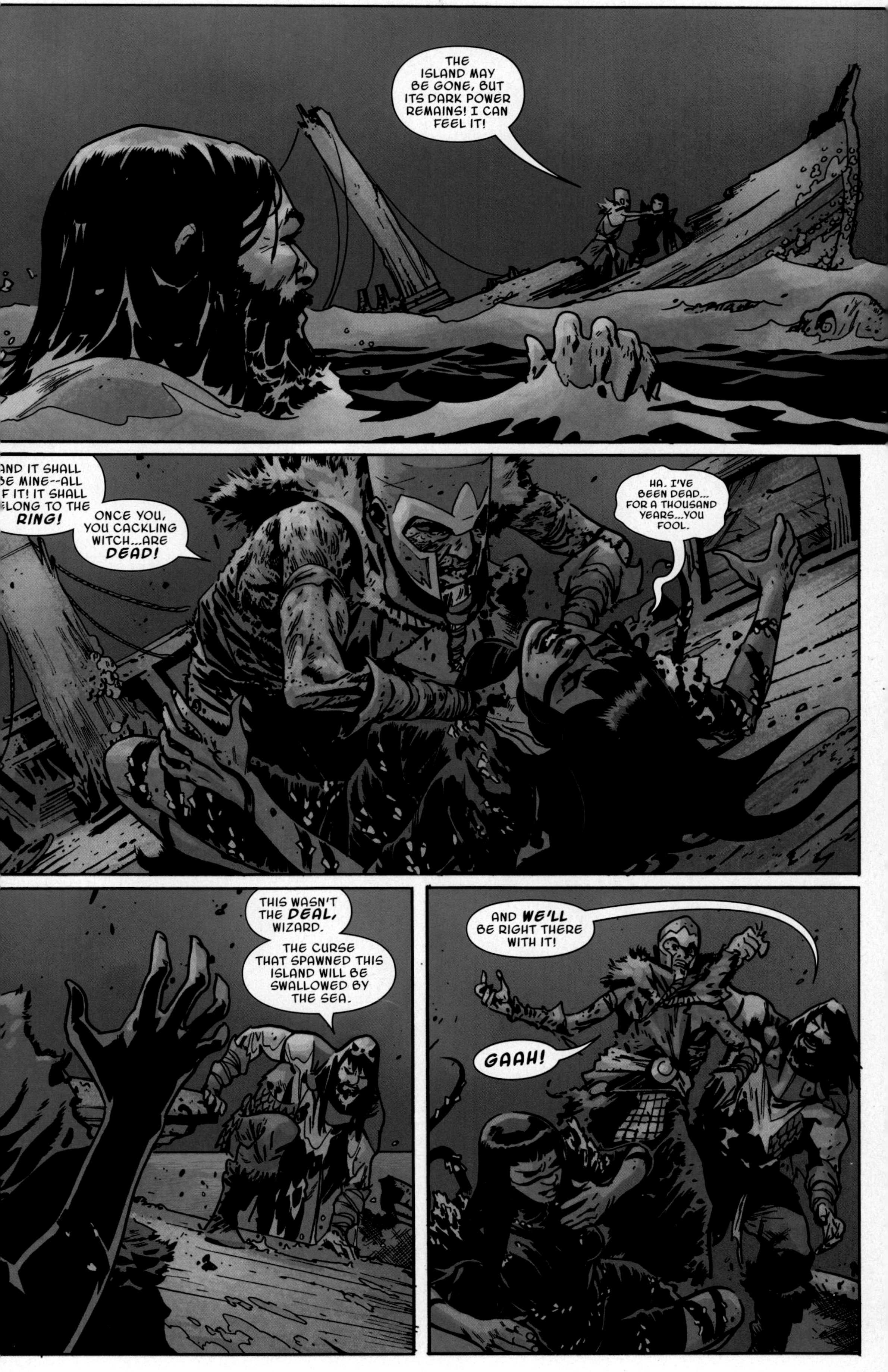
THE ISLAND MAY BE GONE, BUT ITS DARK POWER REMAINS! I CAN FEEL IT!
AND IT SHALL BE MINE--ALL OF IT! IT SHALL BELONG TO THE RING!
ONCE YOU, YOU CACKLING WITCH...ARE DEAD!
HA. I'VE BEEN DEAD... FOR A THOUSAND YEARS...YOU FOOL.
THIS WASN'T THE DEAL, WIZARD.
THE CURSE THAT SPAWNED THIS ISLAND WILL BE SWALLOWED BY THE SEA.
AND WE'LL BE RIGHT THERE WITH IT!
GAAH!

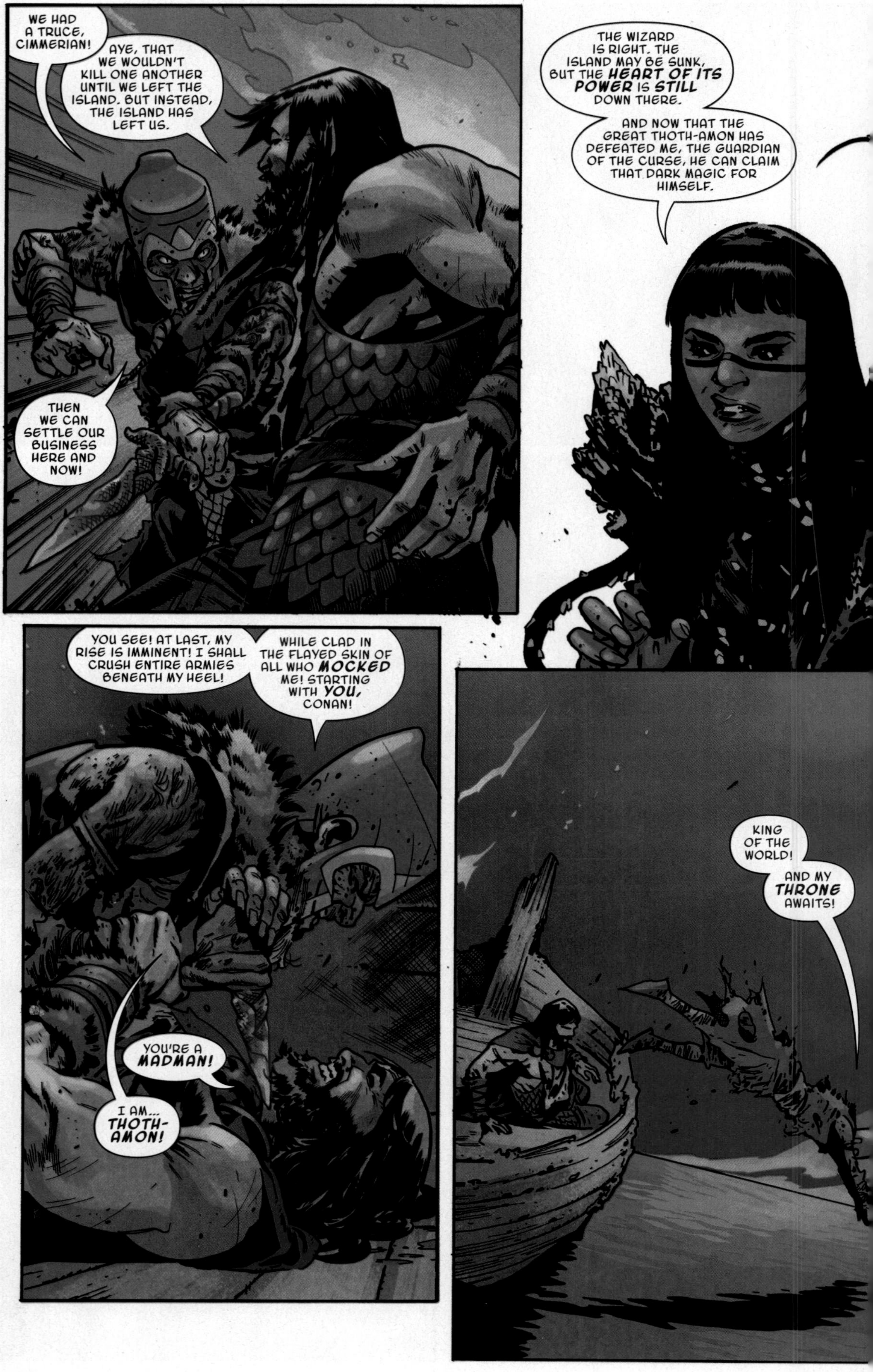
WE HAD A TRUCE, CIMMERIAN!
AYE, THAT WE WOULDN'T KILL ONE ANOTHER UNTIL WE LEFT THE ISLAND. BUT INSTEAD, THE ISLAND HAS LEFT US.
THEN WE CAN SETTLE OUR BUSINESS HERE AND NOW!
THE WIZARD IS RIGHT. THE ISLAND MAY BE SUNK, BUT THE HEART OF ITS POWER IS STILL DOWN THERE.
AND NOW THAT THE GREAT THOTH-AMON HAS DEFEATED ME, THE GUARDIAN OF THE CURSE, HE CAN CLAIM THAT DARK MAGIC FOR HIMSELF.
YOU SEE! AT LAST, MY RISE IS IMMINENT! I SHALL CRUSH ENTIRE ARMIES BENEATH MY HEEL!
WHILE CLAD IN THE FLAYED SKIN OF ALL WHO MOCKED ME! STARTING WITH YOU, CONAN!
YOU'RE A MADMAN!
I AM... THOTH-AMON!
KING OF THE WORLD!
AND MY THRONE AWAITS!

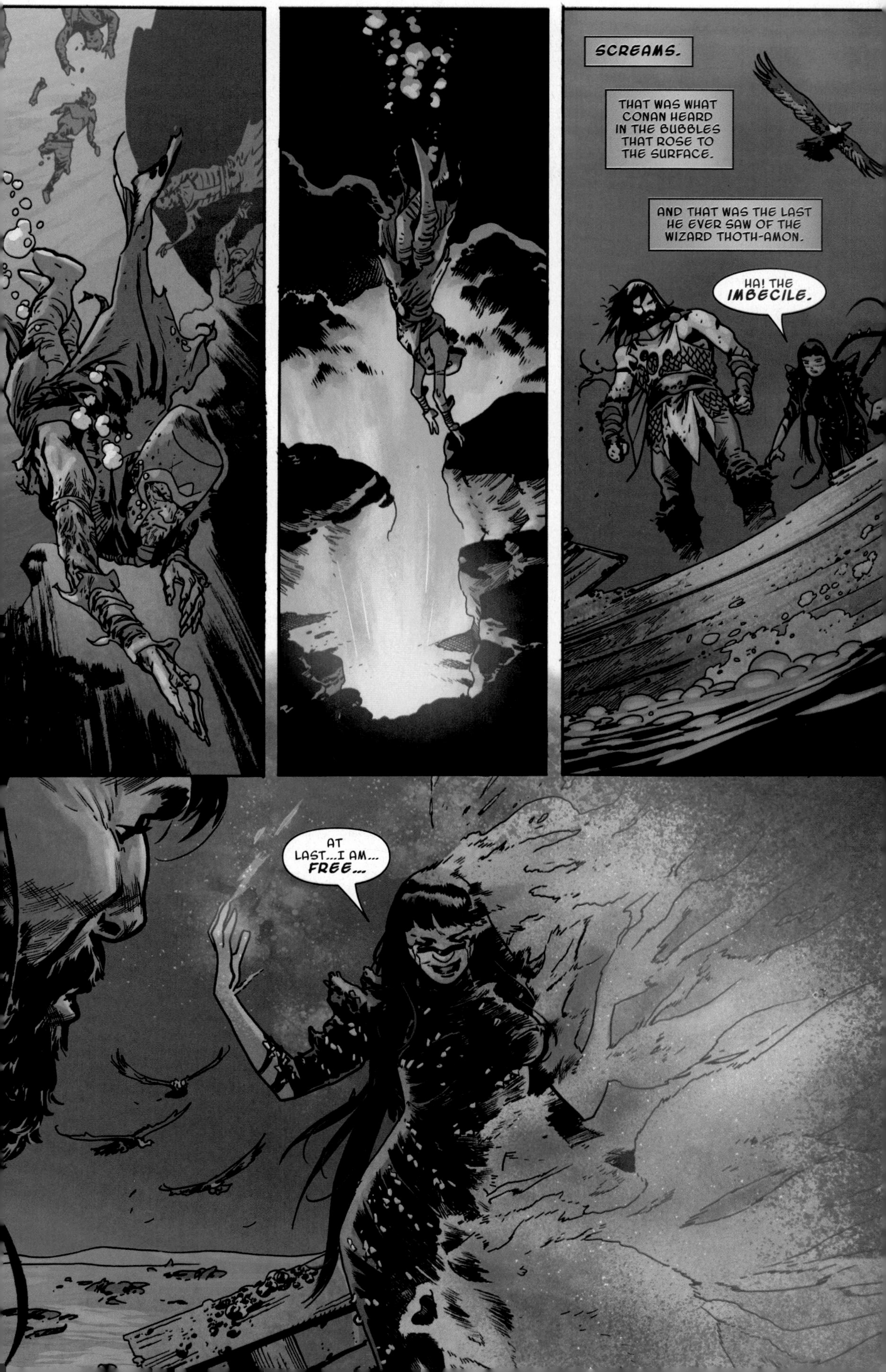
SCREAMS.
THAT WAS WHAT CONAN HEARD IN THE BUBBLES THAT ROSE TO THE SURFACE.
AND THAT WAS THE LAST HE EVER SAW OF THE WIZARD THOTH-AMON.
HA! THE IMBECILE.
AT LAST...I AM... FREE...

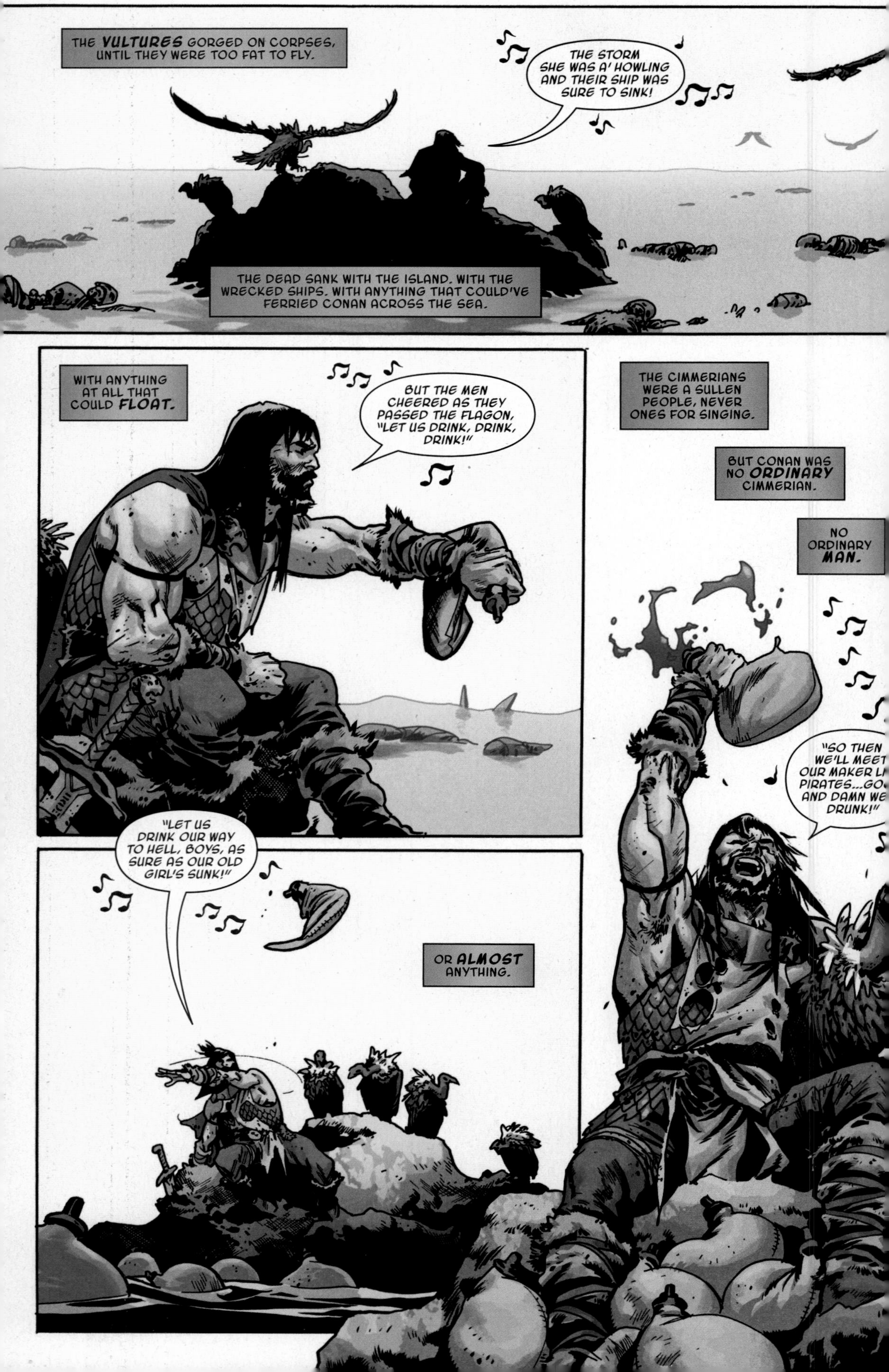

THE VULTURES GORGED ON CORPSES, UNTIL THEY WERE TOO FAT TO FLY.
THE STORM SHE WAS A' HOWLING AND THEIR SHIP WAS SURE TO SINK!
THE DEAD SANK WITH THE ISLAND. WITH THE WRECKED SHIPS. WITH ANYTHING THAT COULD'VE FERRIED CONAN ACROSS THE SEA.
WITH ANYTHING AT ALL THAT COULD FLOAT.
BUT THE MEN CHEERED AS THEY PASSED THE FLAGON, "LET US DRINK, DRINK, DRINK!"
THE CIMMERIANS WERE A SULLEN PEOPLE, NEVER ONES FOR SINGING.
BUT CONAN WAS NO ORDINARY CIMMERIAN.
NO ORDINARY MAN.
"LET US DRINK OUR WAY TO HELL, BOYS, AS SURE AS OUR OLD GIRL'S SUNK!"
OR ALMOST ANYTHING.
"SO THEN WE'LL MEET OUR MAKER LI PIRATES...GO AND DAMN WE DRUNK!"

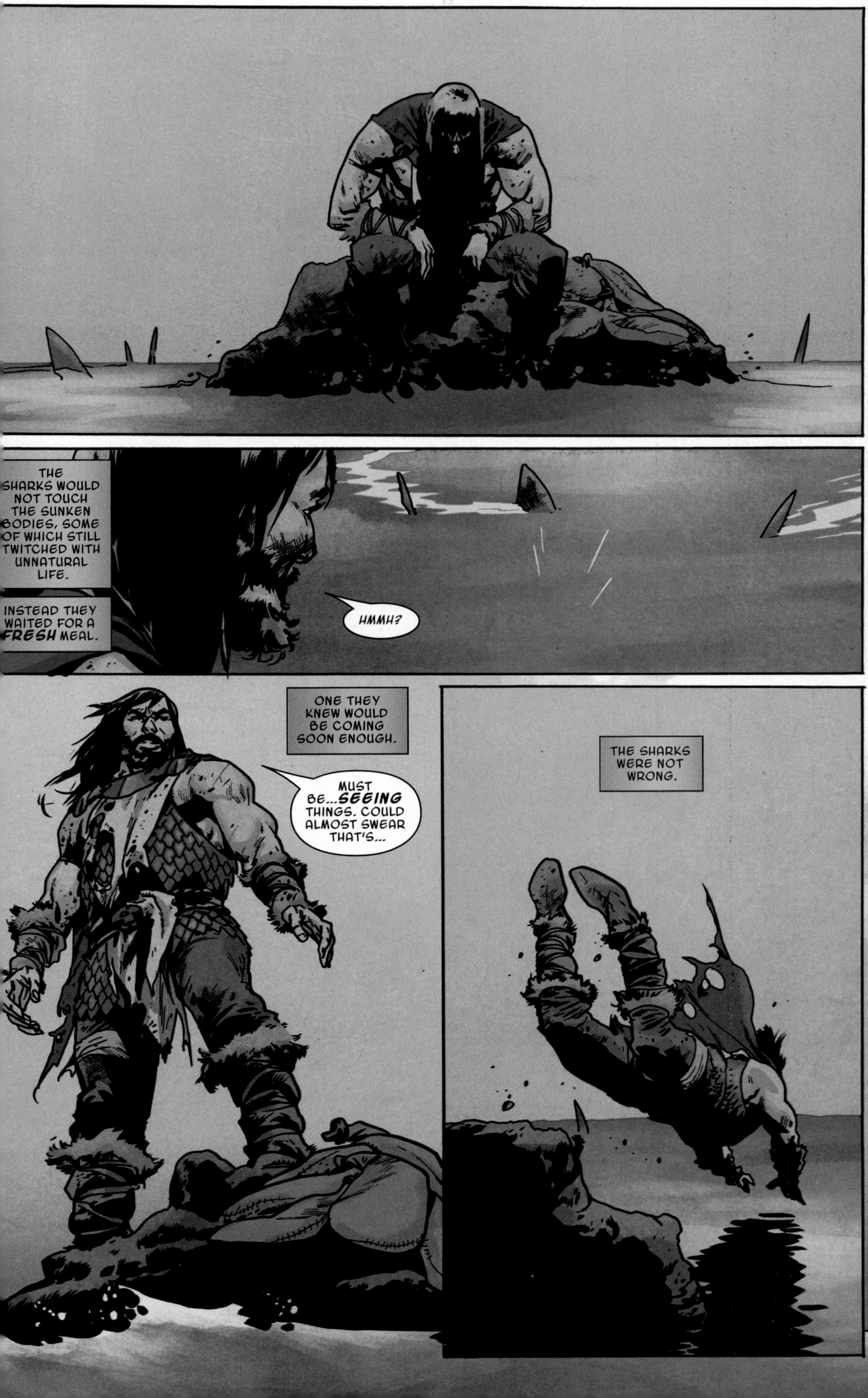
THE SHARKS WOULD NOT TOUCH THE SUNKEN BODIES, SOME OF WHICH STILL TWITCHED WITH UNNATURAL LIFE.
INSTEAD THEY WAITED FOR A FRESH MEAL.
HMMH?
ONE THEY KNEW WOULD BE COMING SOON ENOUGH.
MUST BE...SEEING THINGS. COULD ALMOST SWEAR THAT'S...
THE SHARKS WERE NOT WRONG.

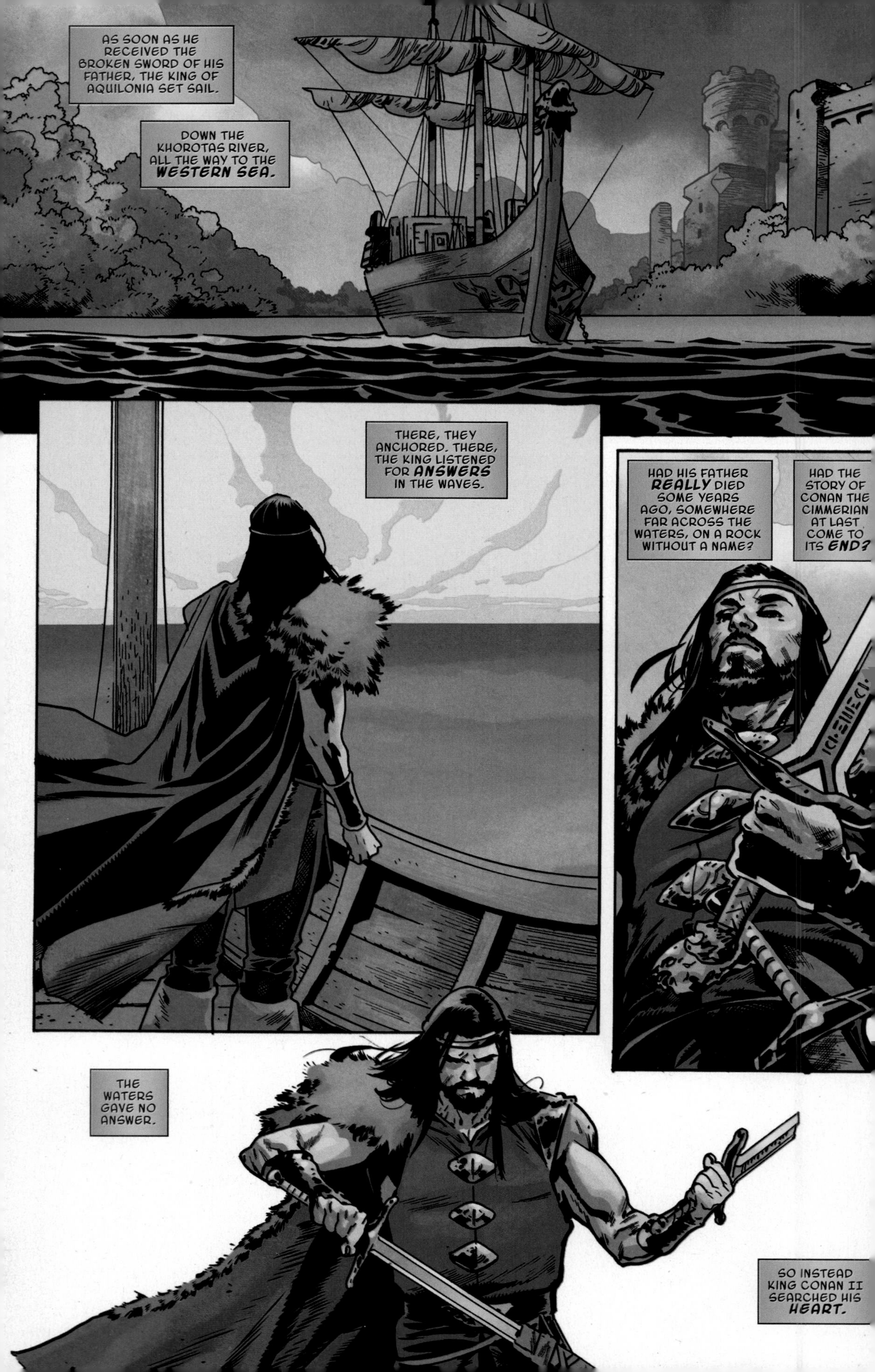
AS SOON AS HE RECEIVED THE BROKEN SWORD OF HIS FATHER, THE KING OF AQUILONIA SET SAIL.
DOWN THE KHOROTAS RIVER, ALL THE WAY TO THE WESTERN SEA.
THERE, THEY ANCHORED. THERE, THE KING LISTENED FOR ANSWERS IN THE WAVES.
HAD HIS FATHER REALLY DIED SOME YEARS AGO, SOMEWHERE FAR ACROSS THE WATERS, ON A ROCK WITHOUT A NAME?
HAD THE STORY OF CONAN THE CIMMERIAN AT LAST COME TO ITS END?
THE WATERS GAVE NO ANSWER.
SO INSTEAD KING CONAN II SEARCHED HIS HEART.

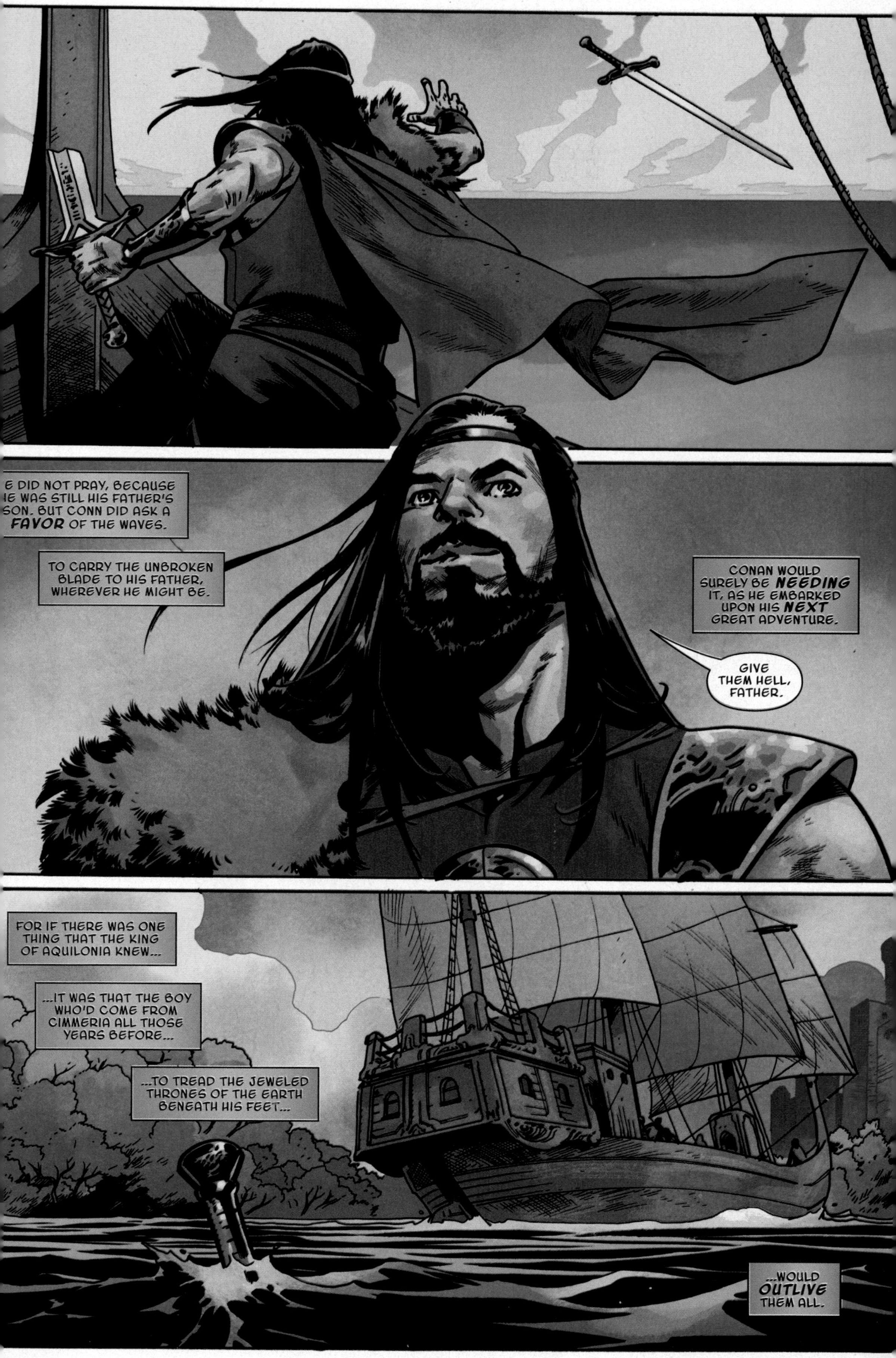
E DID NOT PRAY, BECAUSE HE WAS STILL HIS FATHER'S SON. BUT CONN DID ASK A FAVOR OF THE WAVES.
TO CARRY THE UNBROKEN BLADE TO HIS FATHER, WHEREVER HE MIGHT BE.
CONAN WOULD SURELY BE NEEDING IT, AS HE EMBARKED UPON HIS NEXT GREAT ADVENTURE.
GIVE THEM HELL, FATHER.
FOR IF THERE WAS ONE THING THAT THE KING OF AQUILONIA KNEW...
...IT WAS THAT THE BOY WHO'D COME FROM CIMMERIA ALL THOSE YEARS BEFORE...
...TO TREAD THE JEWELED THRONES OF THE EARTH BENEATH HIS FEET...
...WOULD OUTLIVE THEM ALL.

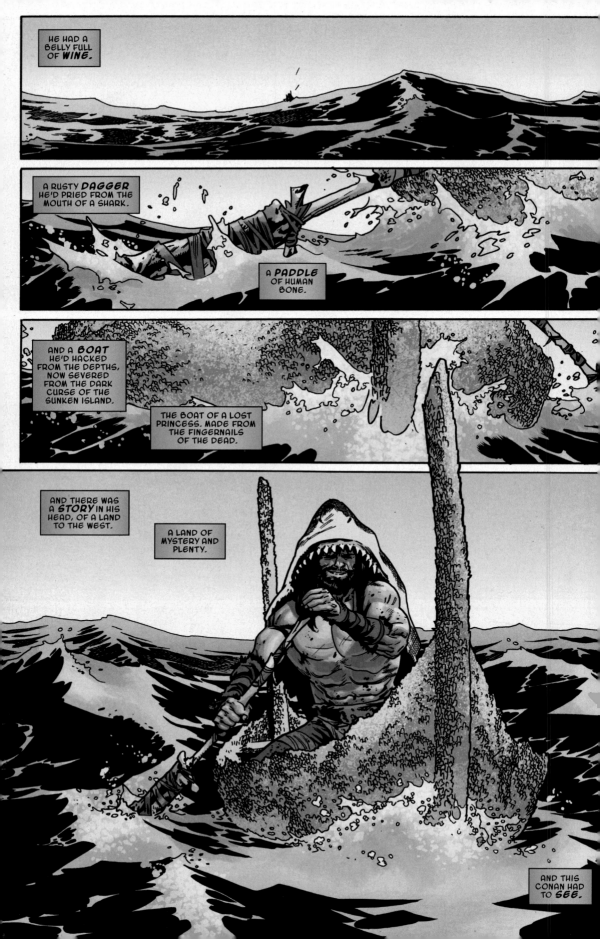

HE HAD A BELLY FULL OF *WINE.*

A RUSTY *DAGGER* HE'D PRIED FROM THE MOUTH OF A SHARK.

A *PADDLE* OF HUMAN BONE.

AND A *BOAT* HE'D HACKED FROM THE DEPTHS, NOW SEVERED FROM THE DARK CURSE OF THE SUNKEN ISLAND.

THE BOAT OF A LOST PRINCESS. MADE FROM THE FINGERNAILS OF THE DEAD.

AND THERE WAS A *STORY* IN HIS HEAD, OF A LAND TO THE WEST.

A LAND OF MYSTERY AND PLENTY.

AND THIS CONAN HAD TO *SEE.*

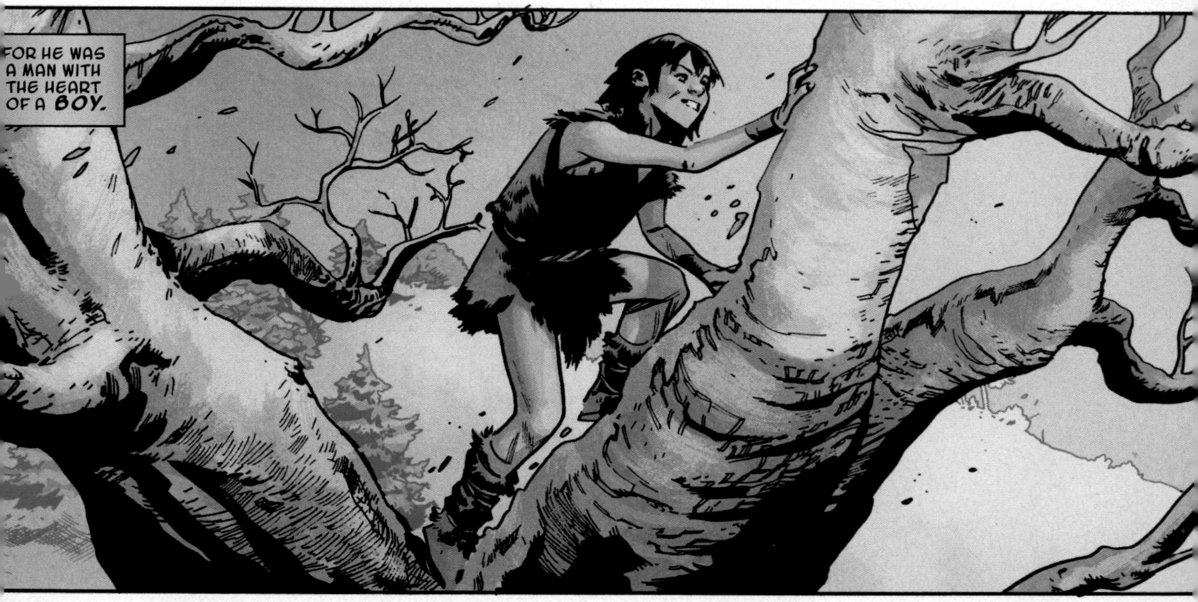
FOR HE WAS A MAN WITH THE HEART OF A BOY.

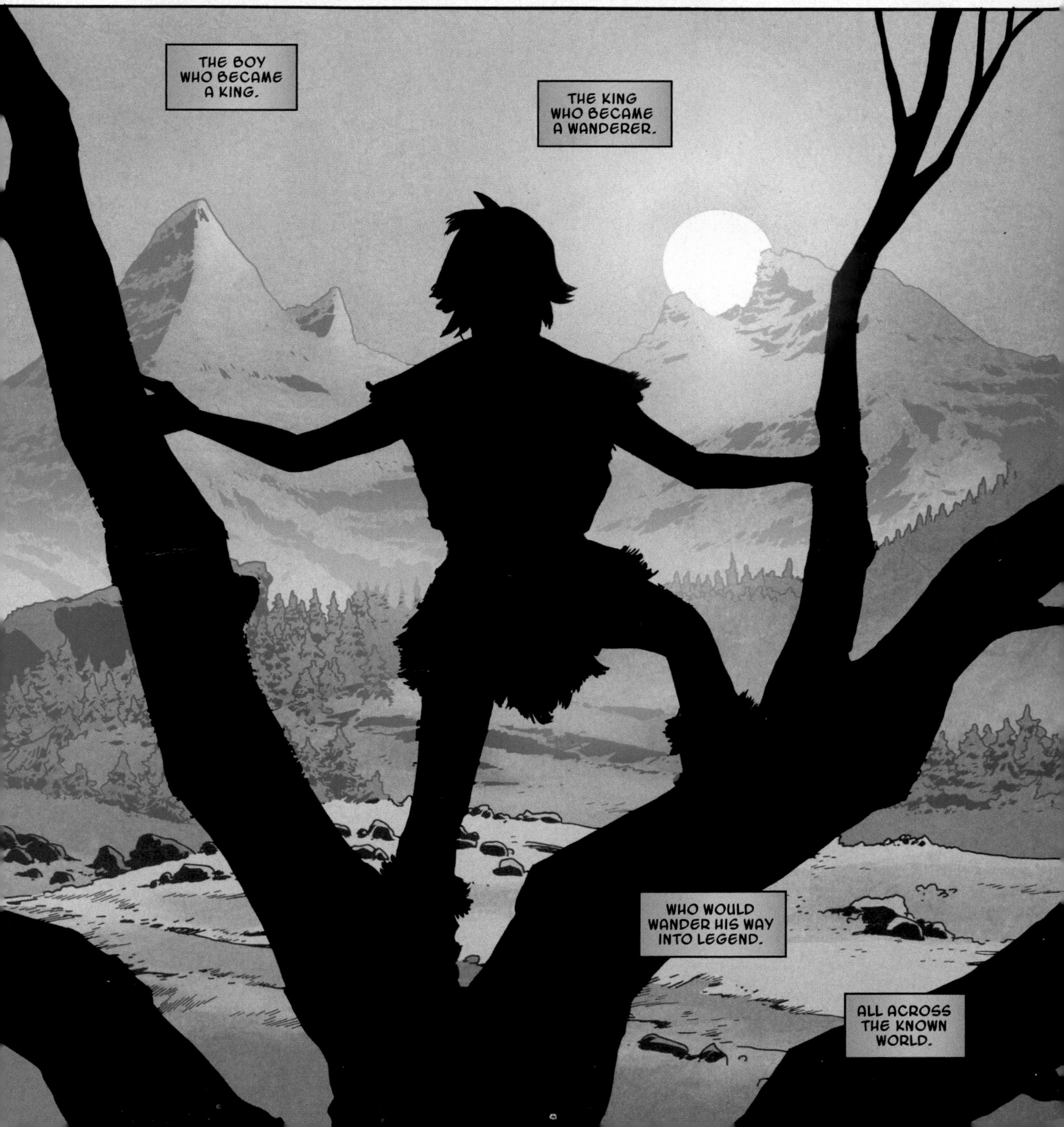
THE BOY WHO BECAME A KING.
THE KING WHO BECAME A WANDERER.
WHO WOULD WANDER HIS WAY INTO LEGEND.
ALL ACROSS THE KNOWN WORLD.

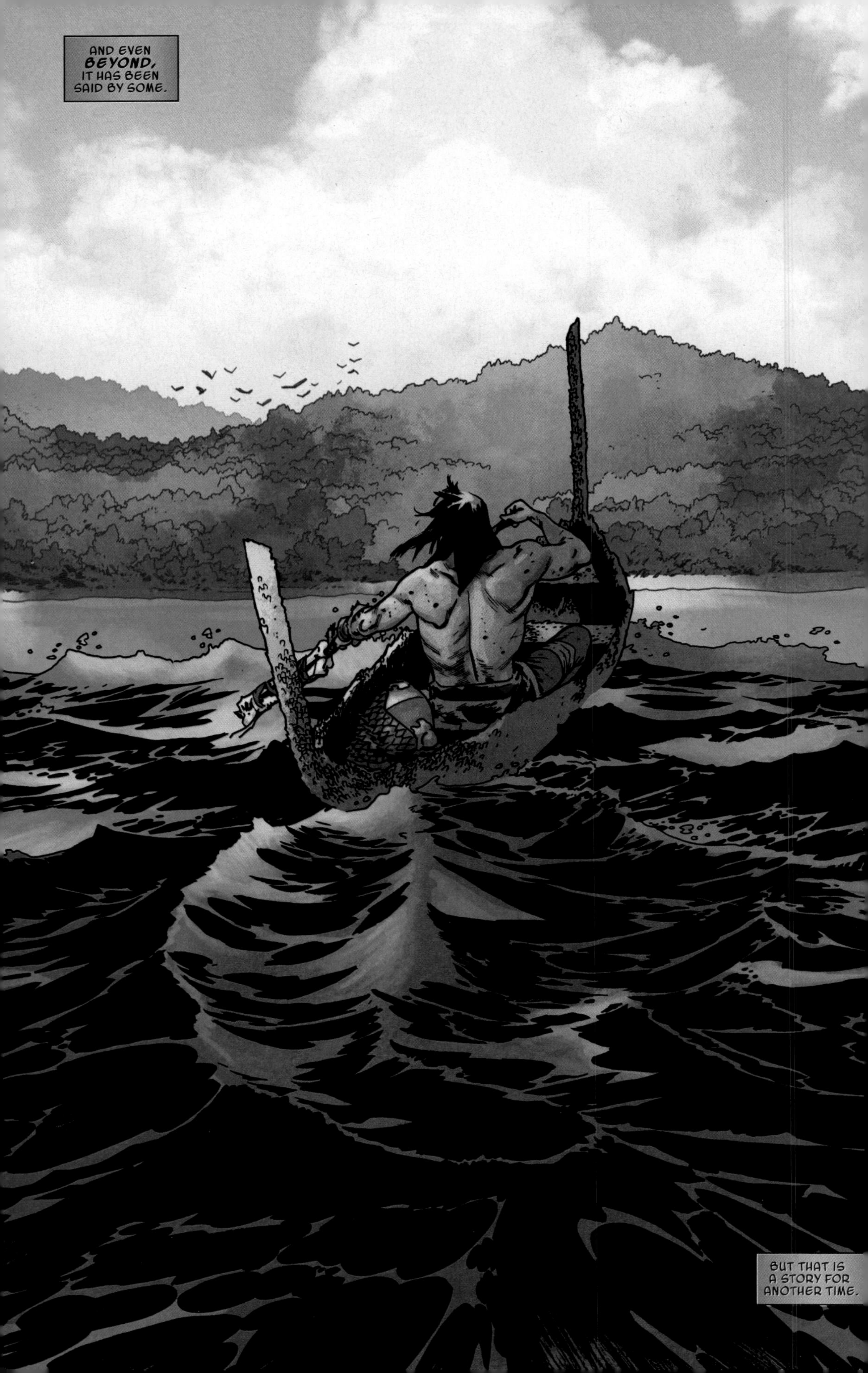
AND EVEN BEYOND, IT HAS BEEN SAID BY SOME.
BUT THAT IS A STORY FOR ANOTHER TIME.

#2 VARIANT BY DAVE WILKINS

#4 VARIANT BY DECLAN SHALVEY

#5 VARIANT BY
PASQUAL FERRY & MATTHEW WILSON

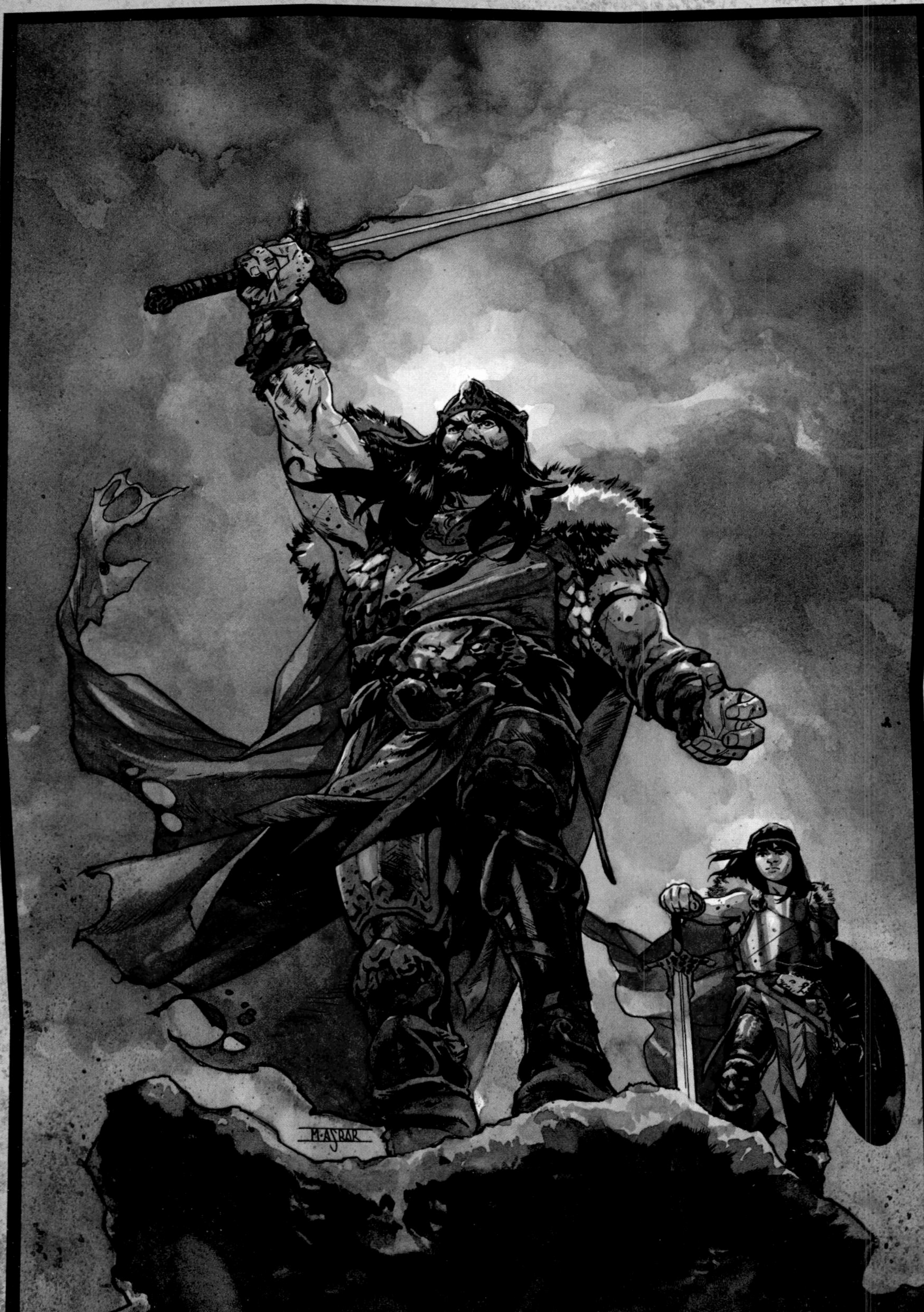
M·ASRAR

#6 VARIANT BY **MAHMUD ASRAR**